· THE ·
CAROLINA
WAY

· THE ·

CAROLINA
WAY

LEADERSHIP LESSONS
FROM A LIFE IN COACHING

DEAN SMITH

and GERALD D. BELL *with* JOHN KILGO

Preface by Roy Williams

THE PENGUIN PRESS
NEW YORK
2004

THE PENGUIN PRESS
a member of
Penguin Group (USA) Inc.
375 Hudson Street
New York, New York 10014

Library of Congress Cataloging-in-Publication Data

Smith, Dean
The Carolina way : leadership lessons from a life in coaching / Dean Smith
and Gerald D. Bell with John Kilgo ; preface by Roy Williams.
p. cm.
Includes index.
ISBN 1-59420-005-X
1. Basketball—Coaching.   2. Coaching (Athletics)—Philosophy.   I. Bell,
Gerald D.   II. Kilgo, John.   III. Title.
GV885.3.S59 2004
796.323'07'7—dc22   2003053664

This book is printed on acid-free paper. ∞

Printed in the United States of America
1   3   5   7   9   10   8   6   4   2

Designed by Stephanie Huntwork

Sincere thanks to those who played for me at North Carolina and at the Air Force Academy; to all the coaches for whom I worked and played; to the brilliant coaches who served as my assistants at North Carolina and contributed greatly to our success; and to the dedicated members of the administrative staff in the North Carolina basketball office who went well beyond the call of duty on behalf of the players and coaches.

CONTENTS

by Roy Williams, head basketball coach,
University of North Carolina

Coach Dean Smith is the greatest on-the-court basketball coach there ever was, and in his dealings with his players and others off the court, he was equally effective. He set a high standard for excellence, integrity, and sportsmanship that inspired his North Carolina teams for thirty-six years, and as you will learn in this book, his teachings continue to help his former players in their far-ranging professions as teachers, doctors, coaches, business leaders, professional athletes, lawyers, and politicians.

Always generous in the way he shared his vast knowledge with his friends and colleagues, Coach Smith now shares with a wider audience how he came about his philosophy of teaching and coaching and why he taught the things that he did. It's an inspiring book not only for coaches and athletes but for people in all walks of life who believe that it is possible for good guys to finish on top.

I joined Coach Smith's staff at North Carolina twenty-five years ago. I certainly didn't come for the money because there was very little available in those days for the position I had. In fact I drove tapes of his weekly television show to stations around North Carolina early each Sunday morning in basketball season and did other odd jobs just to make ends meet. I joined his staff so I could learn from a master teacher. It was one of the best decisions of my life. I've listened to Coach Smith talk about basketball and life in general for more than twenty-five years. I watched him run his program with honesty as the basic foundation for everything he did. I soaked it up. Now, through the pages of this book, you get a front-row seat for yourself and learn why his way of teaching and leading is so extraordinarily special and effective. You will learn how he dealt with winning and losing with his players, what techniques and rituals he used to help get competitive, strong-willed individuals to put the team first, and why he never feared change.

After ten years as Coach Smith's assistant, I left Chapel Hill to take my first college head coaching job at the University of Kansas, his alma mater. Coach Smith's advice then was for me to be myself and not to be tied so strongly to his philosophy that I wouldn't be willing to change to suit my personnel. As usual, his advice was golden. I took what he taught me, added my own wrinkles, and found it worked pretty well at Kansas. Coach Smith is always looking for better ways to do something. After ten years at his side I went to Kansas as my own man, and although I believe the game should be played a certain way, I adapted it each year to fit our personnel.

The philosophy works. I had countless people during the fifteen years I was coach at Kansas tell me that they used the same principles in their businesses that we did with our teams to get their employees to work together unselfishly and feel like family. When you think about it, that's quite a compliment. *The Carolina Way* is about basketball, but not *just* basketball. It's also about life and fairness and people striving to serve others. For example, TJ Pugh, a former player of mine at Kansas, who is a student in medical school now, directed his remarks at our chancellor during one of our basketball banquets: "Chancellor, I just want you to know that Coach Williams is the best teacher I've had in my four years here." The remark made me feel good, of course, and later that night I told my wife that it would certainly make Coach Smith feel good too because everything he teaches is a perfect model for people to follow in all walks of life.

I agree with Coach's description of himself when he says that as a coach he was part benevolent dictator and part servant to the players. He is honest and fair and plays no favorites. He pushes, but he understands different situations. He's a disciplinarian, but he understands that all individuals are not the same. He requires people to look at team goals, but he understands that individuals have their own goals and needs too. He listened to his players in one-on-one meetings and heard their suggestions and then gave them great latitude to think for themselves on the court. But when it came time to approve the overall picture, he was a strong leader who said, "Okay, men, I've heard you. Now, here's the way we're going to do it. Let's get to work for the good of the team." The best leaders have the strong convictions that have marked Coach Smith's career. As important as basketball is and was to Coach Smith and his former players, they all knew from day one that it wasn't the reason they were at the University of North Carolina. The players were there to learn, to experience college life in its fullest form, and academics trumped basketball. They were true student-athletes who earned their degrees. Coach had a saying that went like this: "During the season, everything for the team; out of season, everything for the individual." Whether it was advising one of his star underclassmen that he might consider leaving college basketball early to sign a lucrative NBA contract or helping a nonscholarship player through a tough personal situation, Coach Smith was a servant to his players. He cares for them deeply, and his devotion to them continues to this day. Phil Ford, one of his former great players, said, after he went through Coach's program, "I knew when I signed with North Carolina that I was getting a great coach for four years, but in addition, I got a great friend for a lifetime." That pretty much sums up the relationship Coach Smith has with his players. His leadership skills are so superb that I'm absolutely convinced that he would have been a huge success as a doctor, a businessman, a politician, a college professor, or the math teacher and high school coach that as a youth he thought he would become.

The hardest thing for a coach, and I suspect for leaders in other professions as well, is to start out with new players or employees. They don't know you. They can say, "We trust you, Coach," but it's truly hard to trust any leader until you've been with him or her for some time to see how he or she reacts to different situations. I'm sure employees at a big company are all different, and I know players are. Although our basketball staff spends a lot of time recruiting and trying to bring in the right people, we don't know for sure until we get them on campus whether the team or the individual is the more important thing to them. Getting them to believe in a philosophy that puts the team first is no easy task. I've had players tell me that they react to my passion for doing things the right way and standing for what I believe in. Coach Smith brings that passion to the office daily. He coached in what might be the most pressurized position in all college basketball for thirty-six years, won 78 percent of his games, graduated more than 96 percent of his players, and never ran afoul of the many NCAA rules and regulations.

As head basketball coach at Kansas I found that teaching what Coach Smith had taught me was easy because I believe in it so strongly. I have the conviction that no opponent can shake our confidence in what we are doing. The players respect that because there are no iffy situations, no doubting what our philosophy is, no second-guessing our approach. I deeply believe that what we do will be successful. Coach Smith talks in this book about the value of the one-on-one meetings he had with his players, as well as the team meetings. Sometimes my players laugh when they first hear me say this, but in the first meeting I have with them each year I tell them that the easiest way for them to be successful and to keep me off their backs is for them to do what I tell them to do. "It would be silly for us to battle," I say, "because I'm going to win. Whether you're a McDonald's All-American or someone who thinks you invented basketball, I'm going to win any battle that we might have. So let's not waste any time battling."

Sure, I listen to the players when they talk to me and make suggestions, just as Coach Smith did. But when it's time to make a decision for the good of the team, like Coach Smith, I'm a benevolent dictator. Great leaders know what it means to make tough decisions, even if they sometimes aren't popular with the people they're leading.

I wasn't a very good player—let's get that on the record now—but I tried to make sure that no one ever played harder than I did. It remains my style as a head coach. I've had players tell me that one reason they work so hard is that I do. I guess you could call that leading by example. I tell my teams that I won't spend time coaching effort. I expect that to be a given. Coach Smith believes, as I do, that if you do your absolute best, you can live with the result, regardless of what it is. The seniors on Coach Smith's teams were a great help in selling that principle to the rest of the players. We call it senior leadership, the value of which Coach talks about in the book.

A lot of coaches have been able to get players to sacrifice for a common goal, but Coach Smith did it better than anybody else because he made his players feel good about doing it. He emphasized it so much that no matter what role a player had, he knew it was extremely important. If it was a small role in the overall scheme of things, Coach Smith still was able to convince the player that if he didn't do it well, the team would not be successful. He frequently found ways to thank players for performing their roles well, especially those who worked hard in practice but didn't get much playing time in games. He wanted these players in particular to know that they were very much a part of the team's success and were appreciated. It's emphatically true that each person on teams coached by Dean Smith was important, and was treated with respect, and that included the men and women who were student managers. His philosophy didn't allow for a star system. It was all about Team.

Our teams won 418 games while I was at Kansas, nine conference championships, went to four Final Fours, won a lot of other tournaments along the way, but I never went out on the court with my team to receive a trophy. I sent my seniors out because I believed it was their trophy. I got that directly from Coach Smith, who took the blame for the losses and gave the players credit for the victories. Just like him, I found that my reward came from seeing the players succeed. You can ask any player to recall highlights of his career, and he will answer that it was some moment when the team accomplished something great. Their lasting memories are not about individual things but about *team* things.

Everyone who reads this book and comes to understand the things that Coach Smith taught and why he taught them will benefit in a significant way. When it came to building a team and getting a group of divergent personalities that spanned four distinctly different decades to unite for a common cause, he's the best ever. *The Carolina Way* has countless nuggets that people in all walks of life will find extremely helpful and inspirational.

INTRODUCTION

Is coaching management? I've been asked the question many times and still don't have a definitive answer. However, Dr. Jerry Bell, my collaborator on this book and a business professor, consultant, and leader with impeccable credentials, says emphatically that coaching *is* management. He argues that good leadership qualities are transferable from one occupation to another, so I'm going to yield to his considerable wisdom and experience.

Our basketball program at North Carolina certainly had a strong philosophy and mission, which produced extraordinary results over a long period of time, thanks to the terrific players and people we attracted to our program. We believed in following a process instead of dwelling on winning or worrying about consequences. We asked our players to concern themselves only with things within their control, so our mission statement was: Play hard; play smart; play together. We knew if we did those things, we would be successful a large percentage of the time. We wanted the players' focus and attention and tried to help them avoid distractions. In addition to winning hundreds of games, our players graduated and went on to great careers, and while at Chapel Hill they proved to me, beyond a shadow of a doubt, that when talented individuals sacrifice for the team, everybody wins.

When I wrote my memoirs several years ago, two chapters in the book attracted much attention, judging by the mail I received. One of them, "I Might Be Wrong but . . . ," dealt with what I think about matters of theology and in other areas of life. The other chapter, "The Carolina Way," was a brief review of the things we taught and why. After hearing from so many businesspeople who asked questions about the Carolina Way, I began to understand that maybe coaching is management after all. That seed had first been planted in 1990, when Jerry Bell invited me to be on the faculty of the Young Presidents' Organization University at St. Moritz, Switzerland. He was chairman of the faculty of this particular session. The YPO is comprised of leaders who became presidents of their organizations before they reached the age of thirty-nine and whose companies were of at least a certain minimal size. The suggested title for my session was "Coaching Is Management." I persuaded Jerry to make the title a question instead of a statement. The Young Presidents asked many good questions after my talk, such as "What do you do with a prima donna who gets the job done but is not a team player?" I replied that in my role as a basketball coach, I wouldn't enjoy having such a person on the team if he didn't change, so I'd probably hope that he'd transfer. The Young Presidents were particularly interested in questioning me about two other areas of concern: How did we motivate our players to play hard and accept discipline? And how did we get them to put aside individual goals for the good of the team? There I was in this business environment talking to these dynamic young leaders about motivation, teamwork, and how to get people to work hard for team goals, and it suddenly seemed abundantly clear that coaching a college basketball team and managing a business do have some common issues. Also, although I didn't know it at the time, I later learned that the Young Presidents graded the faculty and seemed to be highly interested in what I had to say. Dr. Bell knew all along that coaching is management. I'm leaning in that direction now.

There are some differences, of course. For example, our players at North Carolina loved playing basketball and wanted to be at practice and were willing to put in the hard work to succeed. They were talented at it, or they wouldn't have been on our team. North Carolina plays basketball at a very high level. Not every manager can coach such an eager team. Maybe it was easier for me to lead my players, who wanted to be there, than it is for a business manager to lead members of her sales department who feel they have to be there. If I taught eighth grade, I'd prefer teaching an elective subject rather than a course that the students were required to take.

The idea for this book came from John Kilgo, a writer and longtime observer of our North Carolina basketball program, who earlier helped me write my memoirs. He too thought that the qualities that made our program successful would benefit people in other professions. Again, I was slow coming to that conclusion. One of my former players, Dr. David Chadwick, wrote a book several years ago titled *Twelve Leadership Principles of Dean Smith*. Well, I never knew that I had twelve principles of leadership and suggested to Dave that maybe they were what he thought *might* be my leadership principles based on what he had observed. Still, we all have a philosophy, whether we know it or not, and I've come around a little. Kilgo believes that readers can take things from our philosophy and benefit from them, and I agree that *could* be the case. Whether you're leading a basketball team, a nurses' school, a small insurance office, or a large corporation, there are certain common denominators. Honesty, integrity, discipline administered fairly, not playing favorites, recruiting the right people, effective practice and training, and caring are foundations that any organization would be wise to have in place. The most important thing in good leadership is truly caring. The best leaders in any profession care about the people they lead, and the people who are being led know when the caring is genuine and when it's faked or not there at all. I was a demanding coach, but my players knew that I cared for them and that my caring didn't stop when they graduated and went off to their careers. My parents taught me as a boy that all people are equally loved by the Creator and deserving of respect. They imbued me with core values and provided the opportunity for me to have a spiritual foundation, which placed great emphasis on being of service to others. If I've failed in any way to follow through on that, then it's my fault, because the training was there.

I believe it's accurate to say that the most effective leaders have these things in common: the talent to create a sound strategy for their teams or businesses; knowledge of the importance of recruiting good people who wish to improve their personal skills and believe in the companies' or teams' philosophy; understanding that whether they like it or not, they lead by example; belief in the importance of being light enough on their feet to adapt to changing conditions; and the ability to honor their commitments, admit their mistakes, and take responsibility for their failures.

It's also true that leaders in virtually all professions must learn how to compete. Obviously I'm a competitive person, or I wouldn't have coached basketball at North Carolina for thirty-six years. I enjoyed having our team go against the best teams in the nation. The games were like a test. We used the games to measure our progress and see how we stacked up against the best teams in America. All leaders, not just coaches, must learn how to compete effectively, because the competition is looking for ways to beat them. While we talked with our players about the process and not about winning, that didn't mean we didn't want to win. Winning was important to us, very important. But when we did our best and lost, we accepted it, congratulated our opponent, and worked hard to improve. Leaders must know how to bring their teams back from defeat.

Even though I was convinced (with some reservations) that this book done properly could be useful, I wouldn't have done it without Jerry's contribution. I'm a coach, not a businessperson, an artist, or a doctor, and it would have been presumptuous of me to tell people in those and other professions how they could make the Carolina Way work for them. Jerry has worked closely with leaders in business and many other professions, and he's well qualified to examine what we taught and explain how it could be transferred to other professions. He's done that brilliantly in this book, which I'm proud to coauthor with him.

My role was to write about the things we taught at North Carolina, and why. Jerry, under the heading of "Business Perspective," explains how others can take those lessons and training strategies and put them to good use in their own jobs and leadership activities. When you read the section on teamwork and team building, you'll see that we had many rituals that we used. They didn't start out as rituals but were initially put into play to answer needs. They became part of our program and eventually as familiar as Thanskgiving dinner with the family. I do think rituals assist in team building.

The player perspectives that appear in each chapter were the idea of John Kilgo, who gave this book its form. When he first approached me about having the players give their lasting impressions of the way we taught, I vetoed it, even though I knew the information could be interesting and valuable. I just believe these men have been asked about me so much that they must be tired of talking about me after all these years. Nevertheless, John Kilgo was persistent, and with allies Scott Moyers, our editor, and Jerry, I was outvoted 3–1. However, I did ask John not to call on some of our most famous players who have been asked about me time and again for years and years. Having said all that, I am convinced that the players have a perspective that we couldn't get from any other source. Not having them participate would have left a void and made the book less than what it is. I agreed to go along with it, but only with the clear understanding that it was John who chose which players to interview, did the interviewing, and then wrote their comments. I never favored one player over another and wouldn't have known how to include this one and leave that one out.

In retrospect, I'm convinced that having the players be part of this project was a good idea because what they have to say adds a great dimension to the overall work. They were students in the classroom known as North Carolina basketball, and their observations provide the thread that ties the entire book together in a way that would otherwise be impossible. They provide readers with a strong perspective. These are smart, successful men who have made valuable contributions to society in many walks of life, including teaching, medicine, law, athletics, and business. Candor is one of their many good traits. Everyone can learn something valuable from them. Of course I wish we had the space to interview every player who ever played for us at North Carolina. That would be a worthwhile book unto itself. Meanwhile, I hope *The Carolina Way* provides you with some ideas that will help you in your work.

—*Dean Smith*
June 25, 2003

PART ONE

THE
FOUNDATIONS

FIRST PRINCIPLES

I 've been lucky enough to have been around great coaches all my life. Growing up, I watched my father coach football, baseball, basketball, and track at Emporia High School in Kansas.

From an early age I hung around his practices and traveled with his teams to many road games. I developed a love for athletic competition and also took in the enjoyment and fulfillment my father derived from being a teacher and coach. I saw that he respected the sports he coached—he took the rules *very* seriously—and he took an interest in the lives of his players that extended beyond the playing field. He was very competitive, but he never let a yearning to win trump sportsmanship or a need for team discipline. He wasn't afraid to stand up for what he thought was right—in sports and in more important matters of social justice—even if it was unpopular with many and threatened to hurt his career. He was a man of courage and goodwill. His influence on me was such that I knew from the time I started school that I wanted to grow up to be a coach and a teacher.

I confess I was a much more demanding coach than my father. I assume that I inherited that from my mother. She was a teacher, and she ran her classrooms with a firm hand.

She was also good at making sure things were kept in perspective. There's naturally a lot of excitement and anticipation surrounding games in a coaching household, and she had a knack for settling us down and putting things in proper order. The games were fine with her; in fact she enjoyed them. But academics came first. Any neglect of schoolwork, no matter how slight, meant there would be no sports for me until the problem was corrected. It was a simple rule, strictly enforced. I knew from day one that she meant business and that she was right.

Aside from my Kansas upbringing, I was greatly influenced by the coaches for whom I played in high school and college and for whom I later worked. I played basketball at the University of Kansas for Dr. Forrest ("Phog") Allen and his talented assistant coach, Dick Harp. Dr. Allen was a terrific motivator, and Coach Harp was a brilliant strategist and teacher. They formed a powerful coaching tandem. I was fortunate to stay on after graduation as an assistant coach while waiting for my orders to report for duty as a lieutenant in the U.S. Air Force. I worked with Coach Harp in coaching the freshman team and then tried to assist him and Dr. Allen with the varsity practice.

I was in Germany with the Air Force when I was asked by Bob Spear to join him as his assistant coach at the brand-new Air Force Academy, starting with the first class in 1955. It turned out to be a great opportunity for me. Our players at the academy were smart, tough, and dedicated. They learned quickly, and that was good because our practice time was limited as the result of the academic and training demands made on them. The cadets weren't as big or quite as quick or athletic as the players we competed against, so Bob and I did a lot of tinkering and experimenting in searching of ways to level the playing court. He allowed me to put in some of the pressure defense we ran at Kansas, and we came up with a matchup zone that I later took with me to North Carolina. We ran a ball control offense, which included much cutting, screening, and intricate passing, but we also ran the fast break at every available opportunity. It was a basketball laboratory—and great fun. The Air Force Academy under Bob Spear upset many nationally prominent teams.

Bob always encouraged me to go to basketball clinics to learn what other great coaches were teaching. I spent an entire afternoon in 1956 talking with Oklahoma State coaching great Henry Iba. After I asked him a question, he said he remembered me from playing at Kansas and invited me to his room to talk basketball. When that session ended, my notebook was full of notes about Mr. Iba's excellent, sagging man-to-man defense and his ball control offense. While we later preferred the opposite approach at North Carolina—pressure defense and a fast-paced offense— Mr. Iba's style was highly successful. Later, when I was Frank McGuire's assistant at North Carolina, I was privileged to know Long Island University's legendary coach Clair Bee, who taught me some basketball as well as invited me to contribute to the basketball book he was writing for his close friend Coach McGuire.

After I left the Air Force Academy in 1958 to become the assistant coach at North Carolina, Frank McGuire was my head coach for three seasons. He was very much into the psychology of athletics and was quite adept at motivating his players. He had never studied psychology; it just came naturally to him. He also had a keen eye for judging talent, one reason he was such an accomplished recruiter.

Of course my coaching philosophy probably has been most influenced by the men who were my assistant coaches during my thirty-six-year tenure as head coach at North Carolina. We spent hundreds and hundreds of hours together watching tapes, planning practices, working on the practice floor, and just talking basketball.

I took a little bit from all these people and others as well. So what does it all amount to, everything I took away and everything I added? Like most people, I never gave much thought to defining my personal philosophy, but I admit I was stubborn about what I believed to be right. Basketball is a beautiful game, and I had a vision of how it should be played and

how our program should be run. That vision involved our coming together as a team, putting team ahead of self, first and foremost, and being
smart and hardworking.

We were tough on our freshmen, as you'll read in a later chapter on recruiting. We believed we had to take them out of the bad habits they had
formed in high school, often with their coaches' blessing. It was under-
standable because the young men we're talking about were almost always
the best players on their high school teams. In ridding them of bad habits,
we tore them down in order to build them back up.

Unlike business offices, where the same staffs might be together for
several years or longer, college basketball teams change each year. In my
thirty-six years as North Carolina's head coach we never had the same
team return. The addition or subtraction of just one player can have an
enormous impact on a team's chemistry, not to mention its ability. With
input from my assistant coaches, I decided what offense, defense, and
overall plan we would try to use with each particular team. We made adjustments each year, depending on our personnel, and an annual goal was
to disguise our team's weaknesses and accentuate its strengths.

For instance, our 1996 team was extremely young. Rasheed Wallace
and Jerry Stackhouse, with my full blessing, had decided to sign lucrative
NBA contracts after they completed their sophomore seasons in 1995.
(Jerry has since earned his college degree, while Rasheed is still working
on his.) It was a wise decision for Jerry and Rasheed. Nevertheless, their
departure left us with a lot of holes. We had three freshmen in our top six
players.

We decided that our best approach for that particular team was to sim-
plify things. We didn't put in our complicated defensive traps and presses
until much later in the season, and not all of them even then. Offensively
we generally believed in a freelance approach, by which I do *not* just mean
going one-on-one. Our freelance offense had few rules, but it was not easy
for young players to grasp because it involved much moving without the

ball and screening. It may seem counterintuitive, but for this young team, we put in a more structured offense.

Our coaches and players preferred to pressure and trap on defense and to push the ball on offense. The style was fun to teach and play. But when the personnel wasn't suited for that style, we didn't hesitate to change to something the players could do better, although we always looked to fast break for easy baskets. That was one of our staples. We didn't fear change even in the midst of the season. When your goal is to put your players in the best position possible for them to be successful, there's a time to be stubborn and a time to be flexible.

In teaching our players, I tried to concentrate on the process rather than the result. I think it's the best way to teach. If a coach starts out on the first day of practice talking about winning, that approach can actually get in the way of winning.

Building a team takes patience and planning. We went through the process step by step, no shortcuts. We repeated drills until good habits were established. We stressed sound fundamentals. We drove home the point that basketball is a team game and the team members need to depend on one another. We talked about the soundness of putting the team first. We taught the players not to dwell on the consequences of failure. We valued each possession, and I encouraged the players not to look at the scoreboard until it became smart to do so with a few minutes left, although that was difficult for them to do. We went to great lengths to reward unselfish behavior, and we profusely praised those acts that we wanted to see repeated.

Of course confidence helps, no matter what you're trying to accomplish, but false confidence and hubris don't pay off. I've seen basketball players strut around and act cocky when in reality they are scared out of their wits. I wanted our players to be quietly confident. False praise as a weapon to build confidence? I didn't believe in it. Certainly I wasn't going to tell a poor rebounder that he was doing a good job rebounding. That is more manipulation than effective teaching. A person isn't going to wake up one morning and suddenly become confident. It's not that easy. Words aren't going to do the trick. Confidence must be earned. It takes time, work, dedication—on the part of the teacher and the pupil.

A former college player told me his college coach had belittled his shooting for four years, admonishing him, "Don't shoot unless you have a layup because you're the worst shooter I've ever coached." During the player's senior season his team was down one point to a conference opponent with one second to play, and he was on the foul line to shoot a one-and-one that would decide the game's outcome. During a time-out called by the opposing bench the player's coach suddenly told him a different story: "You're the best shooter I've ever seen. There's no doubt in my mind you're going to knock these shots in. Just go out there and be confident."

The player took his place on the foul line and looked over at his bench. He saw his coach slumped over in his chair, eyes closed, fingers on both hands crossed. The player burst out laughing. His first shot was so hard that it bounced off the backboard and into the basket. He also made the second shot to help his team win by one point. In practice the next day the coach said, "Nice going last night, but I still don't want you shooting anything but layups."

Confidence can be as fragile as an eggshell. Coaches can't talk players into being confident, although praising players when praise is deserved can help them become more confident. But they can do the reverse if they tear players down with criticism. Then self-confidence may never bloom. It's entirely possible that I was too critical, especially early in my coaching career. I was too much of a perfectionist. At some point I realized that our execution wasn't going to be perfect. Basketball is not a game of perfection. Mistakes are part of it.

Thorough preparation does wonders for anyone's confidence. We tried to put our players through every situation in practice that they might experience in a game. For instance, we would give our second team a fifteen-point lead with five minutes on the clock to see if our starters could go to their "hurry-up" offense and overcome it. The first team pressed and gambled on defense, shot three-pointers on offense, and if it missed, it fouled the defensive rebounder. (A team's best rebounders usually are not its best foul shooters.)

When a situation came up like this in a game, I could say to them, "We've done this before in practice. Let's go out and repeat it now." In such a situation, players can gain confidence from their coach because they have been prepared to face it.

Hard work that results in success equals confidence. That's the only formula I have. I know of no other way. That's why bad practices really got me down. I never really learned how to handle them. "What did I do wrong to make us go backward the way we did today?" I would ask myself.

Basketball was extremely important to the young men who played it at North Carolina. It had to be in order for them to have worked and practiced as hard as they had over their early years to reach the level of excellence that resulted in scholarships to a great university and basketball program. I tried to impress on them, however, that they couldn't make basketball their entire lives. Some perspective was called for. They all knew their academics came first, even though at times basketball seemed more important. There was much more to their lives than basketball, and we tried to emphasize that. I wanted them to be actively involved in the student body and to have friends who were nonathletes.

My staff and I worked hard to give the players their best chance to succeed. The by-product of this is loyalty, which early on became a cornerstone of our program. Players and coaches, managers and secretaries. We all looked out for one another. We depended on one another. There was a trust there that no one wanted to violate. The feeling of not wanting to let your teammate down is a powerful one. It's an important part of building a team.

This manifested itself in every game, but especially on the road. Of the thousands of people in the building—and we usually played before capacity crowds—only the ones with "North Carolina" printed on their blue jerseys wanted us to be successful. The fact that we won so often made us the big game on the schedule of just about every team we played, especially those in our own league, the Atlantic Coast Conference (ACC). North Carolina was everybody's rival.

Getting to the top is difficult; staying there, or near there, for many years running is even harder. It takes a special group of players to handle that pressure. We prepared for that pressure by the way we practiced. We were greatly concerned about how we would play and much less concerned about what our opponent would do. If we did what we were supposed to do, the end result usually pleased us. There was no substitute for this hard work. There wasn't going to be any magic five minutes just before the game, no spellbinding pep talk from me that would catapult us to victory.

As our players gathered in the dressing room before games, they didn't see me until five or six minutes before they went out to warm up. I came in to go over the individual matchups that had been written on the chalkboard by an assistant coach, informing our players whom they would guard. We quickly reviewed what we wanted to accomplish. Then I would say something to them like "You've worked hard for this moment. We've prepared well. Now let's go out and play with great effort, unselfishly, and make smart decisions."

Some coaches say they could tell if their teams were ready to play by the way their players acted in the dressing room before the game or how they were at the pregame meal four hours before tip-off. I never could figure that out. I had teams play well that were loud at the pregame meal, and others that played well when they were quiet and focused at pregame.

At home and away we protected the sanctity of our locker room. It was for our players, coaches, managers—our basketball family. The media made many requests over the years to be allowed into our locker room to tape our pregame or halftime talks. We had chancellors of the university ask for permission to come in and speak. A North Carolina governor once wanted to come in to observe what we did in our last-minute pregame preparation. All those requests were denied. I didn't want our players looking up to see a stranger in their locker room, and certainly not a stranger holding a television camera. If the president of the United States had asked permission to visit with us in our locker room before the game or at halftime, I would have denied it. The North Carolina locker room was for the players. They were the most important people in our program, no exceptions.

I didn't plan special things for halftime. It all depended on how the first half had gone. My halftime sessions were mostly impromptu. Certainly, if the team hadn't played well, I didn't praise their execution. I analyzed what had transpired in the first half. I tried to keep it positive, especially for road games. It was hard enough on the players without my dealing in the minutiae of their mistakes. The crowd was against them, the other team was fired up, and it was time for us to band together as one. We talked about keeping our poise. Our reserves were really active on the bench, cheering for the players on the court. It was all part of supporting one another in tough times.

If we had particularly good senior leadership, as we usually did, and we had played poorly in the first half, I might cut my talk short and say to them before departing, "You guys get together and decide how you're going to play better. It's your team."

Our players usually responded with superb play on the road in front of hostile crowds. We won as a team or lost as a team. There was no finger-pointing. I might have plenty of critical things to say to a player in a team or individual meeting. It might be tough criticism. But I would never criticize a player in public. A leader should take the blame for losses and give the players credit for victories. I strongly believe that.

After a game my responsibility was to my players. After shaking hands with the opposing coach and some of his players, I ran to the dressing room. It was a time for me to be with my players and assistant coaches. Sometimes a television producer intercepted me on the way to the dressing room and said his network wanted me for a quick interview. I almost always declined. TV didn't understand, but my players did.

You seldom saw North Carolina players arguing with one another or scolding one another on the court. Now, a senior might speak up if he saw something he didn't like. But it was done in the right way. I didn't embarrass them publicly, and they didn't point fingers at one another. It was our cast-the-first-stone theory.

Even though I came out of college accredited to teach high school math, I wasn't hung up on statistics. We used them to prove a point, but seldom for any other purpose. They can be very misleading. For example, if a player was credited with three steals, that might look good on a stat sheet, but he could have played poorly on defense. He could have gambled three or four other times and failed to get a steal and given his opponent easy baskets. That kind of defensive inconsistency wasn't good for the team, no matter what statistics indicated.

I was interested in how many points North Carolina scored, but not in individual scoring. Let's say an opposing player took thirty shots and made nine. He led the game in scoring and might have been named player of the game by television announcers. But that shooting percentage—nine shots made out of thirty taken—was good for North Carolina. We didn't care how many points an opposing player scored as long as his shooting percentage was low. Our coaches graded every possession of each game. It was tedious work and took more than five hours to grade game tapes, but we thought it was important. We rewarded unselfish acts that helped the team: good defense, setting effective screens, diving on the floor in pursuit of the ball, assists, blocked shots, deflected passes. We didn't even want the official game statistics kept for the media to be given to our players because they stressed points scored over all other aspects of the game.

We kept many statistics in practice. Our managers recorded three-point shots attempted and made in each practice. We did the same for foul shots. We wanted to know who our best shooters were over an extended period of time. This was our way of using solid information to guide our strategies.

I believed in being honest with our players. I wasn't going to con them, that was for sure. Sometimes it meant saying things that I didn't enjoy. I told one player after his sophomore season that he might want to transfer to another school where he'd have a better chance to play. He was a terrific young man who had been an outstanding football player in high school and had been offered scholarships by some big-time football programs. His love was basketball, though, and he had accepted our scholarship offer after we scouted him and liked his potential. However, things had not gone that well for him in basketball during his freshman and sophomore seasons. I knew how competitive he was and was concerned that he might be unhappy sitting on our bench for four years. "You're great for our team, and we'd love for you to stay," I told him before he left Chapel Hill for summer vacation after his sophomore year. "But you're our thirteenth man, and I don't see things improving much for you as far as playing time goes. Think about it for a week, and let me know what you decide. We'll support your decision either way."

He called me in a week and said he was going to return to North Carolina. I was delighted. He spent hours and hours each day that summer working on his shot, his ballhandling, all his basketball skills. I couldn't believe my eyes when practice opened on October 15. He was vastly improved. He won a starting position for us and made All-ACC first team before he graduated. He also played professionally in the old American Basketball Association.

I learned from my players too. I never penciled in a starting lineup during our planning work in the summer. That would have been unfair to players who had worked hard in the off-season and improved. It's amazing how much some young people can improve from one year to the next.

I was always excited to open practice on October 15. Our players were fired up and anxious to get started. They started out even in my eyes. The six weeks of preseason practice was my favorite time of the year. It was a special time to teach and build a team from scratch. Our team chemistry as well as other important elements was determined during those six weeks.

To sum up, if you asked me to define my coaching and leadership style, I'd describe myself as an open-minded dictator. My basketball philosophy boils down to six words: Play hard; play together; play smart.

PLAYER PERSPECTIVES

Charles McNairy,
class of 1997, M.B.A. student at Harvard

How was Carolina basketball able to reach a level of excellence year after year? The answer lies in Coach Smith's philosophy of life, which is one of personal decency, of treating people equally, of embracing learning and change, and of expecting excellence. Coach believes that all people are created equal, and that is the foundation of the way he treats people. Basketball was an extension of his philosophy of life, and he used it to serve as one giant learning experience for himself and his players.

Coach Smith's personal and basketball philosophies connected with us as players. He believed nothing was as bad or as good as it seemed. He prepared his players for every possible late-game situation, and he expected discipline from us in learning the fundamentals.

We knew as players that he and his coaching staff always gave total effort in coaching and preparing us, so we prepared and worked in a like manner. In the process, he made the game incredibly enjoyable. It didn't matter if a player performed well or poorly; Coach's respect for him remained constant. He never made criticism personal. He preferred positive reinforcement as a tool to influence behavior rather than condemnation. The by-product was a more confident player who had a deep loyalty to the team, the program, and the coach. It's hard to put my finger on exactly why this is, but there's something about him that makes people associated with him try very hard not to let the program down.

North Carolina's game against the great Tim Duncan and Wake Forest in Winston-Salem on January 28, 1995, is a prime example of Coach Smith's ability to get the best performance from his players. Carolina basketball had staged many comebacks under Coach Smith's direction, but this game was different because we couldn't make a shot. For the longest time we simply couldn't score. We got good shots and missed them. We had two different stretches in the second half when we went five minutes without scoring. How could we rally against a great team if we couldn't score? Coach Smith figured it out.

We trailed, 55–45, with 5:45 to play. Making up ten points in a short time against a terrific opponent is a monumental task if you can't make a shot. Wake's capacity crowd of nearly fifteen thousand fans made so much noise that the building seemed to shake beneath our feet. Their students had left their seats and encircled the court, to be ready for the victory celebration that seemed just minutes away.

We'd get the deficit down to six, and Wake Forest would answer. It was a very frustrating day for us. During a time-out Coach Smith, always encouraging, told us that if we cut the deficit to fewer than ten points with four minutes to go, we'd be fine. We did it and trailed by 57–51 with 3:04 to play. During a television time-out Coach Smith told us that "we're in good position." I recall thinking that being six points behind with three minutes to play, on the road against the sixteenth-ranked team in the nation, didn't seem like such favorable odds. Then Coach told us he'd rather be in our shoes than Wake's, and he added that we should enjoy the rest of the game. "Have some fun," as he often said.

We still trailed, 61–57, with only thirty-nine seconds to play, when Wake Forest Coach Dave Odom took time-out to set his defense and secure the victory against his school's number-one rival. The entire Wake Forest crowd was standing and making so much noise that it was deafening. On our bench Coach Smith designed a double screen to free Dante Calabria, one of our best perimeter shooters, so he could take a three-point shot. One of the things Coach taught us was to keep our poise and have options if the original plan broke down, as this one had. Coach's double screen got Calabria wide open as designed, but by mistake, one of our players swung the ball to the wrong side of the court. Making the best out of what could have been a horrible situation, point guard Jeff McInnis threw the ball inside to Jerry Stackhouse, who scored, was fouled, and made the free throw. We got our three points, but by going to an option off a broken play. Wake Forest led by 61–60 with twenty-six seconds left. Our shoes suddenly felt more comfortable.

Coach Smith called time-out to set our defense and to make some substitutions. He put Pearce Landry, a valuable substitute and determined defender, into the game for starter Donald Williams with orders not to let Wake Forest star guard Randolph Childress, the team's best free throw shooter, touch the ball. He put freshman Shammond Williams, who had great quickness, into the game to replace McInnis. "Let's not let them get the ball inbounds," he told our players as they left the bench to return to the court. Landry covered Childress, a defensive ploy he practiced every day during simulated late-game situations. When Wake Forest couldn't get the ball inbounds within the allotted five seconds, it became our ball. It was a long five seconds too. After the game, in talking to the media, Coach Smith got that point across by saying, "We did play six seconds of good defense there." Did I mention that he could sometimes be as subtle as a train derailment?

Coach Smith took another time-out to get Williams and McInnis back in the game. He didn't designate one man to shoot, but instead told those two to penetrate the defense and take the ball to the basket or to pass to one of our talented inside players, Stackhouse or Rasheed Wallace. McInnis penetrated and passed to Williams, who made a shot from twelve feet. Our comeback was complete. The stunned Wake Forest crowd was left standing in silence.

Playing for Coach Smith completely changed my approach to handling adversity. Whether we won or lost, he taught us that we should embrace the process of testing ourselves and have fun doing it. We believed that we could achieve the improbable, and even if we failed, he made us feel that our dignity and self-respect would remain intact. It was one reason his players performed consistently at such high levels of excellence.

The older I get, the more I understand the effect that Coach Smith's leadership has had on my life. His character, the respect he holds for all people regardless of their status in society, his eagerness to learn new things, and his sheer enjoyment in competing all have affected the way I approach my life.

When I make a mistake, I know I should "recognize it, admit it, learn from it, and then forget it." It was one of Coach Smith's Thoughts for the Day, things unrelated to basketball that he expected us to remember and be able to recite if called upon. He gave them to us each day before practice. If I'm tempted to judge another person, I recall another of those thoughts: "I will not judge another until I have walked in his moccasins for a fortnight."

If ever faced with a daunting task that appears to have a high chance of failure, I think back to Coach Smith's message that regardless of whether the goal is achieved, my worth as a person is constant and I should relish the challenge of testing myself. Each of these truths not only affected me deeply while I played for Coach Smith but continue to impact my life.

When things appear dark, I will think back to that January

night in 1995 when our coach directed us to an improbable come-back victory.

Woody Coley,

class of 1977, now senior managing director,
Trammell Crow Company, Orlando, Florida

When Coach Smith spoke, he expected your full attention. Anything less resulted in a reminder that not paying attention could affect the outcome of a game.

His behavior during time-outs in close games was a lifetime lesson. Sure, he'd discuss the upcoming sequence of events and what would be required to make them successful, but he always started with the bigger picture. If we were down three points with a minute to play, he'd enter our huddle with a smile. "Isn't this fun?" he'd ask. "Just remember, if your first business venture fails, you can come back from it just as we've done here in the second half."

Then his tone would become completely positive and confident: "When Kuester makes the shot . . ." Listing all the dramatic come-back victories directed by Coach Smith would fill a long chapter in this book. He trained us to assume that we could accomplish anything, and it is a lesson that lives within us all to this day.

BUSINESS PERSPECTIVE BY JERRY BELL

I give talks on leadership and team building to all sorts of companies around the world, and I try to do as much listening as talking. While every walk of life has its own unique issues, the elements of successful leadership remain remarkably consistent across the entire range of organizations, business-related and nonbusiness-related alike. Dean Smith's success as a leader is particularly widely relevant because his program taught as its core that the fundamentals of good basketball are the fundamentals of good character.

But I'm not Dean Smith! Isn't it easier to learn how to diagram a trick play than to develop character? Sure it is, but if you can apply his philosophies in your own work and aren't looking for shortcuts or quick, easy solutions, Dean Smith's program has much to offer you.

All great leaders know you can't just talk about good character; you have to live it. To become an extraordinary leader, you must build your own personality skills. This comes first. You must be what you want your followers to become. No shortcuts, no magic, no easy formula. Effective leaders build themselves fundamentally. They develop healthy personality characteristics. They love people, care about them, are interested in them, and enjoy interacting with them. Instead of avoiding people, they move toward them. They become good psychologists. They learn to work well with all kinds of people.

Good leaders don't fool themselves either. They can work with a large variety of people, but not with everyone. Some bosses may say of someone they don't like, "Well, I don't like him or enjoy being around him, but I can make myself work with him. After all, I don't have to go out to dinner with him." Don't deceive yourself because that line of thinking usually doesn't work well. A leader doesn't want to see such a person, much less work with him. If the boss doesn't like employees well enough to enjoy going to dinner with them, he or she shouldn't hire those people in the first place. Running a business or a profession is hard enough when the boss likes his or her employees. Why complicate matters? It's almost impossible to respect someone whom you don't like or don't respect.

The greatest leaders I've known are absolutely devoted to their people. There's no way to fake it. They put their people in the center of their thinking. They treat their employees with dignity and respect, and they don't embarrass them or berate them. Even though they have a knack of bringing out the best in their employees, conflicts still arise, and turf battles surface. It's inevitable when you're leading human beings. Effective leaders know how to referee these conflicts and render fair, quick decisions. They quickly pick up clues that allow them to anticipate problems and deal with them before they rage out of control and damage their companies. They're able to do this because they have humility and effective communication skills.

A leader won't accomplish much, or even be happy, unless he or she is willing to compete. Leaders should love competition and not be stifled by it. They must give everything they have to achieve their personal and companies' goals, as long as it's done with honesty and integrity and within the rules. Good leaders enjoy putting themselves on the line. Instead of backing off and becoming cautious, they raise their own level of work when the competition raises its. They have a passion to succeed, but they don't believe winning or losing defines their worth as human beings. While winning is the goal in business, effective leaders understand that some losses are natural. They don't give up because of failures. In fact they are uncommonly resilient and become more determined to succeed the next time. Setbacks do not devastate them.

Modesty is also a trait of good leaders. They accept criticism and understand their limitations; it helps immunize them against flattery and the egomania that success can breed. Good leaders love sharing credit for success and understand why it's important. They routinely deflect credit to others, downplay their own accomplishments, and admit to their mistakes. They take blame for the losses and give employees credit for the victories. Effective leaders do not believe that they're more important or valuable than others. They communicate this by their actions, treating others with respect, sharing credit, being able to laugh at themselves, and resisting any urge to brag. Modest leaders put their colleagues and employees at ease. It's no coincidence that Dean Smith is among the most modest men I've ever met.

2

PLAY HARD;
PLAY TOGETHER;
PLAY SMART

I never went into a season as North Carolina's head coach thinking we'd just plug things into the previous year's plan and duplicate our- selves. As I said, we never had the same team return, and there were any number of other variables from one year to the next. We couldn't have had the long run of success that we enjoyed if we'd been too stubborn to change and come up with new ideas and different ways to play the game.

I will repeat this several times in this book: Don't fear change. Some- times change can refresh a stale team; sometimes it's mandated by chang- ing personnel; sometimes the rules of the game change. We adapted each year to hide our weaknesses and accentuate our strengths.

Although we didn't have a system at North Carolina, we certainly had a philosophy. We believed in it strongly and didn't stray very far from it. It pretty much stayed the same from my first year as head coach. It was our mission statement, our strategic plan, our entire approach in a nutshell: Play hard; play smart; play together.

Hard meant with effort, determination, and courage; *together* meant unselfishly, trusting your teammates, and doing everything possible not to let them down; *smart* meant with good execution and poise, treating each possession as if it were the only one in the game.

That was our philosophy; we believed that if we kept our focus on those tenets, success would follow. Our North Carolina players seldom heard me or my assistants talk about winning. Winning would be the by-product of the process. There could be no shortcuts.

Making winning the ultimate goal usually isn't good teaching. Tom Osborne, the great former football coach of the University of Nebraska, said that making winning the goal can actually get in the way of winning. I agree. So many things happened in games that were beyond our control: the talent and experience of the teams; bad calls by officials; injuries; bad luck.

By sticking to our philosophy, we asked realistic things from our players. A player could play hard. He could play unselfishly and do things to help his teammates succeed. He could play intelligently if we did the job in practice as coaches. We measured our success by how we did in those areas.

When we put these elements together, the players had fun, one of my goals as their coach. I wanted our players to enjoy the experience of play-ing basketball for North Carolina. Each player on our team knew he was important. Each did a terrific job of sharing the ball, which also made the game enjoyable for more players. All won and lost as a team.

Of course it is easier to talk about playing hard, playing smart, and playing together than it is to do all three. It begins by the recruiting of un-selfish players, who subscribe to the philosophy of team over individual. In a summer physical education class I once taught at the Air Force Academy there was one young man who shot every time he touched the ball. Exas-perated from watching him, I pulled his four teammates off the court. He asked who would throw the ball inbounds to him. "You understand that it takes at least one more player," I said to him.

PLAYING HARD

Maybe a player wasn't the fastest, the tallest, or the most athletic person on the court. In the course of any given game that was out of his control. But each of them could control the effort with which he played. "Never let anyone play harder than you," I told them. "That is part of the game you can control." If another team played harder than we did, we had no excuse for it. None. We worked on it in every practice. If a player didn't give maximum effort, we dealt with it right then. We stopped practice and had the entire team run sprints for the offending player. We played a style of basketball that was physically exhausting and made it impossible for a player to go full throttle for forty minutes. When he got tired, he flashed the tired signal, a raised fist, and we substituted for him. He could put himself back in the game once he had rested. We didn't want tired players on the court because they usually tried to rest on defense. That wouldn't work in our plan. Therefore we watched closely in practice and in games to make sure players played hard. If they slacked off, it was important to catch them and get them out of the game, or if it occurred in practice, to have the entire team run.

PLAYING TOGETHER

One of the first things I did at the beginning of preseason practice was to spell out for our players the importance of team play. Basketball is a game that counts on togetherness. I pointed out that seldom, if ever, did the nation's leading scorer play on a ranked team. He certainly didn't play on a championship team. I made them understand that our plan would fall apart if they didn't take care of one another: set screens; play team defense; box out; pass to the open man. One man who failed to do his job unselfishly could undermine the efforts of the four other players on the court.

PLAYING SMART

We taught and drilled until we made the things we wanted to see become habits. The only way to have a smart team is to have one that is fundamentally sound. We didn't skimp on fundamentals. We worked on them hard in practice and repeated them until they were down cold. We didn't introduce something and then move away from it before we had nailed it. Our entire program was built around practice, which we will talk more about in a later chapter. Practice, competitive games, late-game situations, and my relationship with our players are what I've missed most since I retired from coaching. We expected our team to execute well and with precision. If we practiced well and learned, we could play smart. It was another thing we could control.

PLAYER PERSPECTIVE

Steve Previs,
class of 1972, former ABA player,
now trader, Jeffries International Ltd., London

Playing hard: The essence was summed up by Coach Smith when he said, "Always play as hard as you can. Years from now, when you look back on your career, it would be terrible to think, 'If I had only given a little bit more or sprinted harder, we might have won the game.'" When I heard him speak those words, a chill went down my spine. I've carried that thought with me ever since. Every time I feel myself coasting, it pops into my mind, and off I go again.

Playing smart: Coach Smith could accept physical errors but not mental ones. The preparation, planning, and attention to detail that went into playing smart would astound many people. It took many forms. Take just one, passing the ball up the court instead of dribbling it. With our passing game offense that might entail ten passes on one possession to force the opponent's defense to move until we broke it down. Another was a thorough understanding of the rules. We knew the rules and applied them to our advantage.

Our defense was complicated, and the players had to be smart to learn the multiple defenses that Coach Smith used. He taught us to see man and ball but told us that if necessary, we could lose sight of the ball but not of the man we were guarding. How many times have you seen a man-to-man defense break down because the defender lost sight of his man, who cut to the basket for an easy score?

Playing together: This was the secret to the success of Carolina basketball under Coach Smith. When our class arrived at Carolina in the fall of 1968, our freshman team would have averaged 180 points a game if the six of us had matched our high school scoring averages. Something had to give because that obviously wasn't going to happen.

We learned to play together, unselfishly. No one cared about individual scoring averages or newspaper headlines. The important thing was to play together as a unit to beat the other team. It meant pointing to a teammate to thank him for a good pass that led to a score, taking a charge when you knew you were going to get slammed, passing up a good shot so a teammate could get a better one, diving for loose balls.

It was all about "we," not "me." It was the thread that wove us together. We respected one another and knew we were part of one of the greatest fraternities in the world. We were a unique family, and nothing could drive us apart, certainly not the opposition.

Coach Smith knew that when he asked us to play hard, play smart, and play together, he was giving us a mission that we could control. We could control how hard we played, with how much intelligence, and we could do it unselfishly. It's a philosophy brilliant in its simplicity.

BUSINESS PERSPECTIVE

A leader's job is to develop committed followers. Great leaders, like Coach Smith, inspire their teams to believe so deeply in their mission that they become immersed in what they're doing. They work hard naturally. Average leaders inspire their subordinates to do just enough to get by, just enough to get raises or keep their jobs. They become "transactional employees"; they see their jobs as commodities, so they become focused on the minimal level of acceptable performance, on what they have to do to get paid. Such employees view extra effort as "unfair." If they are offered more pay elsewhere, better "deals," they leave. Bad leaders destroy their followers' sense of commitment.

WORKING HARD

A high-level manager at Toyota leaving his office at the factory one Saturday afternoon saw a man prowling around in a lot full of new cars that were about to be shipped out to dealers. Suspicious, the manager walked closer and saw that the man was examining windshield wipers. It turned out that he was the production worker who had installed the wipers on those particular cars. During the night he had wondered if he had made a mistake on one car, and he had come in on one of his days off to make certain he had done his job properly. Any leader's dream: a team member whose commitment to his work drove him to put in this extra time without a second thought.

But a sense of balance is vital. The lesson to draw from Dean Smith's "Work harder" isn't necessarily to work longer hours but to keep your focus during the hours you work and to manage your time and priorities effectively while you work. Not every player wants to be the CEO because of the all-consuming nature of the job. One manager expressed concern to me that she had an employee who didn't seem to want to be promoted. He worked from 9:00 A.M. to 5:00 P.M. He arrived at work on time, stayed until he was supposed to leave, and then left. When I asked the manager what kind of work the man was turning out, she said, "Fantastic. He's a great employee who works very hard." My recommendation to the manager was to enjoy it. There was no problem. This worker was succeeding. You do not have to be promoted to succeed.

I know of a basketball player at Carolina who was a tremendously impressive individual. He was smart, tough, competitive, talented—a winner. At best, basketball was his fourth priority behind his faith, family, and schoolwork. But in the two hours he spent at practice or in a game nobody worked or competed harder. He gave himself completely to basketball and to his team during those hours. At times managers might need to say to employees who are searching for meaning in their work and lives, "Listen, I'm not asking you to put this job ahead of your faith, your family, or even your hobbies. But I am asking you to commit to giving us everything you have for forty hours a week." Not all employees are alike. Some may not want to be promoted from jobs that they enjoy. This particular basketball player probably could have made a lot of money playing professional basketball, but he decided not to have his name entered in the NBA draft. He chose med school instead and is now a successful doctor.

I break down the idea of working hard into three main components:

1. Pure effort: It may seem paradoxical, but it's the people who bring the same great effort to work every day who don't burn out. If you know you're giving your all, you're much less likely to overrev when you take on greater responsibility, to risk burning yourself out with too much work and too many re-

sponsibilities, destroying your family life, hurting your health, and losing your love for what you're doing. Keep the needle at 100 percent, but know that no matter how great the pressure, it won't go higher than that. Keep balance and perspective.

2. Concentration: In a given day we all move from one issue to another at blinding speed. You go from discussing a problem with a key employee to presenting the boss with a new budget. Then it could be time to prepare a sales pitch for an important client, but first, suddenly, a dissatisfied customer needs attention. You must stay in the present and focus on each task, one at a time. Don't jump ahead to another problem before you finish with the one at hand.

3. Self-discipline: Managers must work until they finish a project. That means having the patience to repeat things until they are done correctly. Usually it's the dreary 5 percent of the wrap-up that's the hardest.

The willingness to delay gratification, to do the things you don't want to do, to work long hours when long hours are needed: These are the habits of mind of great leaders. These habits are formed early in life. That is why it's critical for parents not to make their children's lives too easy by solving their problems for them or letting them escape responsibility.

WORKING TOGETHER

Not all businesses require the same degree of teamwork. *Working together* usually means one of three kinds of interdependence in the business world.

First, there's pooled interdependence, in which independent units collectively form a whole without having to work with one another—members of a sales force organized by regions. Sales reps who work in San Francisco and in Chicago for the Northwestern

Mutual Life Insurance Company have a vested interest in the company's succeeding, but they seldom see or talk to anyone from the other office. Since they don't depend on each other, not much time should be spent asking the two groups to work together.

Second, there's sequential interdependence, the dependence of one unit of a company on the work of another in order to do its own work. The classic example is an assembly line in an automobile factory. One person places the bumper on the car; then someone else bolts it to the car. The work is moderately interdependent, usually at the hand-off stage. It can usually be coordinated by technical processes. It calls for managerial coordination more than true teamwork.

Finally, there's reciprocal interdependence, wherein someone's actions directly impact another's, people depend on one another to produce effective work, and bad things happen if they don't work well together. A surgeon and an anesthetist must work together as a team in the operating room. Here's a true story: A patient was undergoing major surgery in a leading hospital in the Northeast when the surgeon and anesthetist began arguing. Their egos and turf wars fogged their brains to the point they forgot someone was on the operating table with his chest open. They became so angry that they began wrestling on the floor of the operating room. A nurse had to summon help to break up the fight. When personal interests override the team's, the results can be horrible.

Obviously, teamwork is most needed in areas where there is the highest level of reciprocal interdependence. The key to building teamwork is to hire the proper people and then to train them to believe completely in the concept of putting the team first.

Leaders must help their team members discover that the best way for each individual to succeed personally is by being a team player. Many companies preach teamwork and the importance of working together, but when it comes time for financial rewards, they are given on an individual basis. Unselfish behavior must be rewarded. I would award or average bonuses assigning 60 percent on a person's individual performance and 40 percent on how well he or she contributed to the team and worked with their fellow employees. If a company is going to convince its employees to work together, it needs to walk the walk itself. Reward those who work together.

WORKING SMART

Most managers say, "I'm working incredibly long hours and still can't keep up with my workload. I can't work any harder than I'm working now, so what can I do?"

Work smarter. Begin by mastering the *external* environment. I've had to think a lot about why good businesses die. More than anything, they die because senior leaders have lost touch with the outside world. All the external factors that affect an organization can be divided into eight categories:

- Customers
- Competitors
- Technological changes
- Changing government regulations, laws, and rules governing the business
- Economic conditions and cycles
- Changes in cultural values, such as racial equality, women's rights, and the global economy
- Vendors and suppliers
- Stakeholders, including owners, stockholders, accounting partners, lawyers, and distributors

These eight elements change each year. Leaders must seek to understand changes in these domains and then alter their organization to stay synchronized with new conditions. If a company doesn't change, it dies.

A second key to working smart is to build your people's talents so they build your business. You must delegate in order to have the time to devise new strategies, to look ahead.

A man in the Washington, D.C., area started a company in his garage eighteen years ago. He nurtured it and built it until it was doing eighty million dollars a year in sales. But he was stuck at this level. He worked sixteen-hour days, six and seven days a week, and strained his family relations and his health. Then he hit the wall. "I can't work harder," he said, "so how can I work smarter? How can I grow my business?"

My advice was for him to help his people become smarter so they could build the business. He had eight vice presidents in his company. He had to determine whether they had the talent and skills to get the company to where he wanted to take it. Three of the eight didn't. Two accepted other jobs in the company, and one left. Three new ones were hired to join the five who stayed in their jobs.

The owner spent four hours each month in one-on-one meetings with each vice president. He taught them how to run the business. He coached them to step back and think about the business, not just operate it. They brought problems to him, and together they solved them. He delegated, allowing his subordinates to use their full talents as managers. He worked fewer hours but accomplished more, and his happiness increased. As for the vice presidents, they said the days they spent with the owner were their most profitable and enjoyable of the month. Their commitment became deeper.

How did the company do once the owner made these changes? In five years, annual sales went from $80 million to $380 million, with a corresponding increase in earnings.

Key lesson: Spend prime time to meet with key people. Leaders spend too much time working and not enough time thinking. They should delegate more to create more. Work on the important things first; your people and their skills are the important things.

3

WINNING

Our goal each season was to win the NCAA championship. We planted that seed within our players without dwelling on the ultimate goal. I certainly didn't meet the team on the first day of practice and proclaim, "We're going to win it all." We had much work to do before we were ready to dwell on a championship or even talk about one. I knew it, and so did the players.

To get to where we wanted to be as a team in April, we had a process to go through. We knew it would be long, and we knew it wouldn't be easy at any step. We also knew we couldn't afford to sidestep any of the issues that we needed to face to make us a good team.

The best way to win is to make it a by-product of the process. In any competition, the participants are better off if they get their minds off the final outcome and onto a ritual. For example, when one of our players went to the foul line late in a close game, I wanted him to be thinking about his ritual, not about the consequences of missing. From the mid-1960s on I asked each player to have a ritual on the foul line. It didn't have to be uniform throughout the team. I encouraged each player to develop his own.

One player might decide to bounce the ball three times before shooting; another might not dribble it at all. I just wanted them to do the same thing each time they went to the foul line. Their minds would be on the ritual, not the outcome. It helped relieve the pressure of the moment.

After Ireland golfer Paul McGinley sank a difficult ten-foot putt to clinch the tense 2002 Ryder Cup for the Europeans over the favored team from the United States, his celebration seemed to be delayed. That was because he had concentrated so completely on his routine that it took a second or two for the result of his successful putt to register with him. A reporter asked McGinley if he had thought about the consequences of missing the putt. "Oh, absolutely not," the Irishman replied. "Had I done that, I wouldn't have been able to take the putter back. I just concentrated on my routine." He certainly didn't let his mind wander off in the direction of reminding him, "Hey, Paul, remember, there are millions around the world watching this putt on television."

At least McGinley got to hit his putt in front of a crowd of respectful spectators, most of whom wished him well. They also were ghostly silent as he aimed his putter and fired. So, if it was necessary for him to follow a routine to help in getting his mind off the consequences, imagine how important it is for a twenty-year-old college student who is on the foul line with twenty thousand people screaming and otherwise trying to distract him and maybe millions more watching on television.

It is not easy, even for world-class players. Most need help to calm their nerves. Many amateur golfers who've faced three-foot putts to win five-dollar bets probably know what I'm talking about. When a lot is on the line, rituals can help. Concern yourself with the process, not the result.

It's extremely important to handle success, or winning, correctly. After all, when things are going well and the team is winning, it's easy to overlook mistakes. Some say winning cures all ills. Maybe so, but winning can also make us fall into the trap of overlooking mistakes. "Hey, Jack didn't box out on four occasions, and our shot selection left much to be desired, but we won, so what's the big deal?"

Well, it is a big deal. Maybe we made some tough shots, and the other team missed some good ones, but we still won. Maybe we won even though we became sloppy on defense. Those mistakes could cost dearly in the future if not corrected. Don't let winning overshadow weaknesses or sloppy play. Make the corrections. I dwell more on it in the next chapter when I discuss handling losses, because it does seem true that we learn more from defeat than from victory.

I fought that hard too. My personal goal as head coach was to be pleased after a game, win or lose, as long as our team played well. I told our players not to be affected by the expectations set by outsiders. I never completely mastered this, that was for sure. In sports, we keep score, and others make judgments based on who does best on the scoreboard. I admit there were times when we played poorly and won and I still felt good. I was often upset after a sloppy win, but probably not as upset as I would have been if we had played well and lost.

It's not just the players who need to keep striving; that goes for coaches too. Did we play hard? Did we play together? Did we play smart? If the answers to those questions are yes, there should be satisfaction gained from a successful execution of the plan, regardless of whether it resulted in winning or losing.

It was fine with me if our teams were somewhat understated. I wanted our excellence on the court and our standing as representatives of the University of North Carolina to bespeak achievement. I saw no reason to shout it.

Maybe it was old-fashioned on my part, but I detested showboating. I didn't want a fancy pass when a simple one would work as well or better. I loved for our team to dunk, but I didn't want our players to stand around and scowl at opponents after doing so. I never thought it was cool to show up an opponent on purpose. Now, if they were unduly provoked—and that happened sometimes—that could be a different story. One of Michael Jordan's dunks against Maryland might be an example. Michael felt an injustice had been done against him by a Maryland player, so late in a game at College Park, he felt payback was justified. If you didn't see this particular dunk, I'm sorry I can't describe it to you. People still talk about it when Michael's UNC career is recalled. I believe it was the night that *windmill dunk* became part of basketball's lexicon.

Why strut around after making a basket? I told our players to try to act as if they'd done it before. One of my assistant coaches, Randy Wiel, had a great way of putting it: "A lion never roars after a kill." I'll take Randy's word for that.

One of our highly ranked teams, missing a starting player because of injury, was a decided underdog playing at Duke, which had a team ranked in the nation's top five. We played a sensational game and won. The players were understandably excited near the end of the game. I called them over to our bench and told them, "Finish this off with class—shake their hands and congratulate them—and then we'll celebrate in the dressing room with the door closed."

I wanted our players to be complimentary of the other team in their comments to reporters after the game. Shake hands with your opponent, and don't gloat.

We played against one player who never had anything to say to us after we beat his team. Then, one night after they defeated us, he showed up in our locker room to talk to us and shake hands. When he finally left, I cleared the room of everyone but the players and said, "Now, that's exactly how you shouldn't act after winning. If we win the next time we play them, let's make a point to see if he comes to our locker room to congratulate us." He didn't.

We wanted to win with class. It demonstrated good sportsmanship and was smart. After all, we might play the same team again before the season was over. Why make them angry?

PLAYER PERSPECTIVE

Bobby Jones,

class of 1974, former
NBA Defensive Player of the Year, currently
athletic director and head basketball coach,
Charlotte Christian School

Coach Smith seldom talked about winning. Instead he talked about the things we needed to do to be successful. He never got too high after winning or too low after a loss. He talked to us about what we did well and what we did poorly, regardless of the outcome of the game. He was focused on our daily improvement and used the games as a test to measure our progress.

One of the things I recall best about playing for him came after a heartbreaking loss to Wake Forest in the ACC tournament. He came up to me afterward and thanked me for my effort. That meant a lot to me, to be thanked by my coach after a disappointing loss.

BUSINESS PERSPECTIVE

Winning or losing in business is not typically as clearly defined as it is in college basketball. Company profits are often misleading indicators because there may be a significant difference between the current bottom line and a company's overall health. Profits frequently lag behind the truth. A company can be earning great profits and still be sick. On the other hand, a very strong company may not be doing very well on the bottom line, but in two years, with current policies in place, it will produce excellent profits.

I once asked the top officers of a large bank to apply their philosophies about winning in business to a sport and to write down how they would lead a sports team at these different levels of play: Little League; high school; college; the pros.

In coaching Little Leaguers, the executives said, they would teach the players to have fun, to play for the love of the game, to learn, and not to spend much time worrying about winning and losing. That would take care of itself. The key was to make the game enjoyable for the young people so that they would want to continue to participate.

At the high school level, they said, they would talk to the players mostly about improving, playing together as a team, learning the game, and not treating winning as a life-and-death matter. They would tell them to have fun and enjoy the experience of competition.

College sport, the managers said, was a more serious matter. It was on television; big crowds came to the game; newspapers covered the games; the coaches were focused on their careers. The executives said they would continue to talk to the players about having fun, giving their best, and playing as a team, but winning definitely would be introduced as an important part of the equation. The emphasis would be on performing the fundamentals well and playing their best, as the way to win.

At the professional level, their approach would be: "We have to win. Nothing else will do. The players are being paid to win."

Ironically, the approach the managers said they would take in coaching the Little League team—have fun, play for the love of the sport, learn and improve, play your best, and don't worry about winning or losing—probably would create the best chance of winning. Teaching players to focus on the process is the most effective way to produce victory.

Smart business leaders focus on factors that produce winning rather than on winning itself. They don't put their chief emphasis on quarterly per share earnings because to do so hurts their businesses. CEOs who focus completely on profits end up creating losses. One way for a company to lose money is for managers to focus so heavily on winning that the employees lose their focus on working effectively.

One company had forty-two sales reps in different areas of the United States. The vice president of sales, who lived and worked in San Francisco, held a telephone conference call every Friday at 9:00 P.M. eastern time with all the reps. It was a two-hour call in which each rep was asked to review his or her week. All the reps had to sit through the entire two hours listening to their counterparts describe their week, each of which invariably brought blunt criticism, acerbic side comments, and stern directives from this sales manager, followed by an inevitable "You can do much better than that."

The reps hated the call. It made them miserable, deflated their spirit, accomplished little, and sent them off to the weekend in a horrible frame of mind, not to mention that it kept them away from their families until 11:00 P.M. on Friday. Those reps weren't excited about going to work on Monday. This is a classic case of how to demoralize a sales staff and ruin a business. The sales reps complained to their manager's boss, who did nothing about it, resulting in the resignation of many of the best reps. Finally the sales manager was fired after two years of damaging the company. His campaign to win at all costs failed. If the top managers had listened to the feedback or collected organizational surveys, they would have removed this manager much earlier.

Another organization, a U.S.-based company with an extensive international presence, brought in a new CEO who was so focused on profits that he ignored the processes that led to profits. He told his management team, without consulting them, that their goal, and the goal for their employees, for the coming year and each year thereafter would be to increase sales and revenues by 25 percent.

There were to be no exceptions. When that edict filtered through the ranks, the employees were in disbelief. They already were working as hard as they could and doing their best. They knew the goal was unrealistic, so they asked some top managers to try to persuade the CEO to adopt less ambitious and more realistic numbers, such as growth of 4 to 8 percent. The CEO became furious at the request and said, "You will raise your sales and profits by twenty-five percent, or you will look for another job. You don't know what people can do until you push them. The twenty-five percent goal remains in effect, and those who don't meet it will be terminated. No exceptions."

The employees were demoralized and very worried about keeping their jobs. The situation became worse when several employees were fired for not meeting their goals. This pressure-filled climate made it impossible for employees to do their best work or to care about trying. How could they feel good about a company that treated them this way? Employees went underground. Many faked their numbers. Others hid their inventories or made sales to "illegal customers." The CEO thought he was winning when in reality he was losing badly.

At the end of his second year the bottom fell out when auditors discovered the problems. The company had lost about $250 million in value and barely escaped bankruptcy. It will take many years to resurrect this firm, if it is possible at all.

The CEO, acting on his own, without seeking advice from experienced managers, had focused so much on winning that he ruined the people and processes that produced winning. The moral of the story is: Managers who focus entirely on winning neglect the processes for perfoming well and run over their people, thus usually end up losing. Companies that declare, "Winning is all that counts," often ruin their businesses.

4

LOSING

Even though we worked hard to succeed, we tried to convince our players that losing was not the end of the world. Sometimes we played very well and still lost. Those are the times you shake your opponent's hand, congratulate him, and make a vow to improve. When our players performed well and lost, I thought it was important to let them know that they'd done many things well. Losing shouldn't override that. It didn't do us any good to lose confidence after losing a well-played game against a good opponent.

For example, one of the hardest losses I remember was in 1989, when we faced a great Michigan team in the NCAA tournament round of 16 in Lexington, Kentucky. Rupp Arena was filled, mostly with fans pulling for the Wolverines. Michigan had all the incentive in the world, inasmuch as we had beaten them in 1987 and 1988 in the NCAA tournament Sweet 16 to end their season. We played perhaps our best game of the season in that 1989 tournament game, and Michigan would tell you it played its best game as it went on to win the national championship. We played so well and competed so hard in that game that we should have been happy with our performance. Still, losing the game was a major disappointment, and it should not have been.

Losing after playing poorly was another story. I expected our players to be angry after a poor performance. I wanted them to feel that they couldn't wait to get back on the court and work to make amends. That's the way competitors usually react to playing less than their best, and that is healthy. Fortunately, we didn't have many truly poor performances from our North Carolina teams.

I ought to point out here that after carefully reviewing tapes of our games, we found it was almost always true that we hadn't played as poorly, or as well, as I thought immediately after the game. That was why I was careful about what I said to the players right after a game. I kept my remarks brief if I made any at all. I didn't want to come down hard on the players in the locker room and then have to change my story the next day after I had reviewed the tapes. It was better to wait until I had all the information in hand. That way I could be very specific with my criticism and praise, making it a better learning experience for the players. I learned my lesson after losing at Vanderbilt during the 1967–68 season. I criticized the team after that game. Then, when I studied the game film, I saw that we really had not played poorly. I couldn't take my words back, but I could learn from the experience, as I did. Maybe some good came of it because that North Carolina team went on a twenty-game winning streak before losing to UCLA in Los Angeles in the national championship game.

Is it easier to teach and learn after a loss? Yes, because losing is such a motivating force. Players want to get back out there and show everyone that they're better than that. Not many teams looked forward to playing North Carolina when we were coming off a loss. When we won but didn't play well, I tried to treat that as a loss with the players, but that was hard to sell.

After a loss everyone realizes the need for improvement. Feelings are hurt, competitive juices are flowing, and the team realizes it needs to listen, learn, and improve. Losing sticks with you. We didn't lose many games at North Carolina, but I nevertheless remember the losses much more vividly than I do the victories. Crisis brings each of us face-to-face with our inadequacies. Losing brought about disappointment for all of us. It's a powerful emotion.

Often we don't know if we really failed until we look back on it at a later date, by which time we can add some perspective to the outcome. If a loss helped us become a better team because of what we learned from it, it would be hard to categorize it as a failure. Our 1982 North Carolina team lost to Virginia on February 3 by the score of 74–58. Although it was only our second loss of the season, the margin of defeat, as well as the way it unfolded, made us angry. Our players learned from it and became a more determined group. We went on to win sixteen games in a row, including a win over Virginia for the ACC championship, en route to winning the national championship. Looking back, I'd have to say the loss to Virginia helped us, although we didn't think of it that way at the time.

The really tough losses, usually ones in which the team played a tremendous game but lost in a heartbreaking manner, were hard for me. I felt so bad for the players after they had played hard, played together, played smart, and still lost in almost a fluky way.

One such loss was our ACC tournament championship game against South Carolina in 1971. South Carolina had been picked as high as number one in the nation in some preseason polls, and it was considered a rebuilding year for us. Indeed, some in the media wrote that our program was headed downhill after a series of highly successful seasons. We were picked fifth, sixth, and seventh in the eight-member ACC in preseason polls.

Our players responded in a fantastic manner that year. They beat South Carolina by fifteen points in Chapel Hill and lost to them in a very close game on the road. Our team surprised the experts by winning the regular-season ACC championship with a league record of 11–3. However, in those days only the ACC tournament champion was allowed to go to the NCAA tournament. We played South Carolina in the conference tournament finals for that lone berth and led for most of the game. With five seconds to play, we were ahead, 51–50, when a jump ball was called. South Carolina got the jump ball and scored with a second left on the clock to win, 52–51. Our team had played brilliantly in defeat.

The loss really hurt. I was devastated for the players, who took it hard, real hard. In our locker room after the game I tried to pump them up by congratulating them on a terrific, gutsy performance. "We have to put this one behind us, work hard, and go to New York and do our best to win the NIT." While it was hard for me to put a happy face on that deep disappointment, the players recovered from it with some excellent practices and went to New York and won the NIT championship, which was much more prestigious then than now because in 1971 there were no at-large NCAA tournament bids. The NIT teams were just about on an equal footing with those in the NCAA tournament. One of our NIT wins was over Julius Erving's Massachusetts team by the improbable score of 90–49, and another one was over Duke. I was impressed by the way our players had bounced back from adversity.

South Carolina pulled out of the ACC after the 1971 season, but as fate would have it, our team won the ACC championship the next season and faced South Carolina in the NCAA tournament in West Virginia. We won, 92–69. Some coaches say revenge is not an effective motivating factor because the emotion is short-lived. I'm inclined to disagree in some instances.

Losing can bring outside distractions, create doubt among the team, maybe result in a loss of confidence, and even bring dissension to the ranks. Therefore it has to be dealt with carefully.

I was reminded of that in 1997, in what turned out to be my last year of coaching. After winning nine of our first ten games against excellent competition, we slumped at the beginning of our ACC schedule beginning in early January. The reasons? Bad scheduling on my part, a little bad luck, and some excellent opponents.

We honored one of our foreign players, senior Serge Zwikker, by giving him something close to a home game in the Netherlands over the Christmas holidays. Then we stopped in Italy to play an excellent Italian national team. We arrived back in Chapel Hill on January 2 after a long, tiring trip. Let me be clear when I say we never used one of these trips as an excuse for poor play. I told the players before we went that we would go as long as they understood that they had to be prepared to play when we got back home. We didn't go into this blindfolded.

Nevertheless, two days after returning, we played an excellent nationally ranked Wake Forest team, featuring Tim Duncan, in Winston-Salem. They played great, we didn't play well, and they won, 81–57. To exacerbate matters, one of our starters, sophomore Vince Carter, suffered a hip injury in the game that was to hamper him for a couple of weeks.

After the game Dave Odom, the Wake Forest coach, graciously brought up our Christmas trip. "I thought Carolina looked tired from their overseas trip," he told the press.

At my press conference, I gave Wake Forest credit, which was deserved, even though I was disappointed with our play. "I saw one great basketball team out there, and I hoped to see two. They are better than we are, that's obvious. But it's early in the season, and I hope we can improve."

A few days later we played Maryland in Chapel Hill without Carter, unable to play because of his injury. We led by twenty-two points, but Maryland rallied to win, 85–75. We were 0–2 in the ACC, had lost a twenty-two-point lead at home, and everybody was talking about North Carolina's slump.

It got worse. The next game was at Virginia, where we lost, 75–63. Carolina was 0–3 in the ACC for the first time ever. Norman Nolan, a Virginia player, said, "I don't think they're as intimidating or as good as Carolina teams of the past."

Not that the media needed more ammunition but some reporters heard some players arguing in our locker room after the game. Even though I said afterward, "I feel better about our team than I have at any point in the season," the reporters weren't listening to me. They had their story.

Part of dealing with losing is handling outside forces, which you can't control. The sports pages were filled with stories about our slump and about the shouting in our locker room. Some wrote that the situation was so serious that North Carolina's basketball program would never be the same. We were in the midst of some incredible, record-setting streaks of making the NCAA tournament, not finishing lower than third in the ACC, and of winning more than twenty games in a season. I tried to convince our players to forget about all those streaks and just worry about getting better in practice each day. They listened.

While the media had a field day, some in the ACC gloated about our problems. Forget the NCAA tournament, we were advised by some rivals, and concentrate instead on making the NIT. Many of our own fans and students jumped ship and spoke derisively of our players. It seemed like us against the world, which is not always a bad situation for a group of competitors. The right group will fight back.

Still, it was not a happy time for us; there's no doubt about that. Damage control was necessary. Unfortunately NC State came to Chapel Hill bent on adding to our woes. They led us, 56–47, with two minutes to play in the game. An 0–4 start in the ACC seemed certain. Suddenly our players somehow found a way. We scored the last twelve points of the game and won, 59–56. It was a scintillating comeback.

We gained some confidence by winning a game that seemed lost. We later played extremely well but lost close road games at Florida State and Duke to end the first half of the ACC season with a conference record of 3–5.

"We might lose the rest of them or win the rest of them, but my guess is it'll be something in between," I said at a speech to UNC's Educational Foundation chapter in Raleigh.

We avenged the losses to Virginia and Florida State by winning by lopsided scores. We trailed at Georgia Tech by sixteen points with nine minutes to play in the game and won, 72–68. We rallied to beat NC State in

Raleigh. Our players were playing better and with much more confidence, winning twice over Tim Duncan's Wake Forest team. We beat Maryland in College Park by twelve, won at home against Duke.

We won sixteen games in a row, including the ACC championship and the NCAA East Regionals, en route to the NCAA Final Four. The team, called a failure by many in early January, did not give up. The players improved significantly.

They stuck to the process—play hard; play together; play smart—and dug themselves out of a deep hole. We didn't run from our mistakes. We faced up to them and made the needed corrections and adjustments. From despair to the Final Four as ACC champions, that was the story of that season.

PLAYER PERSPECTIVE

Joe Wolf,
*class of 1987, former NBA player and
now assistant basketball coach at the
College of William and Mary*

Michael Jordan left Carolina for the NBA after his junior season in 1984. I was a sophomore the next season, and our team was very young. Buzz Peterson was our only senior who had played meaningful minutes.

We lost on the road to Clemson, 52–50, on January 30, 1985, for our second straight close loss and the one that sticks in my mind. We were disappointed and frustrated after that loss. I still recall the Clemson coach came into our locker room and told Coach Smith what a great game it had been. That didn't go over well with any of our coaches. All our players witnessed what had taken place, and we all felt deep disappointment, not so much because we had lost, but because we thought we had let our coaches down. That meant more to us than anything because we had such great respect for these men who taught us the fundamentals not only of basketball but also of life.

We made the trip home in silence. The players felt the emptiness that comes with losing and disappointment. Usually when we arrived back in Chapel Hill after a road game, all of us just filed off the bus. This time, as the bus driver got off to open the baggage compartments, Coach Smith stood up at his seat. The rest of us took the signal and sat down. Quickly and with some emotion he told us we wouldn't be losing many more. He asked each of us to come to practice the next day with a winning outlook. We looked at one another with renewed hope and enthusiasm. After a bitter defeat our coach had stood up and told us we wouldn't be losing much for the rest of the season. We were invigorated.

We thought we had let the coaching staff down with our play, but Coach Smith's message was that we were going to get better. He made it clear that we hadn't let him down. I'm not certain of the exact words that Coach Smith used that night, but I am sure of the way he made me and my teammates feel.

From that point on our young team played with more confidence because he let us know that we had not disappointed him. We won thirteen games after that for a total of twenty-seven victories for the season. In a year when many experts predicted we'd be down after losing Michael Jordan to the NBA, we tied for the ACC regular-season championship. Even though we lost guard Steve Hale, one of our most important players and leaders, to injury in the first game of the NCAA tournament, we went on to beat Notre Dame on its home court and Auburn in front of its loud fans in Birmingham, Alabama, before losing a close game to the eventual national champion, Villanova, in the Elite Eight.

As a footnote, we were ready when Clemson came to Chapel

Hill for a return game on February 23. We won, 84–50. To my knowledge, Coach Smith didn't go to the Clemson dressing room afterward. It wasn't his style.

Before someone is hired or promoted to a position in top management, it should be determined if he or she has the skills it takes to be a gracious loser. If the answer is no, that individual shouldn't be in top management.

It's an absolute necessity for a leader to be able to handle losing. The bigger a person's job, the more losses he or she will have, and the more costly they will be. All businesspeople know how it feels to lose, whether it comes in the form of poor quarterly sales, introduction of a bad product, poor operating performance, losing to a competitor's good work, or just bad luck.

Good leaders don't want to lose, and they work hard to avoid it. However, they are not afraid to fail. When Brad Faxon, considered by many to be the best putter on the PGA Tour, was asked the secret to his excellent putting, he replied, "I'm not afraid to miss." Losing isn't the end of the world—if it's handled properly. In fact most effective managers don't waste time worrying about losing as long as they know in their hearts that they did their best. On the other hand, if losses occur because of poor effort or sloppy planning, it's a horrible feeling, one that's difficult to shake. These are the types of losses we play over and over in our mind and thus tend to affect our work on the next projects.

Here's how the most effective managers handle losing:

- They recognize a loss when it occurs, admit it quickly, and never try to cover it up. Trying to hide the loss or cover it up is the worst thing to do.
- They move to patch things up as quickly as possible and correct the mistakes that led to the loss. There is no time for excuses.
- They meet with everyone involved in the loss to figure out the lessons they can learn from it.
- They ask everyone involved to write down five actions they will take to avoid a similar loss in the future and then implement those five steps that same day.
- They forgive themselves and others involved 100 percent. "We will not experience one more ounce of guilt about this mistake. It is over."
- They vow never to think about it again after learning everything they can from the loss. They move on to the next project unafraid to take smart, calculated risks. They don't fall into the fear of failure trap, which prevents people from performing at their best.

EXAMPLE OF TURNING LOSS INTO VICTORY

Coca-Cola spent millions and millions of dollars in research, product development, and marketing before it launched New Coke, which was to take the place of its popular "old faithful." The company thought the new formula would be an improvement over the longtime favorite soft drink. Otherwise it wouldn't have moved forward with this monumental change, one that involved many risks.

Coca-Cola knows how to put a new product on the market and make it succeed. The introduction of diet Coke, for instance, was one of the most successful launches of a new product ever. Similar or better results were expected for New Coke.

Sometimes even the best plans of the most successful companies don't work. Replacing "old faithful" with New Coke was a failure from day one. Responses flowed in quickly. Consumers didn't like the changes and wanted the old Coke back. Furthermore, they were confused about why such a good thing had been changed in the first place.

Although stunned by public reaction, Coca-Cola executives let it all soak in. Don Keough, the excellent company president at the time, knew soon after the launch that his company had made a huge mistake. Although he'd heard enough to convince him of that, some of his leading managers pushed for more time for New Coke to catch on, and Keough reluctantly agreed. After all, this was a major company investment.

Although he was the leader of one of the world's leading companies, Keough's ego was healthy enough, and his mission clear enough, that he didn't need to be someone he wasn't. He often answered his own office telephone. He wanted to know what consumers thought. He didn't hide behind his title or his power. He was available. He knew how to listen, and he wasn't afraid to hear bad news.

Six weeks after the launch of New Coke, by which time Keough was virtually certain that a big mistake had been made, he received a call in his office from a woman who said that his decision to discard "old faithful" and replace it with New Coke had pretty much ruined her life, as well as the lives of her children, neighbors, and friends. She said she'd enjoyed the old Coke since her childhood. During the conversation Keough asked her where she lived and she said she lived in a nursing home in Omaha, Nebraska. That was the final straw.

Soon afterward he brought his top managers together and said the case was closed. The customers had spoken, he said, and Coca-Cola had messed up. It was going to correct the mistake immediately, even though the cost of launching New Coke had been in the multimillions of dollars. The company did so by putting the popular "old faithful" back on the market under the name Coke Classic, while leaving New Coke there for those who preferred it.

The introduction of New Coke at the expense of "old faithful" could have cost Coca-Cola dearly. But instead of hiding the mistake or trying to cover it up or being defensive about it, the company admitted the error, learned from it, and moved quickly to correct it. Because of great leadership, Coca Cola turned what could have been a devastating loss with long-term consequences into a victory. It pays to know how to lose well and to find the opportunity in every loss.

PART TWO

PLAYING

HARD

·5·

CARING

The best leaders really do care about the people entrusted to them and want to see them succeed. They will go the extra mile to help a student, a soldier, an athlete, a parishioner. Military books and journals are filled with examples of how the most inspired officers care for the soldiers under their command. Ernie Pyle, the brilliant newspaper columnist who became famous writing about American soldiers in World War II, wrote one of his most memorable pieces about a captain from Belton, Texas, by the name of Henry T. Waskow, who was killed in action on the front lines in Italy in January 1944.

Pyle wrote: "In this war I have known a lot of officers who were loved and respected by the soldiers under them. But never have I crossed the trail of any man as beloved as Capt. Henry T. Waskow of Belton, Texas. Capt. Waskow was a company commander in the 36th Division. He had led his company since long before it left the States. He was very young, only in his middle twenties, but he carried in him a sincerity and gentleness that made people want to be guided by him."

Pyle was present the night the men brought Captain Waskow's body down by mule train. He was placed at the side of a road along with four other dead American soldiers. Pyle described how the men who had fought under Captain Waskow knelt at his side and grieved. "I sure am sorry, sir," Pyle quoted one soldier as saying.

Pyle continued: "Then the first man squatted down, and he reached down and took the dead hand, and he sat there for a full five minutes, holding the dead hand in his own and looking intently into the dead face, and he never uttered a sound all the time he sat there.

"And finally he put the hand down, and then reached up and gently straightened the points of the captain's shirt collar, and then he sort of re-arranged the tattered edges of his uniform around the wound. And then he got up and walked away down the road in the moonlight, all alone."

Please understand that I would not dare compare leading a basketball team to a captain leading his troops into battle. They are two distinctly different levels of leadership, but both are still leadership. Certainly, I never used war references in talking about my teams or individual players. We didn't talk about "going to war" or "being in the foxhole together" or even "going down a dark alley together." We stuck to basketball. Going into hostile arenas in the ACC was tough, but it wasn't life and death. It wasn't war.

I truly did care about what happened to our players at Carolina and the Air Force Academy while they were in school and after they graduated. I became close to them. Not to care for them would be hypocritical and then some. Young people are not easily fooled. They'll figure out if they're being used or manipulated. Getting them back after that, I'd think, would be virtually impossible. For sure it's no way to build a team. Our players knew I cared about them, and they returned it to me and our program tenfold over the years.

When a player came to us as a freshman, I told him, "We work very hard, as you know, and I'm a disciplinarian. There might be times that you won't like me. But I try to do what's in the team's best interest as well as in yours." I would ask players to recall a teacher who had meant a great deal to them, and most of them would remember teachers who had demanded much but had done a good job preparing them.

I was hard on our players in practice, which I'll talk about in detail in the next chapter. I came from an era in which coaches raised their voices to correct mistakes, and I certainly raised mine. But I didn't use profanity, nor did I allow it in our practices. A violation of the rule resulted in team running, a lot of running. A leader can be tough and still show respect. I expected much from all our players—academically and in basketball. I also paid close attention to the way they conducted themselves as private citizens because the goal was for them to be as much like other students on campus as possible. I encouraged them to be with other students who weren't athletes. Yet they understood if they, or one of their teammates, made a mistake on campus, it would make the newspapers and become a big deal. That was something the other students didn't have to worry about. Call it life in the fishbowl for a scholarship basketball player at a nationally prominent program. There were certainly privileges, but with them went responsibilities.

I also wanted our players to be active in campus political life. Bill Chamberlain was the second black player we were successful in recruiting to our program. He turned down Princeton for Carolina. I did not routinely let players out of practice. However, if a player needed the afternoon to catch up on his studies, he could miss practice. It had to be a valid reason, though. The players knew that. No horsing around here. Practice was serious business at Carolina. It was where the teaching was done. It was where our standards were established. One day Chamberlain asked me if he could miss practice for political reasons. Reluctantly he explained that a civil rights rally was planned on campus that afternoon on behalf of university cafeteria workers. At issue were their low pay and working conditions. Bill felt strongly about the situation and had been asked to speak at the rally. "I think it's a great idea," I told him. "Go do it."

After all, the players were on campus to learn, ask questions, and develop their own convictions. I didn't want to stifle their intellectual curiosity; I wanted to encourage it. If we're going to call them student-athletes, then let them be students as well as basketball players. What was good for our team came right behind academics during the season. We didn't try to hide it. Still, I didn't want basketball to infringe on an individual's beliefs. A fine line to walk? Yes, but a most important area that needed my attention. We couldn't talk to our players about keeping perspective in their lives if we then turned around and put basketball first all the time. A balance was needed.

The relationship that I had with my players while they were at Carolina led me to stay in touch with them after they left. It wasn't something I planned; it just evolved over the years. Happily so. I helped some find jobs in private business. I assisted others in getting jobs in basketball. Even to this day, although I've been out of coaching since 1997, I hear from our former players on a regular basis. I'm happy they trust me to share important milestones in their lives. I know my feelings for them are genuine. It's always a thrill to have one of them drop by to talk. They often bring family members with them. That makes the occasion even more special. These men did great things as representatives of the University of North Carolina, and when they return to Chapel Hill, our extended basketball family welcomes them warmly. I hope they'll always want to come back.

Of course the Carolina basketball family is larger than most partly because I was head coach there for all those years. I know it was the players who made the program, and I'm grateful to them for what they did. If they hadn't won a lot of games and championships, I probably wouldn't have survived as Carolina's head coach for so long. I knew as a young coach that we had to win for me to keep my job. It's the nature of the beast. It was driven home once again when my fourth Carolina team arrived home after a loss to Wake Forest to see a group of seventy-five to a hundred students burning an effigy of me across the street from Woollen Gym. I understand two of our players, Billy Cunningham and Billy Galantai, went over to the crowd and tore down the dummy.

Chuck Erickson, Carolina's athletic director at the time, asked for a meeting with me the next day. He didn't threaten to fire me, but he did express his concern about the loss to Wake Forest, our fourth in a row, all on the road. One could make the case that I was under pressure to keep my job. I was at peace with it. I didn't talk to the team about it. Dumping my problems in the players' laps wouldn't help them play better. To the contrary, it probably would have put them under such pressure that their play could have deteriorated. I also didn't talk to them about winning or the need to win. My job status was not mentioned. There was a lot of stuff swirling around our program, but we stuck to our process: Play hard; play together; play smart. We trusted it.

Two days later we went to Durham for our fifth straight road game and defeated Duke, ranked among the nation's best teams. A big crowd of happy Carolina students greeted our bus. I tried to make sure the players got credit for our victories. The losses were on me. That was the way I believed it should work. If the players did what I asked of them and we still lost, then it was my fault.

If there's such a thing as a Carolina basketball family—and I think there is—the players should be the leading characters. That's why I was persuaded to write my memoirs, which was to be a short history of each team. I insisted that a picture of each of my Carolina teams be included in the book, along with the names and occupations of all the players and managers who earned letters in that era.

Ninety-six percent of them earned their degrees, and almost 40 percent of those went on to graduate or professional schools. That's a pretty impressive combination: a lot of games won, a lot of nets cut down, many championship trophies hoisted—and the players graduated from one of the nation's leading universities.

Caring was a major part of creating the type of environment that made those things possible. I think we showed that winning and learning are compatible.

PLAYER PERSPECTIVES

Michael Norwood,

class of 1987, financial consultant,
New Bern, North Carolina

My wife Caroline and I received devastating news on August 29, 2001, when doctors told us that our two-and-a-half-year-old daughter Nell had a cancerous tumor behind her nose. It was a type of cancer that affects young children. Even though the doctors told us from the outset that the survival rate for this kind of cancer was only 25 percent, we never gave up hope.

We checked into Duke Hospital the day of the diagnosis and did not leave Nell's room for twenty days. When I played for Coach Smith, he once told me that I was born burly so I could play good defense. I realized during that hospital stay that I was built that way so I could hold Nell in my arms for hours each day. She hated lying down in the bed because that's where doctors worked on her, gave her shots, and took blood. I actually thought about Coach Smith's comment as I walked around the room with my daughter in my arms.

Within one week of the diagnosis, I received countless calls from the Carolina family, including Coach Smith, Coach (Bill) Guthridge, Matt Doherty, Joe Wolf, Jeff Lebo, Joe Jenkins, Curtis Hunter, Kenny Smith, and many others. It showed me again just how strong and caring the Carolina family is. We had tremendous support, and it can be attributed to the type of people that Coach Smith brought to his program and how they had grown as men under his leadership.

After the twenty-day hospital stay, we remained in Durham for another six weeks because Nell received radiation treatments each morning and chemotherapy every other Friday. On those mornings that Nell felt up to it, Caroline and I took her over to Chapel Hill and visited the basketball office. Coach Smith would always put down whatever he was doing to spend time with us and Coach Smith's administrative assistants, Linda Woods and Ruth Kirkendall, always greeted us warmly and made us feel right at home. Most of the time Nell wanted me to hold her. By this time she had lost all her hair and wore a hat, usually a Carolina hat. One day Coach Smith signed it for her and wrote something really sweet on it. After that, she always called it her "good" hat, one that we saved for special occasions. I now realize that every day is a special occasion.

We went back home to New Bern in late October 2001, although we had to return to Duke almost weekly for chemotherapy treatments. During that trying time, Coach Smith and Coach Guthridge called often to see how we were doing. It was always funny when Coach Smith called. He's such a humble man that he thinks he has to identify himself, so he would say, "This is Dean Smith calling from Chapel Hill." In the first place, we all know Coach Smith. Second, with that distinctive voice of his, it couldn't possibly be anyone else.

The cancer was too strong for Nell to overcome. She passed away on September 1, 2002. Coach Smith and his staff did everything they could to help us through those trying times. It was an unbelievable year, one that I would not want anyone to have to go through. Some people look at us funny when we talk about the Carolina basketball family. But it is real. In our saddest time, it was there for Caroline and me. I will always be grateful to them.

Steve Krafcisin,

player for UNC in 1977, transferred
to the University of Iowa, where he played
basketball and graduated, now head coach
at North Iowa Area Community College

Coach Smith genuinely cared for everyone associated with Carolina basketball, and still does. He has an unbelievable way of making his former players feel that they are important people in his life, as I'm positive we all are. For example, even though I played for him for only one year, he always wants to know how my mom, aunt, and brother are doing. In his conversations he takes time to ask personal questions because he's truly interested. A person can't fake that.

Now that I'm older, I understand some of the things he had us do as freshmen that maybe I didn't understand as well at the time, such as not dressing in the varsity locker room until after the first game and having freshmen carry the movie projector and game films on the road. I understand that Coach Smith cared enough to teach us life's lessons, not just those concerning hoops. He certainly didn't let us get bigheaded or otherwise full of ourselves, that's for sure.

He made us feel like family, and still does. That comes from caring and the way he treats us. I try to do similar things with my own players now to make them feel special because they chose me and North Iowa Area Community College. My year with Coach Smith at North Carolina was an important year that helped shape me as a man, and isn't that what college is supposed to be all about?

Charles Shaffer,

class of 1964, attorney, Atlanta

———————

I will always remember one comment that Coach Smith made while I was playing for him. It occurred in 1962, during my sophomore year, in a game against Maryland. I had injured my knee in a freshman football game against Clemson, and this Maryland game was one of my first games in eighteen months of recovering from the injury. My knee was heavily taped. Early in the game I fell and bruised my thigh above my injured knee.

John Lacey, our great trainer, and Coach Smith came onto the court to tend to me. When I got up, I limped badly, and at first it couldn't be determined if I had reinjured my knee. As I limped back to the bench, I overheard Coach Smith say to John Lacey, "We're going to do what's best for this boy."

In these days of going directly to the bottom line, here it is: Coach Smith, our teacher and coach, always did what was best for his boys.

BUSINESS PERSPECTIVE

One of the most significant characteristics of effective leaders is that they care about the people they lead. They instinctively like people, enjoy helping others, and are sincere, warmhearted, and considerate. There are few things a leader does that are more important than to commit himself to the well-being of his or her workers. Once people know you're on their side, they trust you, believe in you, and will follow your lead. Supporting people can't be an act or a textbook assignment. Employees pick up on artificial "people-management" techniques quickly.

Employees know when that caring is there and when it isn't. Frankly they will not trust a boss who doesn't care for them, and without this trust there's little chance of getting them to work hard, or work together, or work smart. They will not become a team.

The best leaders consider the people who work for them more important than numbers. This philosophy helps build committed followers. Once employees are given a chance to succeed, are well trained and coached, are supported and encouraged to offer feedback, they are ready to be held accountable by a caring leader. Now, if a leader has done everything possible to train and develop an employee, and the person's work still falls short, every effort should be made to find another job in the company that is a good fit for that person. If another position can't be found, an effort should be made to help the person find a job elsewhere. Good leaders don't carry or protect ineffective people or those whose skills don't match the job. However, the most effective leaders are always focused on how to help the individual as well as their organizations succeed personally.

Good leaders create a work environment that is like a family, where people care for one another, help one another, celebrate the success of their fellow workers. They convey this message to their employees: "You're on my team for the rest of your life. I'm going to try to help you at every step of your career, and I'll continue to do that even if you leave the company to work elsewhere." Of course the more subordinates a leader has, the harder this is to accomplish and the more time-consuming it is.

The best leaders tend to maintain contact with former employees for years. The workers call their old bosses to share the highs and lows of their careers and lives, to ask for advice, or just to check in. They are dedicated to these people for a lifetime.

A woman in a male-dominated company began her career on

the production line of a leading manufacturing firm. She had had a tough childhood, with an alcoholic father, worked her way through school, and then went to work. She worked hard, was eager to learn and advance. She performed well in every job she held, gradually working her way up to a supervisory role, to foreman, to section head, to manager, to vice president and general manager. Then she found herself in tough competition with six male vice presidents for the position of president of the firm.

The founder-CEO of the company, who had focused his attention on profits his entire career, struggled for months with the decision on whom to name president. He was concerned about the female vice president because she would be in charge of a male-dominated company and industry. She was caring and supportive of people and wanted to institute a set of cultural shifts toward focusing on the people as well as improving communications, performance, quality, and customer service programs.

The CEO believed that if he promoted the woman, three of the male vice presidents would quit and the other three would refuse to work for her. To his credit, he was changing his own leadership philosophy and believed the woman embodied what he himself was trying to become.

The CEO and I set up a series of meetings in which we asked the seven candidates for the president's position to assess the future needs of the business, the company's strengths and weaknesses, the changes that should be made in the organization structure, roles, goals, responsibilities, and the leadership characteristics the new president should have. Then I led the seven vice presidents through a series of exercises with the group to assess their own leadership styles, their strengths and weaknesses, and how closely their leadership characteristics matched those the new president would need to have. After many lengthy discussions, the answer became clear to all concerned: The woman was the best person for the job. The caring CEO put his team through an open, honest, participative process and then, after long consideration of all the facts, made a gutsy and wise call. The woman was promoted.

Even though she won the job in fair competition, many people were skeptical about her at first. It was even suggested that since most of the major customers of the firm were men, she should do her job on the inside and not go out of the office to call on customers in person, for fear of how the male customers would react to her. Incredible.

Her style is honest, two-way, considerate, direct, open, and quick to the point. She doesn't waste a lot of time with fake chatter or pretend to be someone she's not. She puts people first. It's a trait that comes naturally to her. She brings a subordinate in and says, "This is my philosophy; this is what I believe and want to do in the company. If you have ideas and suggestions to make it better, please bring them up. I also want you to know that I'm going to do everything in my power to help you reach your goals and do what you want with your life and career, as long as it helps our company."

Then she asks the subordinate to leave and come back later with his or her top ten business and personal goals that he or she wants to accomplish in the next several years. She meets with the employee to discuss each of those goals and asks him or her to develop a more specific draft for a second meeting. "I would love you to develop a plan, and I will do what I can to help you accomplish it," she tells the subordinate. This way the employee gets ownership of his or her business and personal goals and understands that the boss really cares about what happens to him or her. She follows up with all her people once a quarter to help them, check their progress, and coach them to continue building their skills and pursuing their goals.

After one year in the president's chair the woman won over a tough crowd. The employees not only believe in her but would go through walls for her. They don't want to disappoint her. In the process of doing her job, she turned around a large group of hard-line, cantankerous people, some of whom would have rejoiced had she failed early on. The word about this company is out in the community and industry. News of her leadership philosophy, which highlights her caring for people, has spread to the extent that the firm's personnel files bulge with the applications of prospects who want to come to work there.

She's now been president of the firm for five years and is producing great profits and growth. She works closely with all the customers, who have become fans of hers and supporters of the company. They value her style, intelligence, and sincerity. She does what she says she's going to do. Her subordinates want to be like her and are picking up her habits and installing her approaches in their departments.

The six male vice presidents? They support her, have grown in their own leadership skills and responsibilities, and enjoy and respect her immensely. The profit-minded CEO? He trusts her, is called on to work fewer hours in the company, is engaged in industry and community leadership, is happier with his own life, and is making more profits than ever.

This new president not only took advantage of her personal opportunity but also changed the entire culture of the company—for the betterment of all concerned.

So check your leadership practices. How do you view your employees? How focused are you on their well-being and success? Are you harsh or supportive? Do you see them as tools?

Remember, not caring about people is probably one of the deal breakers for successful leadership. If you don't place people first in your sights, they probably don't like working for you.

If you want to motivate people to work hard, work together, and work smart, help them become successful. People give back what they receive.

6

PRACTICING

Practicing was the most important part of our North Carolina program. We, coaches and players, took it very seriously. I didn't want a player in our program who wouldn't work hard in practice. That was the main reason I wanted high school prospects to watch us practice when they came for campus visits. Did they want to work hard? If not, they would be better off at some other school.

I treated practice with such respect that we had an office rule: I could not be interrupted during practice for anything less than a true emergency. In my tenure as head coach I left practice early only once—to attend to a family emergency. The first thing in getting the players to buy into this approach was to have them see how much practice meant to me and my assistant coaches. It was not a slack time.

I didn't believe in just rolling a ball onto the court and making things up as we went along. When I was a player at Kansas, Assistant Coach Dick Harp made up the practice plan, and it was posted in the locker room for all of us to read before practice. When I was assistant coach at the Air Force Academy, Bob Spear and I spent hours making the practice plan since the cadets' time was so limited. When I arrived at North Carolina to serve as assistant coach to Frank McGuire, he asked me to do the practice plan. He always knew what he wanted to accomplish at practice, plus a lot of scrimmaging, but had never written it down in the form of a plan. However, he liked the idea and asked me to do it.

So, when I became head coach at North Carolina, I already held the view that a highly organized practice was necessary to a successful program. Early in my career our budget didn't allow for any of our practices to be filmed, but in my last five years as coach, we taped all of them so we could review them afterward. At night I studied those tapes and then put together a practice plan for the next day. I reviewed it with my assistant coaches the next morning and gave them the freedom to change something if they thought it was necessary. We also devised a master plan before the start of preseason practice that provided us with an overview of how practice would go for the entire season. I didn't hesitate to stray from it if needed, however. If we had trouble handling another team's press, for instance, we might spend more time in practice the next day on our press offense. It was necessary to be flexible.

When the players arrived in the locker room to dress for practice, each of them received a typed copy of the plan for that day. They read through it before they left the locker room to go onto the court, so that they would have a good idea of the things we would be working on that afternoon. I wanted them to have this overview before they heard from me. It saved time and served to get them focused on the work ahead. What they received was very specific, and all segments were timed. The water break lasted two minutes. Seniors drank first, juniors next, followed by sophomores, then freshmen.

At the top of the practice plan was an offensive and defensive Emphasis of the Day, which was basketball-related. It could be something like "Throw the ball inbounds using both hands" and "See man and ball." Once we chose the Emphasis of the Day, we watched carefully to see that it was carried out. It was important to catch the players if they didn't do it properly, or else we would have defeated our reason for doing it. If there's an emphasis but it's not enforced, it becomes counterproductive.

In addition to the Emphasis of the Day, we had a Thought for the Day that ostensibly had nothing to do with basketball. It was a philosophical text that added some perspective to the players' basketball experience. At least that was my intention. These thoughts could be taken from books, magazine articles, newspapers, my church bulletin, or audiotapes as well as other sources. An example might be: "Don't let a day pass when you don't do something for someone who can't repay you." I was careful when using religious thoughts to include all religions.

The players had to learn the Emphasis of the Day and the Thought for the Day. They knew I might call on them in practice to repeat them. If they didn't respond correctly, the entire team ran. If I thought a player was trying to avoid eye contact with me during my opening remarks at practice, I probably would call on him. I often called on freshmen. It was gratifying to observe the young players memorizing the Emphasis of the Day and the Thought for the Day while they stretched before the start of practice.

After the players had stretched and warmed up, I blew a whistle, and they sprinted to midcourt to form a circle around me. I said what I wanted to say about that day's practice. I then chose one player to recite the defensive emphasis, another the offensive emphasis, and a third the Thought for the Day, and we went to work. The practices in the preseason were longer, sometimes lasting two and a half hours, and gradually decreased in time as the season wore on to where late in the season they lasted from one hour to ninety minutes. Many of our players said that games were easy compared with practice, and that was the desired result. The players sprinted to their workstations at the sound of my whistle.

Our practices were closed to the public. It was my classroom, and I demanded complete attention. I didn't know of any English instructors who allowed strangers to wander in and out of their classroom. Why should the basketball classroom be different? We did, however, often have basketball coaches—high school, college, professional—attend our practices on special passes. They thought they could pick up something that would help them coach their own teams, and we were happy to have them. Sometimes football coaches from college and professional ranks dropped in to watch us practice. Our former players were always welcome. Of course these important visitors sat a long way from the court so the players weren't distracted.

We graded carefully at practice. Players earned points that could be used to get out of running. Points could be earned for good defense, diving for loose balls, setting good screens, deflections, drawing charges, and other unselfish acts—winning acts. I believed that if we got the little things right, it would help us get the big things right. You'll notice I didn't mention points scored. There's more to basketball than scoring, and we constantly stressed that with our players. Scorers received too much attention from the media and fans anyhow.

We worked hard on fundamentals in practice. It was where we set our standards. We repeated things until they became habits. I believed that once we introduced something new, we should cover it in practice for several days to make sure the players got it. We hammered it home: repeat, repeat, repeat until we got it right. We didn't make our drills competitive until they were learned. The players would have concentrated on winning instead of learning. Once the drills were learned, we made them competitive.

We didn't have a lot of chatter in practice either. It was a learning session. If I criticized an act, the player wasn't allowed to respond. He would have spent the time trying to convince me that he wasn't wrong. "That might work with your parents," I'd say, "but not with your coach." I told the players, "I will be in my office after practice. If anybody doesn't understand something we did today, come on by." In my years as head coach, maybe three or four players took me up on it. Criticism must be clear and specific. It serves no purpose to tell the players: "We need to get out there and hustle. They want it more than we do." They're looking for more leadership than that.

Our best practices had a distinct rhythm, and I didn't want them disrupted with unnecessary conversation. Too much talk equals not enough concentration. Of course we wanted to hear talking as the players communicated on defense.

We seldom spoke to our teams about the upcoming opponent. We planned to do things to take the opponent out of what they wanted to do. We were going to be the aggressor and force the other team to react to what we did. While I looked at hours of tapes of our opponents, I shared only a small fraction of that with the players. I wanted their focus in the right direction. If we did what we were supposed to do—played hard, played together, played smart—the outcome would usually suit us. I didn't want to overload the players with so much information that they would think themselves into a stupor. We wanted them to have enough freedom to be creative, rather than paint by the numbers.

Although we introduced an offense or a defense by showing tape that gave the entire picture, we believed strongly in part-method teaching. For instance, we began our defensive drills by putting two players against two others. Then we moved on to three-on-three, then to four-on-four, before graduating to five-on-five. The more people on the court, the easier defense should become. Therefore, if a player executes correctly two-on-two and masters the principles, he should excel at five-on-five. Giving it to them in this part-method manner made it easier for the players to grasp the whole when it was introduced.

We did the same on offense: two-on-two, three-on-three, and so forth. We would break into three groups. One would run our freelance offense against a second group, while the third group would be at another station working on shooting under the supervision of an assistant coach. Each shot would be recorded by a manager.

After we completed our part-method work, we played five-on-five half-court, with transition to the other end. Some days we had brief scrimmages. I probably should have scrimmaged our teams more, but my goal was to teach them the proper way to play. Often players in scrimmages reverted to old habits because of their competitive desire to win.

It wasn't just the players who learned at practice; I did too. For example, for many years we ended the practice before a game with the ritual of putting six players at one end of the court and six at the other end. Before they could leave practice, each of the six players at both ends had to make two consecutive free throws. If five made them and the sixth missed, all had to start over. During the 1978 season I stopped the drill after we determined it was producing negative results. Because players didn't want to be responsible for keeping their teammates on the court long after practice had ended, they tried too hard to make their shots so their teammates could go home. In the process they put too much pressure on themselves. For some of them it carried over to the games. We had unintentionally planted a seed that wasn't productive because the players thought too much about the consequences of missing. The ritual had seemed to help our foul shooting in years prior to 1978, but when it no longer did, we discontinued it.

We changed and at every practice had each player shoot fifty foul shots, all of which were recorded by our managers. The shots were taken at different intervals during practice. That was more effective. Our North Carolina players made most of their clutch foul shots, that much I know. They concentrated on their personal ritual, not on the consequences of making or missing.

I never bought in to the notion that some players practiced poorly but played well in games. North Carolina players earned playing time in practice by working hard, improving, and showing me that they deserved to be on the court in games. They treated practice seriously and with respect. Our players improved throughout their college careers, and working hard in practice was one of the reasons for it.

Practice is a mind-set, an attitude. There are things about being head coach at a school like North Carolina that I don't miss. But I miss practice immensely. It was one of my favorite times, a time to teach and see the players improve. It was in practice that we came together as a team.

PLAYER PERSPECTIVE

Charles Shaffer,
class of 1964, attorney, Atlanta

Coach Smith could coach a game as well as any coach ever, but his ability to *teach* the game to his players in practice was truly extraordinary. He was much like a learned Renaissance scholar teaching *The Divine Comedy* to his students. He was patient, thorough, and confident, with an uncommon ability to communicate and get his points across, which in turn gave his student-players confidence.

Four distinct principles marked Coach Smith's philosophy: defense, physical fitness, the passing game and good shot selection on offense, and unselfishness.

DEFENSE
Coach Smith taught a team defense that had many interrelated parts, which required both thought and action. He utilized part-method teaching, which involved five minutes on one aspect of our defense, five minutes on another aspect, then ten minutes on the whole as the parts were combined. These bite-size portions made the defense easier for the players to grasp, and when he put the entire puzzle together, we saw how brilliant his defensive plan was.

Coach Smith's defense also taught us that each man on our team needed to depend on and trust his teammates, while at the same time instilling in us the strong desire not to let a teammate down. This unselfishness, bred on defense, worked its way through all parts of our game and was the hallmark of Carolina basketball. On defense, an individual defender challenged the ballhandler in an attacking, daring manner, knowing if the opponent drove to the basket, a wave of Carolina teammates would be there to help stop him. We were taught that each of the five men on the court had an important job to do, and if one of us failed to carry out an assignment, our team defense would suffer. We would have let our teammates down.

Coach Smith stressed man-to-man defense, and if a player couldn't perform effectively in that area, he sat on the bench. We all learned that early on. The goal for our defense was to take the opponent out of its offense by eliminating its comfort level. Coach orchestrated this primarily by devising a defense that would take away the opponent's two or three favorite offensive sets, the things that it felt most confident doing. The resulting forced improvisation shocked the opponent and played right into the hands of Carolina's defense.

Coach Smith taught us in practice that if we held a team to a low score and forced a poor field goal percentage, we could be successful even on nights when our offense wasn't at its best.

PHYSICAL FITNESS

Most college basketball players are physically fit, but Coach Smith's teams went well beyond the norm. He knew that he couldn't demand forty minutes of aggressive man-to-man defense and a fast-breaking offense without his players' being in the best physical condition possible. To reach that level, the players ran countless sprints, or tours in practice, and we were expected to report to fall practice in good shape. Although conditioning drills were an important part of practice, Coach didn't want them to take away from time that should be devoted to teaching. In November 1962, Coach Smith used a unique treadmill program devised by the UNC physical education department to accelerate our physical fitness. We practiced free throws after we ran sprints, so we could simulate end-of-game conditions, when we might be tired from a long night of heated competition. The result of all this work and planning, and smart substitutions, was that we could run all night. We were expected to sprint to the bench at time-outs, sprint from one end of the court to the other for foul shots, sprint to the bench when a substitute came in. All this running from one station to another could have had a demoralizing effect on our opponents. That was not happenstance. Coach Smith wanted our opponents to look at us and ask, "Don't those Carolina guys ever get tired?"

OFFENSE

Coach taught us the passing game, good shot selection, and placing a value on the ball by eliminating careless turnovers. We ran our offensive sets over and over in practice until we learned the meaning of a good shot, which was defined for us as one that we should make more often than not. A shot that the shooter would be expected to make less than 50 percent of the time was discouraged. The elimination of bad shots enabled us to take full advantage of each possession. Some coaches like to say that their teams "take what the defense gives us." Well, Coach Smith taught us to be stubborn in this area, explaining, "Our opponent doesn't *give* us anything that is good for North Carolina; therefore we choose to take what we want." This was another aspect of his teaching that drove our opponents crazy. They knew we were going to run our offense until we got the shot we wanted.

My first varsity game as a sophomore was at Duke, and as a young player I had not yet learned the definition of a good shot. I took a long shot from deep in the corner that barely missed, and I was somewhat pleased that my first varsity shot had come so close. Coach Smith approached me after the game and said quietly, "That long shot you took from the corner almost went in, but I can get you a much better shot than that." In this brief conversation I learned what a good shot was. Coach Smith was right because his offense produced much better shots for me than that.

Our passing game offense featured more passing than dribbling and led to many layups and other shots close to the basket. We were taught, in practice and from experience, why shoot from twenty-five feet if the passing game can get us a shot from fifteen feet, or even a layup?

Some turnovers in Coach Smith's offense were not dealt with sternly, although careless loss of the ball was unacceptable. His offense was designed to produce good shots; thus he encouraged risk reward. For example, if we had a play designed to go inside for one of our big men, and if we completed it for easy baskets seven times and threw it away three times, that was a 70 percent conversion rate, excellent by any standards. Coach would exchange three calculated turnovers for seven baskets, plus it was another way that he encouraged his players to play freely without being tentative.

UNSELFISHNESS

If Coach Smith's players were physically fit, could play excellent defense, and took good shots, they met three important criteria that were required to play for him. But there was another one—the most important of all—that had to be there before a player could earn playing time for North Carolina. Unselfishness!

Selfish players, no matter how good they were, did not play for Coach Smith. His players had to be "teammates" in the ultimate sense of the word, or they did not play. He taught us that a pass that led to a basket was every bit as important as the basket itself, and the scorer should thank the passer by pointing to him. If a man dived on the floor for a loose ball, his teammates were expected to rush to his side and help him up. Little things that helped us succeed were celebrated under Coach Smith. We were expected to be on time for practice, for pregame meals, for bus trips, for games. No exceptions. Arriving late, in his eyes, was a way of telling someone that your time was more important than his. He taught us, "You are never more selfish than when you keep a group of people waiting." I don't believe there's ever been a Dean Smith player who forgot the lifetime lesson of punctuality.

If you asked all of Coach Smith's players to express the one main lesson they learned from practicing and playing under him, I suspect that unselfishness would top the list by a wide margin. A lifetime lesson, taught and learned.

BUSINESS PERSPECTIVE

Businesses don't spend nearly enough time practicing, training, or rehearsing. In business there's a game every workday. There's little time set aside to practice or plan. There's not enough time devoted to preparing for a big meeting, sales presentation, project, or problem-solving meeting. We scramble from one problem to the next and do our best with what we've got.

Business is quite different from college basketball, that's for sure. In fact, if college basketball teams were run like many businesses, we'd see some sloppy games on television. Most businesses just go to work and then "play the game." There's little time for practice. Unfortunately there's a price to be paid for that process because practice is where employees and their leaders learn how to improve, to work hard, together, and smart.

Practice, through on-the-job and classroom training, is where great companies are built. Let's say that a business has a major presentation to make to a very important client. A three-million-dollar sale is at stake. The smart thing to do would be to bring together everyone involved in the process in order to plan the entire presentation, establish roles, diagnose each individual on the buying team, and articulate each one's needs, fears, and beliefs. A list of twenty questions the client is expected to ask should be prepared and answered. Then each person's presentation should be rehearsed. There should be role playing, questions should be fired at one another, and the entire session should be videotaped. The tape should be viewed by the group and each person's role critiqued. Then the process should be repeated. If you practice working hard, together, and smart, chances increase that you will perform that way when it really counts. Excellent performance is a result of excellent practice.

Before attorneys make final arguments to juries in important cases, the most effective ones rehearse what they're going to say as well as what they're not going to say. They practice and critique themselves and one another. They do their best not to leave anything up in the air. They don't like surprises. They don't go to the courtroom and fly by the seat of their pants.

However, many businesses do. They will go on important sales calls and wing it or will meet to resolve some big problems with little preparation or skill building. Managers rush from meeting to meeting just trying to hold their heads abovewater. With companies downsizing as they have over the last ten years, the workload for employees has exploded while their staffing help and time have shrunk.

Most of the companies that downsized or merged cut staff. They didn't eliminate the workload; they eliminated the people. More work is dumped on fewer people, so practice time is eliminated. How can one practice when there are so many active fires to put out? The result of such thinking is often sloppy work, ineffective communications, lower morale, employee turnover, and lost sales and profits.

The best companies still believe in practice. They train and develop their people so their people can improve the business. The best leaders insist on practice time—training and development, coaching, mentoring, and performance improvement of their people and themselves. It's not an option.

One leader I know has developed an excellent, detailed, well-planned practice program for his organization. First, each month he selects a book that deals with his business and contains valuable leadership suggestions. Employees are paid fifty dollars if they read it and then meet with their bosses for fifteen to twenty minutes to discuss it and suggest how they can apply it to their work. Employees can read ten such books, present reports on them, and earn an extra five hundred dollars a year. It's not a racket that can be abused, mind you. The reading has to be serious, and the reports have to be well researched.

In addition to this voluntary reading program, each company employee is *required* to read one book each quarter selected by a leadership team and report on it in the departmental meeting, where the manager goes around the room and asks different people to discuss the chapters. He or she might say, for instance, "Allison, what are the main conclusions you took from chapter two, and how could we apply them to our work here to make us better? What are three things that we could initiate that would make us more efficient?"

All the employees are required to attend at least two formal training courses a year, courses that last two or three days each. When they come back from the training, they are required to share with their fellow workers what they learned and how it can be applied to their jobs.

Furthermore, every year each company manager holds six half-day training programs that are specific to the job areas of his or her employees. In the case of the sales manager, say, if he or she does a training session on closing a sale, he or she is asked to present the same program to the managers of the other departments. If the people in production and accounting understand the challenges faced by the sales department, it makes the overall company stronger. The same holds true for sales to learn what it takes to run and operate an efficient shipping department. Shared knowledge is a powerful tool. It makes people smarter and increases the chances of their working together as a team. Just as it's very hard to put in a new offense by rolling a basketball on the floor and doing it on the fly, it's very hard to institute changes to a business without a structured training system.

It would be wise if companies had a rule saying that a senior manager could not be hired or promoted from within unless he or she had a love and thirst for learning as well as the ability and willingness to change old outlooks and old ways of doing business.

If a company is not open to evolving, in this global economy, it will at some point face the need for a revolution. Massive changes are risky and often come too late to save an organization. Some competitor and its employees are getting smarter and better today. They are practicing and learning. Instead of resisting the changes you face, you should embrace them. If your company is in the slow lane and thinks practice is a waste of time, you will have to get used to seeing your competitors sprint past you.

7

RECRUITING THE PLAYERS

Putting together a basketball team at North Carolina began of course with recruiting the players. This was always a careful, tedious, and unending process. And no matter how much work we put into it—and that was considerable—we knew that recruiting was an inexact science. In fact much of it was dumb luck.

It's possible to cross every *t,* dot every *i,* do all the work, and still have the prospect decide to go to another school. Finishing second in a recruiting competition is no better than finishing last. It's also possible to sign a player who doesn't fit in with your program. It's the nature of the business. Fortunately we didn't make a great many recruiting mistakes at North Carolina. Our coaches were good judges of talent, and we were careful to seek young men who were good students and of high character.

Our recruiting efforts were enhanced by our university's excellent academic reputation, the beauty of the campus, the quaint town of Chapel Hill, and the national success our basketball program attained beginning in the late 1960s. All those things, combined with testimonials from our current and former players in praise of the program, made it possible for us to get in the front doors of many outstanding student-athletes.

If our recruiting goal simply had been to find twelve talented basketball players, the job would have been easy. But in addition to having basketball talent, the prospects had to have the grades, test scores, and class rankings to gain admittance to UNC. They also had to fit with the players already in our program as well as subscribe to the way we played basketball. Our players worked hard, real hard. That was why we didn't want to sign a prospect until he had seen us practice. If he didn't want to work that hard, then he would be better off at some other school, and a few did choose that path. During my years as North Carolina's head coach, we decided not to recruit many talented prospects who we thought would not complement the players in our program or who might not be comfortable with the program's philosophy.

The physical attributes we looked for in recruiting were size, quickness, speed, and good hands because I don't believe you can't teach those things. You'll notice I didn't say anything about recruiting jumpers. After all, we were recruiting basketball players, not high jumpers for a track team. Still, we certainly welcomed good team players who had the innate ability to jump high. Most young people who were quick and had good speed could usually jump well.

If a prospect didn't have *all* the physical attributes I just mentioned, there was a chance we'd still recruit him. For instance, if he had a natural feel for the game—savvy is what we called it—along with such other qualities as unselfishness, leadership, toughness, and determination, it might make up somewhat for a slight lack of quickness, speed, or size.

We took one young man who was not widely recruited. The rap on him was that he couldn't run very well. It was true. He had trouble keeping up with more athletic players, especially in a fast-paced game, the style we liked to play. Basketball coaches, except for one mid-major program, shied away from him for this reason. We offered him a scholarship because he had tremendous size, a long reach, excellent hands, and an un-selfish and caring attitude. He was a tremendous young man and excellent student who we knew would be popular with his teammates. It didn't hurt that he really wanted to come to North Carolina. We took him on po-tential. It was a recruiting gamble, one that we won. He became a valuable contributor to the North Carolina program and was terrific for our team's chemistry.

Our program's needs played a major part in determining which prospects we would recruit, of course. If we lacked ballhandling guards but had enough forwards and centers, we concentrated our efforts on guards. In a few cases, beginning in the 1980s, we had to factor in how long we thought one of our players was going to choose to maintain his el-igibility to play college basketball. Still, I have seldom seen a high school player who you could accurately declare would be in the NBA someday. If one of our players was ready to go to the NBA after his junior year, and our investigation revealed that he was going to be a top five NBA draft pick, thereby guaranteeing his financial security for life, we certainly un-derstood if he chose to turn pro and return to Chapel Hill in the off-season to earn his degree. I thought it was the correct position for us to take. Se-rious injury could have robbed a player of his chance to sign a lucrative professional basketball contract. In those cases, our team wouldn't be as good. We had to scramble to try to recruit replacements, but obviously it would be hard to replace those who left and were good enough to play in the NBA.

Sometimes we were at least mildly surprised with these early depar-tures—for instance, after the 1995 season, when we lost Rasheed Wallace and Jerry Stackhouse to the NBA after their sophomore seasons, in which they led our team to the NCAA Final Four. We'd thought that we might lose them after their junior years. Losing both after their sophomore sea-sons set us back a bit. But it worked out well for both of them, and North Carolina's program continued to prosper, although our 1996 team was very young, as a result. We were ACC champions and back in the NCAA Final Four in 1997.

Some colleges sign the thirteen most talented players they can find and then worry about how to divide playing time once they arrive on campus. It works for some, but we chose another route. We made a decision early in my head coaching career not to overrecruit. If we had a really good point guard who had three years of eligibility remaining, we weren't out on the recruiting trail trying to sign another high-profile point guard. We didn't think it would be fair either to the player already in our program or to the recruit. Furthermore, we thought having too many talented players could cause morale problems. We're talking about highly competitive young men, all of whom wanted to play. You can play only five at a time, and there's only one basketball. Having too many talented players at the same position is not the way we built our teams. When you look at it over the long term, I think our method made more sense.

Now it's true that no coach can predict injuries or illnesses. We always had one or two nonrecruited players move up from our junior varsity program, which gave us some depth. It served too as a marvelous way for the student body to be part of our team. Also, we occasionally recruited players with the clear understanding that they would come to North Carolina to be backups and good practice players. It takes a special young man to fill that role and be happy doing it. We were careful during the recruitment of those prospects to tell them what their roles would be. Maybe with hard work and development they could work their way into the starting lineup. It happened in our program a few times. We wanted the facts on the table for everyone to understand. If the prospect decided to go to another school, where he might play more, we understood. Recruiting seldom worked out exactly as planned. The perfect scenario would be to sign a talented point guard who would be willing to learn from a veteran for a season before stepping in as the starter the next year, provided he had earned the right.

Phil Ford,

class of 1977, former college Player of the Year,
NBA Rookie of the Year, assistant coach at
North Carolina for thirteen years, now working
with the UNC Educational Foundation

My mother was a French and English teacher and not an avid basketball fan. She didn't follow the game closely and by and large didn't know the college coaches who came to our home in Rocky Mount, North Carolina, to recruit me out of high school. When my father and I told her that Dean Smith was coming from North Carolina to visit, she replied, "How nice for the University of North Carolina to send a dean to talk to us!"

During the first hour of Coach Smith's visit, he never mentioned basketball in the conversation. Not once. He talked to me about such things as citizenship, race relations, academics, and what would be expected of me at the university. He was very laid back and made me and my family feel at ease. What stood out immediately was that he was honest, had a passion for his players, genuinely cared about academics, and was not going to promise anything when it came to basketball.

Other coaches who were recruiting me were telling me I would start and play a lot, have the ball in my hands for four years, things like that. Coach Smith said I might have to play on the junior varsity team my first year. My mom fell in love with Coach Smith and the way he approached recruiting. I was Phil Ford, Jr., and she called me Little Phil.

"Little Phil, none of these coaches who're coming in here know for sure how you'll do in college basketball against the bigger boys," she said. "How can they tell you how much you'll play until we see how you'll do against college players? If you go to North Carolina and learn and improve, and it turns out you're ready to play a lot your sophomore or junior season, you'll know that Coach Smith won't be in someone's living room promising your playing time to a high school player." Basketball fan or not, Mom had this recruiting stuff figured out.

It was a happy day in our house when I signed to play for Coach Smith at North Carolina. I ended up with much more than I bargained for too. I got a great coach for four years and a close friend for a lifetime.

BUSINESS PERSPECTIVE

In business you need to recruit people whose skills match those needed in their jobs and who share your values. Recruitment is one of the most crucial elements in producing a successful business, but you'd never know it from talking about priorities with many business leaders. Poor selection or placing people in jobs that don't fit their talents and skills is the number-one cause of turnover and poor performance when leaders commit to making great selections, leading becomes much easier. Hire smart; manage easy.

Businesses make four major types of selections:

1. They *hire* new people.
2. They *promote* someone already on the payroll.
3. They *redesign* the jobs of people already employed.
4. They *deselect* people.

College basketball coaches know the importance of recruiting, so they work on it year-round. But most businesses treat selection haphazardly though they intend to do otherwise. This is unfortunate because businesses cannot reach their full potential unless managers commit to making selection a top-five priority; learn how to effectively assess applicants' talents, leadership skills, and knowledge; and learn how to assess candidates' abilities to commit to the company in every way.

The only way to have a great company is to have great people working for it. The three ways to get great people are to *select* them in the four processes given above, to *train* them effectively in technical and leadership skills, and to *lead* them well. If you recruit poorly, you spend much of your time and energy leading and training your poor selections: Their clients and customers dislike them and refuse to do business with them; their co-workers are up in arms about their poor performance and ineffective behavior. One malcontent can ruin an entire department. You try to step in to remedy the situation and spend many unnecessary hours listening to the numerous complaints about the poor selection, trying to coach, train, or direct his or her subordinates while in your deepest heart you know the person probably is not going to work out.

For a business to become excellent managers must select people whose skills and interests match those required by their jobs. It is close to impossible to make people do what they don't want to do or to get them to execute tasks for which they lack skills. Nothing will work to bridge a gap between an employee's skills and desires and the requirements of the job.

Most senior officers have been burned in recruiting. What is the cost of making a bad hire? For entry-level employees, it's about two times their annual compensation. For senior-level positions, the cost is more than ten times the person's compensation. A company should hire slowly, researching the candidate objectively and asking all the right questions. But it should fire quickly. It shouldn't compound the problems created by a bad hire by allowing the employee to stay around for months or years and poison the atmosphere or destroy the performance of others.

Every selection in the organization must be made by first-class processes on the same level as building great strategies, customer service, or high-quality safety processes. Every employee should be given advanced training in selection and then be rewarded for making great selections and held accountable for making poor ones.

EXAMPLE

A man worked as president of a major family-owned company. He was not a member of the family himself. The family members who were in key positions weren't very competent.

The man, a great president, decided he might be better off in a nonfamily-controlled business, so he began the process of looking for a new job. With his excellent job performance and his good reputation, he had no trouble getting the interview that he wanted with one of America's biggest and best-known companies.

This particular company believes in honesty in recruiting and in the importance of making sure each selection is a good match. Sensing the president liked everything about his current job and company except the fact that family members kept him from key policy-making decisions, his interviewers took a different tack. They wanted to make sure that if the man joined them, he wouldn't regret leaving his old job and home. Company representatives decided to see if they could help him stay happily in his current position. That was the topic of their second conversation, which lasted nearly three hours.

In the third interview the interviewers asked the man to talk about his true career interests by discussing his behavior around specific jobs and projects. Doing so brought to light perspectives that weren't completely compatible with those of the interviewing company.

In the fourth interview, they talked about the personal losses the man would incur if he relocated to another city and a different job. The man said his children liked the school they attended, his wife had a great job that she enjoyed, and they all loved where they lived.

As a result of these interviews, the man went back to his company and had a serious talk with his chairman. His job was changed to give him more latitude and responsibility, suiting his skills and making him happier in his work. He handled the redesigned job so well that the company profited greatly, and he earned a million-dollar bonus for that first year back in his old job.

It may not seem like it, but this is an example of a successful interview. The man improved his old job significantly, and the interviewing company didn't land a talented prospect who wouldn't have been the right fit. The man was so grateful for the company's honesty and help that he has funneled about forty million dollars' worth of business to it in the last three years and will continue to do so in the future. He also has recommended several other excellent candidates to the company.

·8·

HONESTY

At North Carolina we were brutally honest with the recruiting prospects. In fact my assistants often chided me for being *too* honest. They said I sometimes painted a picture so bleak that it was unduly discouraging to the prospects. Guilty, as charged. We told the young men the truth, as we saw it, and not just what they wanted to hear. We never promised a prospect that he would start or would play a certain number of minutes each game. How would the players already in our program have felt if they had learned we were out promising their positions to high school sensations?

You wouldn't have much of a program, I'll say that. We told the recruiting prospects that they would get a great education at the University of North Carolina, play in a good basketball program, and be given a fair chance. Phil Ford, one of the great players in the history of college basketball, has said that one of the reasons he chose North Carolina was that we were the only school recruiting him that didn't promise him playing time.

We wanted the prospects to know exactly what was in store for them if they chose North Carolina. The academic demands at Carolina, plus dealing with the emotion of being away from home for the first time and the intense competition on the basketball team, would be more than enough for them to handle. They certainly didn't need to come to Chapel Hill to find broken promises added to the pressures.

This meant we sometimes told some pretty good prospects that they wouldn't have much of a chance to win starting positions at North Carolina unless they improved certain parts of their game. We found over the years that sometimes after telling a real competitor this, he would choose us and then try to show us he could do it. It wasn't our intent to mislead anyone, but if we thought a young man would not have much of a chance to play early in his career as a starter, we told him so. Several proved us wrong. They worked hard, improved, and started before they graduated. At least one even went on to have a long, productive career in the NBA.

The longer I coached, the more partial I became to the prospects who really wanted to come to North Carolina. They didn't need to be sold on our program or the university; they wanted to be a part of North Carolina basketball. That made a strong impression on me. It probably was a mistake on my part, but I thought if the player genuinely wanted to be in Chapel Hill, he would be better for the team than someone I had had to convince to come.

When high school prospects came to Chapel Hill on their official recruiting visits, they spent much more time with our players than they did with me and the other coaches. That made sense to us. While the prospects were on campus to check us out, we were also checking them out. We told our players to be honest with the visitors. We wanted our players to answer their questions as well as tell them how they enjoyed the experience of being a Carolina student and basketball player. We also wanted our players to tell the prospects exactly what would be expected of them if they came to Carolina. We weren't out to trick anyone.

Having our players spend most of the time with the prospects made good sense to me for another reason: They could relate to one another. They had common ground and similar interests. Al McGuire once said there's only so much that a fifty-year-old coach and seventeen-year-old kid have in common to talk about. Our players were our best recruiters.

The current players could also veto a recruit if they didn't think he'd fit in with our program. It happened only a couple of times in my years as head coach.

By the early 1980s our program was on national television on a regular basis, and we had built a reputation that enabled us to get in the door with many of the leading prospects. Nevertheless, we continued to check references carefully. We talked to principals, teachers, guidance counselors, assistant coaches, and the players' high school teammates. We sought all the information on the prospects that we could get. One of our assistant coaches might ask a teammate of a young man, "Your buddy shoots a lot. Do you resent it?" Most of the time the answer would be something along the line of "Oh, no. He's a great guy. He's doing what our coach tells him to do."

We signed one player who shot about thirty times a game during his senior year of high school, the complete opposite of the way we played at North Carolina. He was a great young man who knew he would have to change his style of play if he signed with us. It was easy for him to change, thanks to the job his parents did teaching him unselfishness before he ever got to Carolina.

When he was recruiting, one of my former assistant coaches, John Lotz, used to walk the high school hallways to ask the other students about a prospect. That was a great way to get candid references. We sought information from various sources because we found from experience that a player's high school head coach usually would not say anything bad about him. On two occasions after we'd signed a player, the coach pulled me aside and said, "We need to talk." Then he told me something negative about the young man. "Why didn't you tell me this before?" I asked. The coach replied that he knew we could straighten the player out once we got him to North Carolina. I wasn't quite as confident.

We also found out many things about a young man and his family during our home visits. We were able to get a better handle on how important academics were to the player and his parents or guardians, as well as a better grasp of his goals and aspirations. If I witnessed a player being disrespectful to his parents, I was concerned whether or not we should recruit him.

Before the NCAA wisely limited the number of in-person evaluations a school could make of a prospect, many college coaches thought that they needed to be at every high school game the prospect played during his senior season. In the case of the really great prospects, some coaches saw every high school game they played in as a junior and senior. That seemed ridiculous to me, as well as a waste of time and money. I often told a prospect, "Look, I won't be at every game you play, but that shouldn't be taken as a sign that we are less interested than those coaches who come to watch each time you play. They simply are showing great interest in you since they think it will be harder to say no to them. You can play; we don't need to check you out every other night." Most of the prospects understood that. Some didn't.

As a general rule, we didn't recruit junior college players. The one exception was Robert McAdoo, a young man from nearby Greensboro, who grew up a Carolina fan. He played with us for only one year before signing a lucrative professional basketball contract. He was an excellent player and a good fit in our program. We're certainly happy he chose Carolina and remains loyal to our program today. The reason we didn't recruit junior college players is that we didn't want our young players worrying about our going out and signing junior college players to compete with them after they had invested a couple of years of hard work in our program. Not doing so could have been a mistake on our part, but I was comfortable with it.

PLAYER PERSPECTIVE

Bob Bennett,
class of 1966, attorney, Los Angeles

Coach Smith made no promises other than that I would be attending a great university and playing for a good basketball program. He did not promise me that I would start or get a certain number of minutes' playing time each game—not as a sophomore, junior, or senior.

He emphasized that I would be expected to study hard and to put academics first and basketball second. He was so sincere that I knew he was being truthful with me. During my recruiting visit to the campus I met the chancellor, saw the library (Coach Smith knew exactly how many volumes it housed), and talked to some students and faculty. I also saw the basketball facility, but it was last on the tour. Coach sold the university and its academic greatness and spoke glowingly of the educational opportunity I would have. He mentioned basketball only in passing.

Once I arrived on campus as a freshman, I found things exactly as Coach Smith said they would be. The program was clean in every respect, and all the players were treated equally and with respect. We, all of us, competed on a level playing field. If anything, the high school All-Americans were expected to practice harder and set a good example. There were no prima donnas. Criticism, praise, and discipline were applied equally to all of us.

There was no doubt in my mind what would be expected of me in the classroom and on the court. It was also made clear that I was to take my citizenship role seriously and represent the university in a first-class manner. In recruiting, Coach Smith put his emphasis on the development of the total student-athlete, one reason I chose North Carolina.

BUSINESS PERSPECTIVE

Great leaders know if they break their word of honor, they lose everything. They lead with integrity and take pride in doing the right thing. They treat every person with respect and dignity. They place a premium on fairness and kindness.

When leaders behave this way in the recruiting process, they generate a high level of trust from their subordinates. People know that leaders with integrity will do the honorable thing. They don't manipulate people or sabotage them. Relationships built on dishonesty become complex and ambiguous.

When employees know they can trust their leaders, they don't have to spend time being on guard to protect their own interests. They know they will be treated fairly, and they can spend their time being productive and creative. Those who work for leaders with this kind of integrity develop a high degree of respect for them. They admire them so much, and trust them, that they sometimes go so far as to name their children after them.

Here are three action steps leaders can take to enhance their dealings with people:

- Strive every day to reach a higher level of dealing honestly and openly with everyone.
- Take five minutes at the end of each day to list the three major interactions you worked on that day and the actions you took in each one. Score yourself on how you did according to your own standards of integrity. Just how honest were you?
- On the basis of your analysis of those experiences, design one action step you can take the following day to imple-

ment what you have learned and raise your level of integrity.

Raising the level of integrity and honesty increases leadership effectiveness and the entire organization's performance. Good guys really do finish first.

· 9 ·

BREAKING BAD HABITS

Many of the most highly recruited high school players had been pampered and spoiled. They had been told for as long as they could remember how special they were, how great they were going to be. Adults waited on them hand and foot. Most humans like to believe all the nice things said about them. A constant dose of praise can create some giant egos as well as influence some young basketball player to believe that rules are for others.

Many good high school players are taught to be selfish. They're used to being "the Man." They're the best players on their teams, so sometimes the coaches encourage them to take the most shots and not to worry too much about playing defense. These prospects get the newspaper headlines, have their mailboxes filled with recruiting letters from college coaches, and are important people to their high schools. During the summer many of the most talented of these high school players are treated like royalty at various camps and Amateur Athletic Union (AAU) tournaments. It's asking a lot of a young man to be able to handle that adulation and keep some perspective. It's all out of proportion.

Once the freshmen arrived on campus at North Carolina, we worked to break them of habits and characteristics that we thought would be detrimental to our team's success as well as to theirs. We wanted the "Harry High School" mentality checked at the door. I had individual meetings with our players shortly after they arrived on campus to begin the school year. One of the freshmen came to my office wearing his McDonald's High School All-America jacket. "You can box that up and send it home," I told him. "It's great for you to have it, but this is college now."

How quickly freshmen adjusted to Carolina basketball was influenced to some extent by their high school careers. For instance, we had two great players in our program at the same time. One's life had been pretty much a fairy tale. His basketball career through high school had been free of any bumps. The other player had been cut from his high school team. It had been an indignity in his eyes, and he had the memory etched in his mind. He was hungry and determined when he got to Carolina and played like it from day one. The other player became a tremendous player too, but not before going through some tribulations, none of which he had ever experienced in high school. These were learning experiences; one just learned the lesson earlier in life than the other. Both young men had great careers at Carolina and are doing extremely well now.

We believed in making it difficult for the freshmen, no question about that. "As you start, so shall you finish" is the way we looked at it. Freshmen had mandatory study hall, no matter how well they were doing in school. We had a dinner the night before the start of preseason practice to talk about the team's plans for the season. The veterans voted then on which freshman would carry the heaviest piece of equipment on road trips. The freshmen closed their eyes while the upperclassmen voted by a show of hands. The cockiest freshman usually was given the toughest assignment. Sometimes the vote was unanimous.

The freshmen also had to chase down loose balls at our practices. We made this competitive by awarding points to the freshman who got to the loose ball first. A certain number of accumulated points would get them out of running sprints, which meant we had young players competing hard in practice to get to loose balls. One of our best players, James Worthy, was interviewed after his freshman season. He told a newspaper reporter, "In preseason practice, the only time Coach Smith called my name was to say, 'James, go get that loose ball.'"

I frequently called on freshmen to recite our Thought for the Day and our Emphasis of the Day. In other words, we believed in putting them under some pressure. In some ways it's accurate to say we tore them down to build them back up. The freshmen accepted these demands, knowing they would not affect whether or not they played. Once a game began, we were one team, one class.

It's astounding how much attention is paid to recruiting. Some writers follow the top high school players from game to game, inform their readers which colleges they're considering attending this particular week, and compare them with some of the greatest basketball players of all time. "John Doe of Jones High School has a vertical leap higher than Vince Carter and reminds scouts of Michael Jordan." Oh, my. I never talked to the media or boosters about whom we were recruiting. The speculation was often outrageous and almost always wrong or, at the very best, misleading. We once had a writer compare one of our recruits, who struggled with his passing, with Larry Bird, one of the great passers of all time. A broadcaster compared another of our recruits with Jerry West. For the record, I've not seen another Michael Jordan, Jerry West, or Larry Bird.

Some media people even shot videos of the best-known high school players and marketed them. Recruiting news in North Carolina is a sport unto itself. In fact I'm convinced some of our fans worry more about what future North Carolina teams will look like than they do about the current team. I never could understand that. Is it any wonder that some of these young men had big heads and inflated views of themselves? I wouldn't allow our freshman players to be interviewed by the media until after our team had played its first game of the season. I wanted them to get their feet on the ground. Their egos didn't need the additional media attention, and they didn't need more pressure heaped on them than they already faced in trying to live up to these rave reviews and comparisons.

Invariably the media wanted to talk to our freshmen instead of our established veterans. It made no sense to me. *Sports Illustrated* wanted to put our starting five on its cover for its college basketball edition before the 1981–82 season. It pushed hard for me to include freshman Michael Jordan in the photograph. I didn't for several reasons, one being that I didn't know at the time the photograph was taken, before our preseason work, if Michael would be in the starting lineup for our first game. He was, but I didn't know it at the time the picture was taken.

If I were empowered to write the rules concerning college basketball eligibility, we wouldn't have to worry about freshmen getting too much attention. I wouldn't allow freshman eligibility for men's basketball or football. The recruited freshmen would play on freshman teams along with nonscholarship players. They would have no overnight trips to take them away from their studies. Their practice time would not be as long or as intensive, nor would they have to spend as much time talking to the media. It would give them a better chance to adjust to their academic load and to being away from home for the first time. Aren't teachers supposed to support what's best for their students? Freshman ineligibility definitely would be in the best interests of the student-athlete. We don't do it because of money. Spin it any way you choose, but we allow freshman eligibility in men's basketball and football because of money. If colleges give a freshman a basketball scholarship, they want him "earning his keep" on the court right away. It's wrong and shortsighted. But I've fought that battle for years. I know when I'm licked.

We were fortunate at North Carolina to have many great junior and senior leaders. They helped us with the freshmen. Peer pressure is often a wonderful thing.

PLAYER PERSPECTIVE

Tom Zaliagiris,
*class of 1978, currently president
and CEO of Bentley Churchill Furniture, Inc.,
in Taylorsville, North Carolina*

Each person on Coach Smith's teams was important in his eyes. But it's equally true that no one player, from the superstar to the last man on the bench, was more important than the team.

Freshmen learned this early on.

I believe it's significant that Coach Smith gave much honor to his seniors. I still can remember Phil Ford and me as freshmen carrying the heavy film projector on road trips. We lugged that thing through airports all over the country. As freshmen we were required to chase down every loose ball in practice, were last in line to get on the team bus, last in line for team meals, last for water breaks in practice. We were paying our dues.

The emphasis that Coach Smith placed on respecting the seniors has been a lifetime lesson for me. Once we became upperclassmen, it gave us a sense of self-esteem, even if our playing time was limited. I definitely have carried this philosophy into the business world and stress the importance of everyone in our company's working together as one. We also think our "seniors" have earned the right to be respected.

BUSINESS PERSPECTIVE

It's not unusual for some young, bright, well-educated business recruits to have a few things in common with McDonald's High School All-America basketball players. In many instances, they've been spoiled by their early successes, told how smart they are, and given preferential treatment.

It's hard for them to believe that they have things to learn, but the fact is that when recruits come to work, their knowledge is often very limited. They often have great intellectual ability and academic knowledge but little wisdom. They lack the people skills and the judgment to work with others to implement solutions to business problems. There's a large gap between where they are and where they need to be, but they can't see it.

The leader must find a way to get them to see this performance gap, make them understand it and believe it exists, before he or she can break through their know-it-all habits. People won't change their behavior until they change their beliefs. They'll change their beliefs only when they see for themselves that they'll come out better by changing.

Effective leaders have the ability to get people to change their beliefs, then their bad habits, for their own good as well as for the good of the company. If a recruit has great sales potential and technical knowledge but is going about the work in the wrong way and is too cocky to see his or her mistakes, it's a good idea to ask the new hire to write down the ideal ways to sell to different types of customers under challenging and changing conditions. After getting the answers, ask the recruit to write down how he or she is actually selling. This conversation can reveal to the new sales rep a certain degree of the performance gap and ways of closing the gap.

Then role-play with the new hire or take him or her on a series of sales calls, letting the new hire handle the sales presentations. Ask the sales rep to critique each presentation and then ask the customer to critique the presentation, suggesting ways to improve it. Many go through this exercise and conclude, "Okay, I see I need to learn. How can I do that?"

If a star recruit still needs some persuasion to change annoying or ineffective habits, ask him or her to list the four most effective people they have ever met and then to describe five things each of these individuals do well. Ask the new hire to rate themselves on each of these dimensions of leadership and then to give examples of their behavior that demonstrate their conclusions. Finally, they should list the five reasons why they believe they do not have much to improve upon. The leader should then sit down with the star recruit and coach him or her to success. Your goal as a business leader is to create experiences that give your people feedback about the results of their behavior so they will be motivated to learn how to change their actions when the results are negative.

10

FUN, FATIGUE,
AND THE LONG SEASON

The college basketball season lasts a long time, especially if you play deep into the NCAA tournament, as our North Carolina teams usually did. We started practice on October 15, and our season usually didn't end until late March or early April. My assistant coaches and I, and all the players, were always excited about starting practice on October 15. Every team is. The question is, Will you still be excited and determined in February and March? February is the dog days of college basketball. Coaches and players get physically and mentally tired. February is when teams play the second half of their conference schedules, and October 15 seems like long, long ago.

However, this is also a very important time of the season. Conference titles can be decided in the last crucial weeks. Invitations to the NCAA tournament can be won or lost. The good teams find a way to get through it and continue their good play. We spent a good bit of time planning our late-season practice sessions in an attempt to keep our players fresh and excited. The obvious thing was to shorten practices later in the season, as we did. But more is needed.

Because of the long season, coaches run the risk of inadvertently making basketball boring for the players. The routine needs to be broken occasionally. For instance, if one of our practice sessions wasn't going particularly well, we sometimes divided into two teams, which we made as equal as possible, and let them have a competitive scrimmage. We also ran competitive drills late in the season. Players enjoy competition.

If we sensed that the players were tired and having a hard time focusing, we might let them go ahead and dress out for practice, hold a short team meeting with them, and then surprise them: "Take the day off. See you tomorrow."

In my early years as head coach we played volleyball on the Monday after winning the ACC tournament. I wanted the players to get their minds off basketball for a day after an exciting and draining ACC tournament. Only the ACC tournament champion went to the NCAA tournament in those days. Talk about pressure! Playing in the conference tournament took a lot out of the players. The change of pace provided by an afternoon of volleyball had refreshed them when we got back to work the next day preparing for the NCAA tournament.

Sometimes a change in routine resulted in a day of hard work. If we had a week between games and thought the circumstances warranted it, we might bring the players to the gym to what we called a run-and-shooting practice, which didn't require the players to get their ankles taped. These different approaches kept the players from falling into the trap of a boring routine. It also allowed us to work them when they needed the work and to rest them when they were tired.

A coach also must pay attention to his players, to listen to what they say, watch how they practice, and see if any of them stay after practice to work on their shooting. If not, we usually changed the next practice and lightened up. College basketball as we know it today has developed into a tournament sport. Whether that's good or bad could be debated, but it's nonetheless true. It means the most important games occur in March, when the players have every reason to be tired from a long, arduous season.

The coach can help the players get through it, but only if he pays attention to the messages they send him. Sometimes those messages come via words, sometimes by body language, sometimes by performance. I was fortunate to have outstanding senior leaders to help me in this area. Fortunately for us, we handled the late seasons well. Almost all our teams played their best basketball in March. Certainly, they should have with all the work they had done in practice during the long season.

Although we approached the game seriously and worked hard at it, we hoped everything we did would help the game be fun and fulfilling for our players. That's why we wanted all of them to be an important part of our teams. We liked all five players on the court to touch the ball and to feel free to shoot it when they had a good shot. We played our reserves when we could. We stayed at nice places on the road and otherwise traveled well.

The players had worked hard academically and in basketball to receive scholarships to play at Carolina. We wanted them to have a good experience, enjoy their careers, and graduate. Nothing was more important to me as head coach than those things. I would have felt awful if a player had said to me in our last one-on-one meeting, "Coach, I didn't enjoy it here." It never happened, thank goodness.

Most basketball players find the game fun. Give them time off, and they'd be likely to go to another gym and play a game of pickup with their friends.

Here's another tip: If the hard work is also fun, the performance will be enhanced greatly.

Randy Wiel,

class of 1979, former head basketball coach
at UNC-Asheville and Middle Tennessee State

Most of Coach Smith's former players will tell you that one of his greatest gifts was being able to teach effectively and communicate with young men from four distinct decades—the sixties, seventies, eighties, and nineties. Believe me, the players in the sixties had a different mentality from the players in the nineties. Coach Smith didn't miss a beat in his ability to communicate with all of us and to inspire us as well.

When I played in the 1970s, most coaches had the Vince Lombardi approach: "It's my way or the highway." Coach Smith was tough, real tough and demanding. In practice he wouldn't allow us to talk except to communicate on defense. He pushed us hard and expected a lot. But he was the first to praise good deeds.

The basketball season is a long grind. At North Carolina it began on October 15 and usually ran until around April 1. Everybody was excited and fired up to get started in October, and that feeling ran through December. But beginning in mid-January and running into February, it was practice, games, and travel. It was a grind, one that could be very tiring for the players, mentally as well as physically.

Most coaches make practices shorter late in the season. Coach Smith took it several steps beyond that. For example, our offensive practices usually consisted of much passing, screening, cutting, and searching for good shots. To break the routine late in the season, Coach Smith had what he called our pro game, in which we ran a very fast offense and took the first good shot that surfaced, even if it came after only one pass. He sometimes assigned players to coach the two teams in those sessions, to give them a chance to see how coaching felt. It was a refreshing break from the routine, one that the players enjoyed immensely.

Coach Smith always kept the game in perspective. He wanted it to be fun for the players because if it wasn't, why play? Even when it was fun, it was very hard work. During the last two weeks of February he incorporated a lot of shooting drills in practice because players love to shoot. It kept our attitudes and our legs fresh. Also late in the season, Coach Smith might have us watch a tape for thirty minutes and then surprise us by announcing there would be no practice. We'd be in and out of the gym in less than an hour.

Another way that Coach Smith made the game fun was the way he conducted the drills we ran in practice. They weren't long and drawn out. Many coaches would get on a drill and stay on it for thirty minutes if it weren't being done correctly. Coach Smith knew that we'd have practice tomorrow, and we could work on it again. He believed in short, repetitive drills rather than long and boring ones. He also followed a hard drill with one that was fun. Players love to scrimmage, and Coach usually ended practices with short, snappy scrimmages.

He even broke up his short scrimmages. For instance, if we were set to scrimmage for twenty minutes, he'd divide it into two ten-minute halves. He didn't believe in scrimmaging the first team against the second team. Had he done that, the second team, or the blue team, would have been running sprints all the time. Instead he made the teams even. I recall some times when he put Phil Ford and Walter Davis on the blue team, and when I was a sophomore, he put me on the white team (the first team). It gave us all an equal chance to succeed. In addition to making the scrimmages more fun and more competitive, it was another way in which Coach Smith reminded us that no one player was more important than the team. If we were in a Friday practice with a game to follow on Saturday, though, he conducted practice in a way that the leading eight players got more time playing together as a unit.

The way we were taught to play the game at North Carolina was fun. We played unselfishly. Coach believed the team would be stronger if we had four or five players scoring in double figures rather than one or two men getting all the shots. Instead of staying with one defense, Coach Smith believed in changing. We would apply defensive pressure, and then about the time the opponent grew accustomed to it, we'd call it off and go to something else. Our goal was to give the opposing point guard so many different looks that it made him tentative. In watching tapes, we could see sometimes that opposing point guards would be hesitant as they approached the midcourt line, not knowing if we were going to pressure and trap them or fall back into a softer defense.

As I have gone around speaking to basketball coaches, I've learned that they all know basketball. Most of them know it very well as a matter of fact. But when you hear them talk and then watch their teams play, you see that their teams might be playing a very different style from what the coach says he believes in. It's not easy for a coach to communicate to his players how he wants the game to be played and then get them to do it that way. It takes a special person to pull that off. Those who do it best are the ones who have well-coached teams. Coach Smith was the best ever at it.

His ability to make the game fun and keep the players fresh during a long, competitive season is one reason that his teams always seemed to play their best at tournament time. As players we didn't worry so much about winning and losing, but because of the way he taught us and treated us, we didn't want to let him down. He had an unbelievable knack of communicating with us that made us work hard to avoid disappointing him. It remains that way to this day, long after my playing career is over.

BUSINESS PERSPECTIVE

When business operates at peak performance, the leaders and employees work as hard as they can and still focus with clear vision on what they are doing. The demands on them to perform at a high level are so great that they are starved for time. They go from task to task, but after a hard day's work, something important always is left undone.

In the last decade the speed of change and the degree of complexity in business have accelerated greatly. There is so much pressure on business leaders today that they often have grave problems managing their own lives and their own stress. Many of them complain to me, "I have no balance in my life. It's all work." Some neglect their families, their health, their friends, communities, fun, and spiritual development. They don't read enough and have no chance to get away and recharge themselves—physically, mentally, or emotionally. They have E-mail, pagers, voice mail, and cell phones ringing constantly. Many leaders I work with get fifty to a hundred E-mails a day. They can't get away from work. Well, they have to find a way to escape, or they won't survive.

Burnout is a serious problem in today's business world, for leaders and their subordinates. Their "season" is their career; they have forty years of "game days."

How do leaders get their employees to do their best and most productive work for a lifetime? It's a daunting challenge. When a car is driven too fast, it shakes and easily goes out of control. When workers are pushed beyond reasonable bounds, they burn out, quit, or become so overwhelmed with fatigue and stress that they aren't productive. The best bosses know that their workers must have balance in their lives, must be rested and have positive attitudes if they are to sustain peak performance.

The key to making this happen is pacing, and it requires adherence to what I call the four natural phase movements of the life of a group.*

1. THE TASK PHASE:

The members of the group meet as a team to talk about what's before them and how they're going to get the job done. They define roles, clarify information, and establish processes. Their plan has been developed, their day starts, the work begins.

2. GOAL ATTAINMENT PHASE:

The team executes the plan, they make the decisions, choose alternatives, or make the pitch to an important client. They complete their work.

3. SOCIAL-EMOTIONAL PHASE:

After the project is finished, the group members naturally gravitate toward talking about their feelings about their performance. They suppressed their emotions during phases one and two but now their feelings come out, both positive and negative. The hope is that the individuals don't get too high after a win or too low after a loss because such extremes make recovery time longer and more difficult.

4. THE LATENT PHASE:

After the emotions about how things went have been expressed, team members enter a phase of reflection. They withdraw, they rest over a weekend or during an afternoon off, and recharge physically

*Frederick Bales, a Harvard psychologist.

and mentally. Leaders need to understand that people must have time for resting, processing their experiences, and recovering in order to retool to be able to perform their best on the next assignment. When there's a big task ahead that calls for phase one and phase two behavior, employees won't be ready for it if they aren't given sufficient time to recover.

The leader must recognize which phase employees are in. He or she might have to lead them back to the task phase if they're not ready to go there. A meeting could be called where the leader might ask his or her employees to write down the six things they learned from the previous work cycle. That's an inward time, one for reflection—the latent phase. After it's over, the group will be ready for the task phase and to get going again.

Most leaders know that victories should be celebrated. But the completion of a project, even if it didn't result in a positive solution to a problem, should also be celebrated to let the group go through the social-emotional phase. A good idea is to have a "closure party" to lead the team through phase three. Then give them a little time for the latent phase. After a best effort has been given, the performance has been critiqued and analyzed, and all the lessons have been learned, there must be closure, consolidation, and rest.

The best leaders figure out a way to build fun and variety into the jobs of their employees. "Hey, even though we didn't get the job, you made a great presentation this morning. Let's review it, celebrate our efforts, take a break, and come in tomorrow ready to go."

Some leaders refuse to let their employees have any fun. Their style encourages flatness, fatigue, and boredom and almost never produces winning results. It's a poor way to run a business.

Vail Associates owns and operates ski areas in Colorado. It's a seasonal business, much like a college basketball season, running from

October to early April. Workers are always fired up about coming back to work in October after a summer of varied activities and travels. They are ready to go. The slopes are groomed, the snow is beautiful, the equipment is checked out, and the people flock in. Business peaks at Christmas, when employees work from early morning until late at night. January is still very busy, and the work week is long.

I worked with the employees and ski professionals there. Their job performance was excellent in November and December, when they were fresh. It slowed down a little in January, and by February some of them were so fatigued from the long season that they struggled just to go through the motions. By early March it wasn't uncommon to hear "I'm so tired I don't think I can make it until the end of the season." They longed for a latent phase.

February and March were when people quit their jobs, customer relations declined, and customer satisfaction dropped. The employees were burned out.

We attacked the problem by creating miniseasons. We planned some breaks for the employees and instructors for each month beginning in November. We built more fun into their jobs and hired a few more people so we could give everyone more time off during the peak times. It paid off handsomely.

I met with managers and instructors in February and March, and we talked about learning and teaching theories, the different personalities and approaches of the employees and ski instructors, the four phases of work and group life, and how all these affect performance. We got them to look at their individual work and teaching styles. The meetings caused them to be eager to try new approaches. At the end of February, the employees and instructors remained excited about their work, were more eager to test new teaching approaches and experiment with these new ideas and methods.

Job performance was raised significantly in January, February, and March; customer satisfaction increased; employee morale went up; employee turnover was reduced. Sure, there was still some complaining but the employees and instructors learned to anticipate these phases and to laugh at stress instead of getting angry about it.

Workers treat their jobs much differently when they have fun, feel they are learning, and are not worn out. Willard Marriott, founder of the hotel chain, said the way for a company to provide great customer service is to provide excellent employee service first. Employees need to feel valued, to have fun and variety built into their jobs, and to be allowed to adapt to each of the natural phases of work. Only then can they sustain their peak performance.

PART THREE

PLAYING
TOGETHER

11

TEAMWORK

I t's clear from the way we recruited that we made every effort to bring to Carolina players who would enjoy playing in a team environment. For sure, we didn't look at a prospect's scoring average to determine his potential as a college player. In fact, if a player had a scoring average that was inordinately high, it might have served as a danger signal for us. Maybe his definition of good basketball was to shoot every time he touched the ball. If so, we didn't want him.

Beginning in the recruiting process, we talked to our players constantly about the advantages of playing together. There is a real strength derived from depending on one another. It's also fun and satisfying for a player to realize he had done something to help his team. We drilled it into the players during every one-on-one and team meeting, at each practice and game: Play unselfishly; depend on one another; watch your teammate's back; don't worry about who scores as long as it's a North Carolina player.

We constantly thought about ways to make the team concept stronger. We called it chemistry; the better the chemistry among the players, the stronger the team. On road trips, for instance, we assigned two players to room together, but we changed those assignments for each trip. We wanted each player to get to know all his teammates. When freshmen came to Carolina, we assigned them campus roommates for the first semester. After that, they were free to room with whomever they wished. They often chose to stick with their original roommates.

Changing roommates on road trips is a good way to keep cliques from forming, another of our team-building goals. When we were on road trips, the players had some free time to do as they wanted. They could dress casually, shop, visit the sights, and go out with whom they pleased. In those situations I always liked to see two large groups consisting of six players go out. It was a good sign that cliques weren't forming. Fortunately we seldom had trouble with cliques on our North Carolina teams.

In the early days of integration I sometimes walked into the cafeteria and saw four black players eating at one table and four white players eating at another. That disturbed me. Those barriers eventually broke down, thank goodness, and we had interracial wedding parties involving our players. Henrik Rodl, who is white, had George Lynch, who is black, as his best man. Each of them played a vital role on our 1993 NCAA championship team. It was wonderful to see such strong friendships develop.

The NCAA allows college teams to leave the country once every four years to play overseas. We took advantage of it and traveled during the long Christmas break to play national teams from other countries. I did admonish the players that if we took these overseas trips, they had to do whatever it took to be ready to play our next game once we arrived home. We went to Spain, England, Japan, Germany, the Canary Islands, Italy, the Netherlands, and other places. These long trips helped build team chemistry, that's for sure, and they also served as a terrific educational experience for the players. They saw things they'd never seen before and got a taste of different cultures. The players got to know one another well on these trips. Many times the language was different from ours, so the players had to depend on one another. The long flights, time spent waiting in airports, bus rides to arenas and surrounding towns, free time to do as they pleased, eating together: All those things served as effective team-building tools. The players were together, learning about one another as well as understanding more about the environment in which they all grew up.

As far as the basketball part of the trips was concerned, we played against talented players, usually the national teams from the countries we visited. That tremendous caliber of competition, as well as the different styles of play we encountered in foreign countries, helped our players improve and was good experience for what was to come when we arrived back in the States, playing good teams away from home. Our 1971–72 team went to Spain and defeated Real Madrid, which had a great team. It seldom lost on its home turf. We went back to Spain on another trip and fell behind Real Madrid by a large margin in the second half only to fight back to get within three points late in the game. We lost, but it was an impressive comeback by our players. After the game the Real Madrid soccer coach asked, "How do you teach your team not to ever give up?" I told him that we tried to execute well on each possession and fell back on our philosophy of playing hard, playing together, playing smart. "We always believe we have a chance if we do those things," I said.

If the team as a unit played unselfishly, it would usually succeed, and the individuals on the team would also prosper. The players needed to understand this and buy in to it before we could get to where we wanted to be.

PLAYER PERSPECTIVE

Warren Martin,
class of 1986, now a public school teacher and basketball coach in Chapel Hill

---

One reason teamwork prevailed on Coach Smith's teams is that the players, from the most highly recruited down to the least, heard the same thing from him during the recruiting process. He never

promised playing time and didn't say we'd start, get to play a certain number of minutes, or anything of that nature. I once asked
one of my teammates, James Worthy, an All-American and true superstar, how Coach had handled his recruitment. "He promised me
nothing," James said.

When high school recruits came to the campus to visit, Coach
told us to let him know if we didn't want them to be a part of our
team. If we'd had valid reasons why a recruit shouldn't join us, I'm
sure Coach would have listened. Compatibility was a big part of his
program. While he didn't make recruiting promises, he did tell us
exactly what he expected from us. Almost all of us had watched
Carolina play on television for years, so we understood from the beginning the way his teams played—unselfishly—and players who
didn't enjoy that style wouldn't have chosen Carolina in the first
place. He recruited players who believed in teamwork and making
it work.

When I arrived at Carolina in the 1981–82 season as a freshman,
the team had made it to the NCAA championship game in 1981 but
lost to Indiana. It was amazing how every player who returned my
freshman year—and this included the student managers—was
convinced beyond any doubt that we would win the national championship. I mentioned to one of our veterans that it would be great
to get back to the championship game again, and he let me know
that wouldn't be nearly good enough. Get there and win it, that was
what the veterans believed, and they made the rest of us believe it
too. When we won it in New Orleans, I must say that our players
expected it.

Coach never took teamwork for granted. He stressed it each and
every season. In our first practice each year he would look around at
the assembled players and say, "This is not the same team as last
year. I see some new faces here while some who were with us last

year aren't here." It was his way of telling us right out of the gate that we would have to work to develop the teamwork and unselfishness that had characterized the previous North Carolina team. It wouldn't happen automatically.

Coach put us in the mind-set that if we gave up something individually, we would get something much greater in return in the form of team success. He had an unbelievable ability to make young men understand that if we sacrificed individual goals for team goals, we would be much stronger as a unit and eventually much stronger individually. Coach Smith reinforced his teamwork philosophy by treating every man on the team as a human being, even though we were very different in terms of basketball skills.

To me, a perfect example of a Carolina player who demonstrated teamwork and unselfishness was Cecil Exum, who graduated in 1984. Cecil was a good player and athlete, but he didn't play all that much. Many people in his situation would have pouted and complained, but Cecil never protested one minute about a lack of playing time. Everything he brought to the team was positive. He never missed practice; he worked hard; he cheered for his teammates; he competed against the starters in practice to make them better. Cecil was a symbol of Coach Smith's teamwork, in my opinion.

The men who played for Coach Smith have a strong common bond. We came from many different backgrounds, some with great basketball skills, others with not as much, but we were all taught the same things. After graduation we spread out in many different directions, to many different careers. But when I meet former UNC players who played ten or twelve years before I did or the young men who play now, it's all so seamless. I know about them, they know about me, and the conversations between us are natural and easy. It's amazing how we really do feel like brothers.

BUSINESS PERSPECTIVE

I have asked about a thousand leaders to describe the best team-work experience they ever had, and the worst, in my pursuit of the characteristics of high-performing teams and ineffective ones. I've concluded that you can identify how much teamwork exists in your present orgagnization by measuring your team in the following areas: First, *individual peak performance.* On great teams each member typically performs at his or her highest level of ability. Terrible teams, with individuals who might be highly talented, perform below the talents of their members.

Second, *selflessness.* In great teams the individuals become so committed to the mission and goals and purpose of their teams they lose themselves in the process of working to achieve their teams' mission. They find their personal satisfaction, pleasure, and reward in achieving the teams' goals more than their own interests. Indeed, in this process they become honest about their own strengths and limitations and what they can do and cannot do. The members of a successful team compete to contribute to the team rather than to beat one another.

The members of ineffective teams become so frustrated with the teams that they focus mainly on their own interests and couldn't care less about what happens to the overall teams. They retain their individual priorities. As long as they are able to blend in personally with the teams, that is good enough for them; they become internally competitive, wanting to win against one another. At this point you have concealment, fighting, and sabotaging, not cooperation.

Third, *high morale.* People love coming to work; they enjoy one another's company and have fun executing their roles. Energy is high; they come to work full of enthusiasm, and passion for the work prevails. On terrible teams, people are miserable coming to work; the spirit is dead.

Fourth, *no fear of failure*. On high-performing teams, members are not afraid to fail. Though they may face major risks and obstacles, they still perform without fear of failure, punishment, or shame if they make mistakes. They have learned that all they can do is their best and that the other team members and the leaders will accept them for their best efforts, even if they make mistakes. On terrible teams the members are afraid to fail, so they become cautious, avoiding risk, but they feel stressed, under pressure, and perform even more poorly.

Fifth, *mutual care and support*. Members of great teams care about one another and support one another personally. They are close and value their friendships as well as their working relationships. On terrible teams people typically don't like one another, they fight against one another, and they openly convey their mutual disrespect.

Coach Dean Smith's teams exhibited each of these indicators of great teamwork: individual peak performance; selflessness; high morale, satisfaction, and positive spirit; no fear of failure; and mutual care and support. These indicators are so fundamental to well-functioning teams that you can adapt them as goals for any team you lead so the members focus all their energy on achieving positive results.

12

DEFINING AND
UNDERSTANDING ROLES

Putting a talented, compatible team together is never easy. Problems, some predictable and others unforeseen, almost always surface at some point.

The young men who played basketball at North Carolina and at other ACC schools worked hard for years to get to accomplish what they did in the sport. There's no telling how many social events they missed growing up so they could devote time to basketball. The game obviously meant a lot to them, or they wouldn't have worked so hard at it for so many years. These were world-class basketball players as well as very competitive young men. Most of them had never had to worry about playing time; they had been the stars on their teams for as long as they could remember. Everybody on our roster wanted to play. Most expected to play. It was their competitive nature.

We always hoped that roles for the players would unfold naturally and be defined in practice. These were intelligent young men. They usually knew which players were doing best in practice. Their own strengths and weaknesses were exposed. All of them knew that playing time at Carolina was earned by practice performance. But sometimes roles weren't so easily identified. Sometimes the competition for playing time was extremely close, as was the talent of the players involved, and players honestly didn't know where they stood. On such occasions I had to step in and help the players understand their roles as well as what was expected of them. That was usually accomplished with candid, one-on-one conversations between the player and me.

After the first blue-white scrimmage, which was usually held about three weeks after the start of practice on October 15, I met individually with each player. Because we often had to juggle practice around afternoon classes and labs, it took about four days to conduct all the individual player meetings. I told each player where he stood at that particular time and what he could expect as far as playing time was concerned. I emphasized that things could change, so he should strive to improve with each practice. I tried to be specific in telling him the areas where he needed the most work. Giving up, pouting, excessive griping, or complacency were not options.

During these one-on-one talks I never set up a player to be in direct competition with a teammate for playing time, never said, "In order to beat out so-and-so, you must do the following things . . ." We didn't do it that way. It would have made it hard for those two players to share the same goals for the team. They would have been too self-focused and concerned about doing better than their teammates in order to win playing time. Individual goals would have surpassed team goals, to the detriment of the whole. We would have torpedoed the part of our philosophy that promoted playing together and playing smart. The key was to get the players locked in on team goals and shared dreams, not on individual competition with teammates.

I thought it was important for our players to understand their roles clearly. Basketball is a sport that demands it. In football an offensive tackle knows without anyone's telling him that he isn't going to be handed the ball on the opponent's one-yard line; his role is to block. But in basketball each player can choose to shoot, pass, or dribble. Once, in an NCAA tournament game, one of our big players missed an open shot from about seventeen feet from the basket. During a time-out shortly afterward I asked him why he had taken the shot. "Coach, I was wide open," he said. To which I replied, "There's a reason you were wide open. They wanted you to take that shot." There's a bromide in basketball that goes like this: "We took what they gave us." Well, I never thought any of our opponents ever willingly gave us anything that was good for us. We preferred to be stubborn. Instead of taking what they gave us, we took what we wanted. Having this particular big man shoot from seventeen feet was what the opponent wanted, not what we wanted. It was part of understanding individual roles for the good of the team.

Understanding roles was essential to the way we built our teams and played at North Carolina. It would be very hard to have a true team if the players didn't know what their status was going to be from game to game. Letting them know was in their best interests, as well as the team's.

Once we had gone through the long, careful process of selecting a starting lineup and the leading substitutes, I wasn't quick to change it. I didn't want the players to feel pressured that they would be removed from the game and even have their roles changed if they made a mistake. It would have made basketball robots out of them.

This doesn't mean that we didn't sometimes make changes during the season in our starting lineup and in our substitution pattern. We certainly did, but we didn't do it capriciously. If one of the reserves kept improving in practice and deserved playing time, I tried to make sure he got it. One of the hardest things I ever had to do as a coach was to tell a young man that he was being replaced in our starting lineup. He may have taken the news well, but it was still an unpleasant experience for me.

We believed in attacking our opponent on offense and defense. I didn't want our players to perform tentatively, as they might have if they had it in the back of their minds that I would yank them out of a game for making a mistake. We took some calculated risks. We gambled some on defense and made some tough passes to our big men in hopes of getting a layup. We threw alley-oops to certain players for a dunk. Sometimes those things backfired, as we knew they would. That was one of the reasons I never substituted for mistakes, because sometimes making a mistake is part of the process. Early one season I noticed that one of our players wouldn't pass the ball to a teammate. When I questioned him about it, he said, "He doesn't catch it, and I don't want to get charged with a turnover." I told him it was my job to worry about things like that.

Another reason I didn't substitute for mistakes is that nobody— whether he or she is from business, athletics, entertainment, or politics— likes to be embarrassed in public. Embarrassing a player by screaming at him in front of twenty-one thousand fans and millions more watching on television doesn't help him or the team. However, I didn't hesitate to chew out a player in private or in a team meeting when he deserved it. If we were in a team setting watching tapes, I might say to a player, "Your failure to box out on those three occasions let your teammates down." Sometimes to hear criticism in front of teammates can end in a positive result. Peer pressure can be a valuable weapon.

We learned over the years that the better the players understood their roles—and accepted them for the good of the team—the better off North Carolina basketball would be.

PLAYER PERSPECTIVE

Ralph Meekins,
head manager of UNC's 1983 basketball team,
now an attorney in Shelby, North Carolina

In 1983 we were about to play NC State in the semifinals of the ACC tournament in Atlanta. Ten minutes from the Omni Coliseum, where the tournament was being held, and a full thirty minutes from our hotel at Lake Lanier, I turned to one of my assistant managers to confirm that he had loaded our team's game uniforms on the bus. We had played the day before in our white uniforms and had to wear the same ones again, and I had asked an assistant manager to wash the uniforms and have them ready for the NC State game.

When I asked him, he immediately looked horrified, and I knew we had a problem. I had to go to the front of the bus and tell Assistant Coach Bill Guthridge that we had left the uniforms in the hotel. I did not take the time to explain to him who left the uniforms because I knew it didn't matter to him or Coach Smith. Coach Smith taught us never to think about blame for blame's sake; that wasn't the point. I understood my role as head manager and knew that when something went wrong, the worst thing to do was to blame it on someone under my command. It was my responsibility to make sure the uniforms were on the bus and that was all that mattered. I should have asked about the uniforms before we'd got on the bus at the hotel. We stopped the bus and called the hotel. A hotel employee was kind enough to locate the uniforms and rush them to the Omni. He was late, however, and our players had to go out on the court to warm up wearing nothing but their athletic supporters underneath their warm-up suits.

We ended up losing the game in overtime, and NC State, which had to win the ACC tournament to go to the NCAA tournament, ended up winning the national championship. The minor change in the players' routine surely cost us at least a point; therefore, I take full credit for NC State's 1983 national championship.

Now, as an attorney, I know that I am responsible for all of my work. Blaming others for mistakes not only doesn't correct them but compounds them.

Business Perspective

Part of Dean Smith's greatness as a leader lies in his ability to get his players to get beyond understanding their roles to *embracing* them. But their commitment starts with clarity. If employees don't understand their roles, their specific areas of responsibility, it's almost impossible for the company to work well as a team. Confusion will reign. Divided responsibility ends up being nobody's responsibility.

A huge real estate development company specializes in building resorts, office parks, and other large and complex projects. The company policy puts one person in charge of each project. For instance, in building a ski resort, one manager is in charge of hotel construction, another has to oversee the construction of the golf course, and yet another supervises roads and transportation. Each manager knows that he or she is completely, 100 percent in control of that one project and *only* that project. All of them know exactly what they are supposed to do as well as what they aren't supposed to do. It's important to teach people what their jobs aren't. The hotel supervisor, for instance, is not supposed to meddle with the building of the golf course. He or she can and should offer suggestions and help but stay focused on his or her role.

In assigning roles, the company must do these four things:

- Design a set of complementary roles
- Define specific responsibilities
- Communicate them clearly
- If people are put into jobs that they are good at but might not love, give them hope for the future. Tell them that they have a chance to change their roles at some point, but

not now: Tell them until conditions change, this is how we'll set it up. "It doesn't mean this is forever. You have hope to change or add to your role in the future."

If you want their best work, it is vitally important for people to maintain hope when they want an advancement or more responsibility. Marriage counselors say that counseling seldom works if one partner has totally given up on the marriage: "Why change? This marriage is gone!" There's no hope left, no end to the storm. I give up.

Every person who holds a job has a set of tasks that he or she does well and tasks he or she doesn't do well. It's the leader's role to decide what the "best-fit job" is for an employee and put him or her in it. Job descriptions are often out-of-date almost as soon as they're published, because of internal or external changes.

How does a leader find out what job best fits a person?

- Determine what technical skills they have.
- Learn enough about them to know what they love to do, what their interests are, and what they are good at.
- Find out if their personality fits the specifics of the job. In basketball, some players do better coming off the bench than they do starting. Some employees also do better working in lower-profile jobs, or being second in command, or being inside persons while others excel at more complex jobs, at taking the heat, and at external relations.
- Finally, after getting the answers to these questions, assign those persons a job and a role and tell them exactly what they are supposed to do and not supposed to do. Provide clarity.

When companies do this successfully, they make leading easy. They build focused and dedicated employees who are happy with their role on the team. Their work will show it.

Everybody has a best-fit job, and both sides win when it's identified and implemented. *There's a key, though!* The person's best-fit job *must* be needed by the company. The company has to ask the questions: "Do we need that particular skill? Is it worth the cost to the company?" If the answer to either question is no, then the company needs to help the person find another job, even if it means they leave the company.

A big manufacturing company sells machines to other manufacturing firms and then services them when they break. A man within the company was promoted to manager of the repair division. His new job called on him to work with customers, bring in equipment that needed repairs, assign the work to different departments under his command, and make sure the work was completed in a timely and effective manner.

When the manager assigned work, he got what we call in business push back. He worked with engineers and designers who had strong opinions. The manager was such a "pleaser" he would back off when his subordinates raised objections. The result: Machines weren't getting fixed on time, and when they were finally shipped back, the repairs had not been done correctly. The engineers and designers were blaming the company's customers for not installing the machines properly. The manager was stymied.

After eight months of the company's operating this way, customers were angry and threatened to take their business elsewhere. The company CEO had no choice but to remove the manager from his job. He gave him a thirty-day paid leave and asked him to come back after that time to talk about reassignment within the company.

The leader acknowledged he had made a mistake when he promoted the man in the first place because he had put him in a role that he was not good at. He had not diagnosed the man's best-fit job.

"I put him in a terrible job," the CEO said, "and in the process hurt our customers, hurt him, hurt me, and hurt the company."

The man was a good employee and was excellent in dealing with people in a low-key fashion. A job that was open in customer service fitted him well. But it came with a 30 percent pay cut. Instead of hitting him with the pay cut all at once, the CEO factored it in over several years, making it more palatable. The man does a great job in customer service and is happy. The company is winning because it finally learned that this particular teammate does better coming off the bench than he does as a starter. He found a perfect role to play for himself and the team.

If the CEO had learned this before putting him in a role that didn't suit his skills or interests, the company could have avoided eight months of tension, customer dissatisfaction, and financial losses.

13

WHY UNSELFISHNESS WORKS

Good people are happy when something good happens to someone else. In a team sport such as basketball, it's particularly satisfying to see teammates rejoice in the successes of their buddies. It's part of what makes coaching a meaningful profession.

To build teamwork, it certainly helps to start with good people. As head coach I was very partial to young men who genuinely wanted to play at North Carolina, who needed no sales job to persuade them. They wanted to wear the light blue uniform, and some of them had dreamed of it since they were in grade school, shooting baskets at rims without nets in their backyards. It was a good indication that they had watched us play on television, liked the unselfish way that our teams played, and wanted to play that way themselves.

We didn't necessarily recruit unselfishness per se. It takes some people longer to understand and grasp the personal benefits associated with putting the team first. We usually thought we could change a self-centered behavor pattern once we got the players to North Carolina. We did, however, observe closely to see how the players interacted with their teammates and whether they treated others with respect. We weren't know-ingly going to recruit a problem player, no matter how much basketball talent he had. One person's selfish attitude could poison the locker room and make it hard, if not impossible, to establish teamwork. We didn't make many recruiting mistakes in this area, but when we did, we either saw change or helped the player find another school. This happened only twice in my time as North Carolina's head coach. Had we acted otherwise, we would have violated the very philosophy we taught to our players. We weren't going to allow someone's selfish interests to supersede what was good for the team. That simply was not going to happen.

Building teamwork is harder than it ought to be, simply because of both our society's fascination with individual success and the emphasis it places on winning no matter how it is achieved. For example, when a child comes home from a basketball game, the first thing he or she is likely to hear from parents is "Did you win?," followed by "How many points did you score?" More appropriate questions would be "Did you have fun?" and "How did you play on defense?" and "Did you follow the coach's in-structions?" Our emphasis on winning and creating stars certainly makes building teamwork a daunting challenge. However, it's worth the irrita-tion because it works. It absolutely works.

Basketball is a beautiful game when the five players on the court play with one heartbeat. Passing, screening, cutting, and movement away from the ball: The game can be almost balletic in its grace and simplicity. A team can accomplish great things when the individual members don't worry about who gets credit.

I was a dinner guest of Jack Nicklaus's one night at his beautiful home. The conversation turned to the long-term, no-cut contracts of NBA play-ers. Jack speculated on how the game of professional basketball would change if the NBA operated on the same basis as the PGA Tour, as it re-lates to the competitors' being paid. Professional golfers don't make any-thing if they don't play well enough in a tournament to make the weekend cut. Their paychecks are based on performance. When they play well, they are handsomely rewarded; when they perform below the high standards of the tour, they get no checks, and even have to pay their own way home.

Let's suppose the NBA operated under a system whereby the players on the winning team were paid big salaries, based on a sliding scale of the individual players, with the most talented rated number one and receiving the most money and the least talented ranked number twelve and receiving the smallest amount. Players on the losing team would operate on a similar system by ranking the best to the least talented player but would be paid at a much lower rate. If we go back to those great Chicago Bulls championship teams, we might find Michael Jordan, the most valuable player, being paid, say, $150,000 for a winning game, while Scottie Pippen, rated number two on the team, would get $110,000, on down to the twelfth man, who would get $25,000 for a victory.

All the individual bonuses paid for such things as points scored, rebounds, assists, steals, and minutes played would be abolished. The only monetary rewards would be for team success, not individual honors. I'm agreeing with Jack. Can you imagine what a beautiful game the best basketball players in the world would produce under this system? There would be no selfish play, because all the players would understand, and buy in to, the philosophy that playing hard, playing together, and playing smart would give them the best chance of winning—and large paychecks.

Played correctly, basketball calls for teamwork and rewards the teams and players that play that way. I used to point out to our players that the leading scorer in college basketball very seldom plays for a good team and rarely on a team that competes in the NCAA tournament. In college basketball it's possible to stop any one person from scoring. It might come at a steep price, but it can be done.

The NBA is learning the merits of measuring and rewarding team play over individual achievements. Fewer and fewer professional basketball contracts contain clauses that pay bonuses for individual play, which could promote selfish behavior that is detrimental to the team's success. I know of one former NBA player who had a rebounding clause in his contract. If he retrieved a certain number of rebounds, he received a big bonus. Late in the last game of his season he was one rebound short of earning the bonus. With an opponent on the foul line, the rebounder asked a teammate positioned across the lane not to go for the rebound in case of a miss. He wanted the bonus check. His contract encouraged selfish behavior, even though the young man is a caring, unselfish person by nature. A poor reward system encouraged selfishness. Individual bonuses often reward selfish acts. An example would be for a Major League Baseball team to pay a big bonus to a pitcher for innings pitched. That pitcher might not be honest with his manager if he needed to stay on the mound and get his innings so he could make the bonus.

One of the reasons we made team defense the cornerstone of our North Carolina program was that it demands unselfish play and the ability to trust one's teammates. One individual failing to do his job can cause the defense to fail. If we built this unselfishness on defense, along with a strong desire to support all teammates, we knew this same spirit would carry over to the offense and all parts of the game. We always believed that our offensive plan, executed properly, would produce good shots and a high scoring average for North Carolina. That was usually the case, and statistics bore it out. Nationally North Carolina often was near the top in field goal percentage for college basketball teams and generally was close to the top nationally and in the ACC points scored. In fact we had only four seasons in thirty-six years when we didn't shoot higher than 50 percent from the field, an extraordinary achievement on the part of our players. If our team defense forced the opponent to take poor shots, the result of the game would be pleasing to us a very high percentage of the time.

Whereas our defense was based on team play, some other coaches had success teaching individual defense. Players were told not to switch off the men they were guarding, no matter what. That way the coach could look at points scored and say, "Joe, your man scored eighteen points. You didn't play well on defense." Our style asked players to perform in a different way, and we wanted them to know that a teammate would be there to back them up. We chose our lineups by rewarding defense. The top seven players at this level of basketball should be able to score. North Carolina players earned playing time when they showed us they could play team defense well.

We didn't recruit players on the basis of their scoring averages, and we didn't emphasize individual points scored once they joined our North Carolina team. TV announcers might praise the game's high scorer by naming him player of the game, but team field goal percentage, good ball-handling, setting good screens, and offensive rebounding, not a single player's scoring average, determine how effective an offense is. If a player scores twenty-six points but needs thirty-two shots to do it, he hurts his team.

One way we encouraged good shot selection, in itself a sign of team-work and unselfishness, was to have our players sit together in a room and watch one of our game tapes. We made them grade each shot we took and rate it a good or bad shot. This not only brought more emphasis to our philosophy of taking good shots but also brought peer pressure into the equation. It wasn't a pleasant experience for a player to sit with his team-mates as they graded one of his poor shots. The grading was done anony-mously, so the players would be candid. Many times only the player who had taken the poor shot marked it down as a good one.

From the start of my head coaching career, I believed that teamwork would be enhanced if we punished the team for on-court mistakes. In the U.S. Marine Corps, if one guy messes up, every person in the platoon hikes at 5:00 A.M. When mistakes were made in practice, the whole team ran. "We're running for Jack," I'd say at the sound of my whistle. If Jack kept making mistakes, he got some dirty looks from his teammates. No one, at least no one I wanted on our team, wants to let a teammate down. In most instances a player felt awful if his mistake caused his teammates to be punished.

For sure, something magic happens when a team has one goal and everyone buys in. When our players believed deep down that making the extra pass, helping on defense, and boxing out on rebounds was cool, the team had a chance to be special, very special. Fortunately we had young men on our teams who were unselfish and team-oriented. It is indeed inspirational to see a teammate genuinely excited about your good play. When you help somebody, you help yourself. The family becomes stronger when selfish acts give way to team goals.

Teamwork and togetherness can be destroyed by finger-pointing. It's usually fatal in a team atmosphere. We didn't have much of it at North Carolina, but if it did arise, we corrected it immediately. Watching his former team, the Los Angeles Lakers, get off to a slow start in the 2002–03 season, Magic Johnson explained it this way: "Some of the players are blaming their teammates, and that never works in a team game like basketball."

Our veteran players played a key role each season in helping the coaches build teamwork and promote unselfish behavior. After all, these veteran players spent much more time with the young players than the coaches did. They ran around together, played pickup games together in the summer, ate together. Our veterans were not hesitant to let the young players know: "This is the way we play, and nothing less will be acceptable."

Our former players who went to the NBA also were an enormous help. Many of them came back to Chapel Hill in the summer to get in shape for their season by playing pickup games with UNC's players. While NCAA rules didn't allow coaches to watch these summer games involving current players, a writer was present one afternoon when one of our returning players took an ill-advised shot in a scrimmage against the pros. James Worthy, one of our all-time greats, grabbed the missed shot, stopped play, and said, "If Coach didn't want me taking that shot, do you think he's going to want you to take it? Shape up." That criticism coming from James, who has a drawer full of NBA championship rings, was much more effective than anything I could have said.

Our veterans had been in the program and knew what we needed to do to have an unselfish, successful team. We depended on them, maybe more than many programs did. But although the veterans had an exalted leadership position, when it came to playing time, the best players, regardless of class rank, got it. Everyone in our program knew that was the way it would be. I can't think of another college basketball program that was almost always in the nation's top ten that started as many freshman players as we did at North Carolina.

We did stress having fun. Sure, players came to North Carolina for the chance to play in big games, but we wanted the entire experience to be enjoyable. There was more than enough pressure applied by the fans and the media, to say nothing of what good players always placed on themselves. I didn't need to pile more on as their head coach. I wanted the players to depend on one another, trust one another, do their best—all in the context of having fun. Why invest all the time, effort, and energy that it takes to become a basketball player at North Carolina and then not enjoy the dream once it's achieved? College basketball has become a big business, but it's still a game, not a job for the players, and that's how they should view it.

The best way to experience this feeling is through teamwork and a willingness on the part of the individual to put the team first. Team goals supersede individual goals. It takes a special person to do that, but once players commit to it, they learn that team success makes each individual stronger. The coach's job is to be part servant in helping each player reach his goals within the team concept. In the off-season, things change to focus on each individual. We had a saying, "During the season, everything for the team; out of season, everything for the individual." If we learned in the spring that one of our underclassmen stood to be drafted high in the first round by an NBA team, thereby securing his financial security for life, we put what was best for the individual first. He could still return to college in the NBA's off-season to earn his degree, as was the case with six of our nine players who left college basketball early for NBA careers.

I never compared any of my North Carolina teams or tried to rank them first in this or that, and I won't do it now. However, I will say that our 1971 team represents a great example of teamwork and unselfishness resulting in success. All the great players who had been on the 1967–69 teams that won three straight ACC regular-season championships and three straight ACC tournament championships and gone on to three straight NCAA Final Fours had graduated. The record of the 1969–70 team was 18–9 (the last of our teams that failed to win at least 21 games), and we lost All-American Charles Scott and valuable players Eddie Fogler and Jim Delany to graduation. We were understandably unranked in the preseason national polls and picked to finish anywhere from fourth to seventh in the eight-team ACC.

We'd also had a nationally publicized recruiting setback when the most recognized player in that year's high school class chose another league school after first indicating he was coming to North Carolina. With all this information in their notebooks, writers and commentators speculated on whether our program would sustain its national ranking or slip into mediocrity. We were said to be at the crossroads for the 1971 season. To make our prospects even dimmer, league opponent South Carolina was picked preseason number one in the nation and was an overwhelming choice to win the ACC regular season.

Our players ignored the experts and went about the business of building a team that developed the strength of steel. Play hard, play together, play smart? That group excelled in all areas. We beat South Carolina, 79–64, in Chapel Hill, lost a fiercely competitive game to it at its place, 72–66, and won the ACC regular-season championship with a conference record of 11–3. We were denied a trip to the NCAA tournament (only one team from a conference could go in those days, and we crowned our champion in the league tournament instead of the regular season) when

South Carolina scored just before the final buzzer to beat us, 52–51. Our team went on to win what then was a very prestigious NIT and finished the season ranked thirteenth in the nation. The unselfishness the team displayed was inspiring even to the most casual basketball fan. Because of its unselfishness, the team got great shots and made 52.2 percent of them. The players took team defense to another level, inspired by guards Steve Previs and George Karl, two of the smartest, toughest, most unselfish and competitive players a coach could ever dream of having on his team. They had ample help from starters Bill Chamberlain, Dennis Wuycik, and Lee Dedmon, as well as key reserves Kim Huband, Donn Johnston, Dave Chadwick, Dale Gipple, and Bill Chambers.

Those players believed in their souls that if they committed 100 percent to our philosophy, we would have a strong team. They exceeded all expectations and defiantly answered the pundits who had wondered out loud if North Carolina basketball was about to exit the national stage.

That team of talented, unselfish competitors was key to sustaining North Carolina basketball as a national power. It has to be one of the most important teams in Carolina basketball history, and it gave new meaning to teamwork, sacrifice, unselfishness, togetherness, and winning. There were no so-called great individual stars on that team, yet Wuycik and Chamberlain earned All-America honors. Five players on the team had more than eighty assists each for the season. Four averaged scoring in double figures. Each starter led us in scoring in at least one game. We had a whole team of go-to guys. Their unselfishness made us extremely hard to guard.

This team not only set a standard for excellence through teamwork but also proved that when people sacrifice for the good of the entire unit, they make themselves stronger. Very much so.

The team that experts predicted would finish near the bottom of the pack in the ACC won twenty-six games and lost only six. Why do teamwork and unselfishness work? The 1971 North Carolina team answered the question—emphatically.

PLAYER PERSPECTIVE

Steve Previs,

class of 1972, former ABA player, trader,
Jeffries International Inc., London

Our 1971 team received no respect in the preseason. At least one daily newspaper picked us to finish the season seventh in an eight-team Atlantic Coast Conference, while our student newspaper, the *Daily Tar Heel,* picked us to finish last.

All the great players who had led North Carolina to three straight ACC championships and three NCAA Final Fours during the 1967–69 seasons had graduated, along with All-America Charlie Scott after the 1970 season. The media thought Carolina basketball would leave the national stage and become mediocre. Besides, South Carolina was in the ACC then and was picked in the preseason to be number one in the conference and in the nation.

UNC's players, and Coach Smith, had different thoughts. We didn't have any superstars on the team, although we received great leadership from seniors Lee Dedmon, Dave Chadwick, Don Eggleston, Dale Gipple, and Richard Tuttle. To me, those guys were real leaders, heroes, winners. We looked up to our seniors and depended on them for leadership.

We had so much fun on that team. We played hard, together, and smart—and enjoyed it immensely. Of course our players were sky-high emotionally when South Carolina came to Chapel Hill to play us on January 4, 1971. It was ranked number two in the nation at the time, and nobody gave us much of a chance to win, even though our team had played well all through December. It was a classic game, fiercely contested. The players on both teams went at one another with an intensity that couldn't have been higher. For sure, we weren't going to back down. We won the game, 79–64, and people had to begin to take us seriously.

Shown little respect in the preseason, we confounded the critics by winning the ACC regular-season championship with a league record of 11–3. We were heartbroken after we lost the ACC tournament championship game to South Carolina, 52–51. It scored a basket with one second left to beat us. Unfortunately, in those days only one team per conference could go to the NCAA tournament, and the ACC chose its champion not by which team did best in the fourteen-game home-and-home conference season but by what happened in the three days of the conference tournament. It wasn't fair, but we understood the rules going in and had no excuses.

Our team was selected to go to the National Invitational Tournament in New York, which then was just about on an equal footing with the NCAA tournament in regard to strength of field and prestige. We played great in New York, won four straight games and captured Coach Smith's first "national" championship. It was a rewarding season in every way for those of us in the Carolina basketball family. We sustained the Carolina program as a national power. There was no mistake about that. The Tar Heels didn't disappear.

We really wanted a shot at South Carolina the next season, but unfortunately the school left the ACC after the 1971 season in a controversial move. But as fate would have it, both our team and theirs qualified for the NCAA tournament the next season. We met South Carolina in the NCAA East Regional in Morgantown, West Virginia, in March 1972. We avenged the loss from the previous year in the ACC tournament—with interest. On our way to the NCAA Final Four, our margin of victory was 92–69.

The unselfishness of the players and coaches paid huge dividends for us, and it still influences us in the way we try to lead our lives now.

BUSINESS PERSPECTIVE

Building teamwork in a business is harder than it may seem. It is in the nature of humans to come to work focused on their best interests and goals, with a little selfishness in their souls. "What can I do for me to be successful?" Such an attitude is normal. Don't get angry with employees for having their self-interests at heart. Find what those interests are and then help employees fulfill them by contributing to your team.

Trying to get employees to be selfless and play for "the team" is a hard sell because it appears to go against the grain of human nature. Furthermore, people think they'll help the team most if they are featured prominently in its plans. Their intentions are good, but the results often are not.

Just look at this typical scenario for a manufacturing company, focusing on the conflicting goals of the various managers:

The vice president for manufacturing has the goal of producing excellent products as cheaply and efficiently as possible and on deadline.

The vice president for human resources wants the needs of employees to be met and their compensation, benefits, power, and communications to be effective and common across departments.

The vice president for sales wants to sell as many units as possible for the highest price possible. To satisfy the changing needs of customers, they want a big inventory with great variety immediately available in all sizes.

The inventory and warehouse managers want as small an inventory as possible and suggest limiting it to ten items. They prefer deliveries to be scheduled months in advance and no special orders to be requested.

The vice president of accounting pushes to count every penny and for detailed reports filled out at ten-minute intervals while the salespeople are squawking, "We hate filling out reports."

The CEO is in the corner office saying, "I want them to do all this but to get along, help each other."

You can understand why the CEO might walk out of the office and say to these squabblers, "We have no teamwork here! All of you are focused on your own success instead of on the company's best interests. How can we become a team?"

Somehow a leader has to show all of his managers and employees, most of whom are dedicated but have doubting attitudes, that they'll come out ahead if they cooperate with their teammates and adapt their behavior to help others. It's not easy, especially when many of them don't believe it will be good for them as individuals or for their careers. Here are some dos and don'ts:

- Don't promote anyone in the company who doesn't have a history of working together with his or her colleagues.
- Don't select or promote anyone who doesn't recognize and reward teamwork or who encourages selfish behavior that hurts the company.
- Do preach teamwork and do act accordingly. Instead of rewarding individual performance with a bonus, measure both individual performance and the person's ability to work together with his or her colleagues. Reward teamwork as well as individual performance. Punish poor teamwork behavior. That puts a value on it that even the most selfish person can understand.
- Do have all employees keep records of their contributions to teamwork.
- Keep the need for teamwork fresh in their minds at all times.

- If sales make a request of manufacturing for a special order that would be costly for manufacturing to fulfill, then
  disperse the added expense throughout the company. It
  would be hard to get manufacturing to cooperate or to feel
  good about it if it had to take the whole financial hit for
  helping sales be successful. If manufacturing helps sales
  succeed, sales should share the rewards and vice versa.

Dean Smith and his players demonstrated for thirty-six years
that unselfishness pays. It makes the team *and* the individual
stronger. It's a lesson every business, no matter how large or small,
should learn and teach. Remember to reward unselfish behavior. If
managers allow unselfishness to go unnoticed, employees will assume that you don't value it.

· 14 ·

TEAM-BUILDING
TECHNIQUES

Early in my head coaching career at North Carolina, we developed rituals that helped us build unselfish and hardworking teams, though I didn't think of them as rituals at the time.

Many years after instituting these rituals, I heard my friend Dr. Anthony Campolo, professor emeritus at Eastern University in St. Davids, Pennsylvania, define the term. A church communion is a ritual. A Thanksgiving dinner with family is a ritual. Tony believes that going through the motions of a ritual helps in bonding. I think so too. I encourage rituals because they assist in promoting closeness and unselfishness.

There also should be rewards, ways to recognize and show appreciation for good work and unselfishness that help the team succeed. Here are some of the rituals and rewards we used:

REWARDING THE PLAYERS

We gave our players the option of telling us what types of hotel they wanted to stay in on our long road trips. They were free to choose first-class facilities, such as the Mansion on Turtle Creek in Dallas, Texas, or they could decide to stay in more modest facilities. We told them, however, if they chose the nicer places, they had to dress and act the way others at the hotel did. If that meant wearing a coat and tie when venturing into the hotel's lobby, then so be it.

Our players almost always chose the higher-priced hotels. I'm pleased that they did. Staying at those places was well within the rules, and it served as a reward for the way the players conducted themselves and how hard they worked.

When I first became head coach, colleges were allowed to buy the players travel blazers. It was a good idea because some of our players came from families that couldn't afford to send their children spending money, much less buy them traveling outfits. Then, in a cost-cutting gesture, the NCAA outlawed the team blazers in 1972, yet another rule that was contrary to the best interests of the student-athlete.

The basketball program at North Carolina made a great amount of money, which helped all of UNC's sports programs, male and female. So if I could reward the players by letting them experience a stay at a luxury hotel, I didn't hesitate. Moreover, it was a good educational experience for them. The players also ate at nice restaurants, where they dressed accordingly.

When we traveled by commercial airline, the seniors were given the first-class seats. If there were seats left in first class, they went to the tallest players. Cramped airline seats can be very uncomfortable for a seven-footer. Coaches and managers were seated at the back of the plane.

At my press conferences after games I always tried to praise those on our team who had played well but in a way that wasn't reflected in the game statistics. I knew they wouldn't get mentioned in the newspaper the next morning or show up on ESPN's Sports Center. Still, the things they did helped us succeed, and I wanted to show my appreciation by pointing them out to the reporters. However, I do remember one headline in the *Durham Morning Herald* that read PREVIS AND KARL LEAD NORTH CAROLINA

TO VICTORY. Neither player was the high scorer in the game, but the head-line was accurate because they led our winning effort with their great defense.

As long as they played hard and unselfishly, we did our best to show respect to the players and not embarrass them publicly. As I said, I didn't substitute for mistakes because no one likes to be embarrassed in front of a large crowd. My college coach, Doc Allen, often substituted for mistakes, and I didn't like it. I decided I wouldn't do it when I became a head coach. However, as I said, players came out immediately for not playing hard or for being selfish. Sometimes turning down a good shot could be a selfish act because it hurt the team. If a player was in a shooting slump or had temporarily lost his confidence, there were things he could still control, such as playing great team defense, setting good screens, making good passes, and playing smart and unselfishly.

Players could also get out of running some sprints by demonstrating smart, unselfish play.

PLAYER PERSPECTIVE

Scott Williams,
class of 1990, player on three NBA championship teams in Chicago, still active in the NBA

My experience in basketball at every level has taught me that the most successful teams are the ones that have the best team chemistry. That was true on my teams at North Carolina, where the chemistry was always good, as well as in the NBA with Chicago. In both those places the players pulled so hard for one another that it energized everyone on the team. On the other hand, some of the worst experiences I've had in the pros was playing on talented teams that lacked chemistry. It's such a waste.

At North Carolina, Coach Smith didn't have a so-called system because he treated each team he had differently. But there were some basic fibers that were always present, and from those came his philosophy. For example, he rewarded his seniors by letting them help make team rules, allowing them to be first on the bus and airplane and first in line for water breaks at practice, and putting them in a role to mentor the younger players. It was his way of thanking them for what they'd done for the program for four years.

On road trips Coach rewarded us by having us stay at the best hotels. He arranged for charter flights to take us back to Chapel Hill after night road games played far away, so we could be in class the next morning. It amazed our professors to see us in their 8:00 A.M. classes, alert and paying attention, after they had watched us play on television late the night before at a place that was a long way from home. I recall one night we played during the week at Clemson and were behind at halftime by a significant margin. Kenny Smith dropped forty-one points on Clemson that night, and we came back and won. (I remember the details of my college games like they were yesterday.) I was in one of my mass communications classes the next morning at eight o'clock, and the professor came up to me and said, "I saw you guys play last night. Good job."

Things didn't occur by happenstance at North Carolina. There was an educational value attached, by design, to just about everything we did in the basketball program. Coach made it a point to schedule games in places that most of us had never been, such as Hawaii, Alaska, and London. He taught us life's lessons as we traveled. Believe me, it was educational for a young man who had grown up in Los Angeles to go to the Deep South to play basketball and experience the customs there or for a young man from a small town in North Carolina to visit New York City.

I feel bad for some of my teammates in the pros who don't have the relationship with their college coach that I have retained with mine. Even when he was recruiting me out of high school, I always felt that Coach Smith cared more about each individual player on his team than he did about winning games. Winning was very important at Carolina, and there was much pressure to win, but Coach cared more about our getting a sound education and turning into good citizens than he did about winning.

Also, and this was very important to the players, Coach Smith never took credit for our wins but went out of his way to take the blame for all the losses, claiming he hadn't prepared us properly. Well, as players we knew he had prepared us extremely well, but maybe we just didn't come through or had a poor shooting game. But when Coach went before the reporters after a loss, he put the blame on himself. The players picked up on it, and it took an enormous amount of pressure off our shoulders. For one thing, we didn't have reporters coming up to us after games asking, "What was the matter with you guys tonight? Why didn't you get it done?" I didn't have a reporter asking me, "Hey, Scott, their biggest man is six-six. Why didn't you get more points inside tonight?" Coach's philosophy was that the coach should take a backseat to the players. He took the responsibility for losing when he shouldn't have.

My relationship with Coach Smith remains special, maybe even more so because of the tragedy I suffered when I lost both my parents while I was a student at Carolina. My mother had become extremely impressed with Coach Smith during the recruiting process and felt from the beginning that he was much more interested in me as a person than just as a basketball player. Since the day I lost my parents, Coach Smith has been a father figure to me. When there's a major decision to be made in my life, I don't hesitate to call and ask for his advice. His opinion is so valuable—what he has to say means so much to me—that it's great that I can call him to this day and talk things out. Even when I don't take all his advice, what he has to say is invaluable, and always will be. There were rewards when I played for him, and they continue to this day, thirteen years after my graduation.

BUSINESS PERSPECTIVE

Dean's point that true performance can't be measured simply by numbers applies to all walks of life. There are inevitably too many variables to reduce performance to a number. It's often much better if the manager uses his or her judgment rather than an overly complicated, semiobjective formula in deciding bonuses, especially as they pertain to teamwork. A good manager's judgment is much more effective than most formulas that someone cooks up. Even if the formula is perfect, if the employees don't trust their manager's judgment, the employees will reject it. Actually, if a manager is incapable of making good, fair judgments, he or she probably should be removed from the job. As much data as possible should be used in forming judgments, but don't use metrics to escape responsibility for making the call on employee contributions. All too often, businesses reward their employees on the basis of some formula that is obsolete or unrelated to an individual's true performance.

PRAISE AND CRITICISM

It was important to know how to treat each player because the players were not all alike. If I was critical of one, he might go downhill for the rest of practice. After criticizing him, I tried to find a reason to praise him, although it wouldn't be false praise. At best false praise results in short-term benefits. How are work ethic and self-esteem enhanced through false praise?

They aren't. I waited until he did something well, even if it meant waiting for days. It wasn't good teaching to allow mistakes to go uncorrected.

Some players responded to my criticism by getting angry and playing better. Each player responded differently. It was up to me to find out the best way to deal with each on an individual basis.

During my one-on-one meetings with the players I asked each one if it would bother him if I criticized him in front of his teammates. I told him that if it would, I could bring him to the office after practice and do it. Waiting until after practice to criticize wouldn't have been as effective, of course, but it was an option. I can't recall any player's choosing to do it that way.

We certainly didn't want our players to criticize a teammate for making a mistake. One of the major elements of our team-building efforts was an understanding that the players support one another. This was part of our cast-the-first-stone theory.

Of course, it's just as important to praise as it is to criticize. We were careful in practice to praise unselfish acts, good execution, and effort. Praise behavior you want to see repeated. Positive reinforcement is crucial to team building.

PLAYER PERSPECTIVE

Dr. Joseph Jenkins,
class of 1988, doctor in New Bern,
North Carolina

Coach Smith had a knack for tailoring his teaching to each individual player, from the walk-on to the superstar. Some needed heavy-handed discipline while others needed quiet encouragement. Others needed both and more. Somehow he managed to find out what each of us needed and provided it.

He inspired all of us to be the best players, people, and ambassadors for the university that we could be. I was a walk-on, and I can honestly say that Coach treated all of his players equally—I received the same treatment and privileges as the star players. Coach Smith motivated each player individually but with the same emphasis and goals in mind: team improvement through individual improvement. He never scolded in anger and never without good cause. He commanded respect by his actions, looks, and demeanor rather than by harsh words. When he did raise his voice, he was serious and to the point. There was no ambiguity.

Coach's actions fostered confidence and humility, which were paramount for the team's success. The experience I gained playing for him is indescribable. He changed my life and made me a better person, which has helped me succeed to this day. I'm grateful for the opportunity to elaborate on a truly great man.

Woody Coley,
class of 1977, senior managing director,
Trammell Crow Company, Orlando, Florida

Players lived to receive a compliment from Coach Smith. While he didn't believe in false praise, he knew when a player needed encouragement. The way he gave compliments lasted for hours, even days. He made a big production out of it too. He blew his whistle, stopped practice, and came down to the court from where he had been observing everything. He then recognized the exemplary performance of a player and told the rest of the team that he expected the same from all of us.

The player receiving the compliment might receive some good-natured ribbing from his teammates in the showers after practice, but that was okay. Just knowing that we had measured up to Coach Smith's expectations for even one instant was reward enough.

BUSINESS PERSPECTIVE

One manager has figured it out as well as anyone I know. Twice a year she brings her twelve key people together for a meeting. Each of them is required to prepare and tell the group ten goals for the next six months and how he or she is going to reach them. They all make their presentations in a colorful, humorous way. The conversations are extremely candid and honest. Each person also tells the team which of the goals presented six months earlier he or she has met and which not. It's not unusual to hear a presenter say, "I'm doing well with these goals, but frankly I've not accomplished numbers four and five and don't know how I'm going to get them done. I messed up."

Each member has to be self-critical because the climate in each meeting is designed to help all of them improve and not hide weaknesses or mistakes. Every person has to own up to his or her mistakes, and if he or she doesn't, the others in the room pick up on it immediately. As it turns out, almost all the criticism ends up being self-criticism. Defenses are broken down: "I'm not sure I'm doing this right. Could someone help me?"

Self- and group control is 100 percent more powerful than boss control. The response from the other eleven members is almost always encouraging and helpful: "How can we help you accomplish numbers four and five?" People learn to compete to contribute and not to beat one another.

Moreover, when the presenter talks about his or her successes, the others applaud and cheer. Group praise fires them all up because they are genuinely happy for their teammates' personal successes.

There's also a very important by-product to these meetings. When the presenters talk about their successes, they almost always add something like this: "I want you to know I couldn't have done it without Susan's help."

Getting this praise in front of her boss has Susan feeling like a million dollars. Sharing credit is a powerful force, and it makes the person on the receiving end eager to help again. It is difficult to complete most jobs without aid from others. If they are never rewarded for their contributions to your success, their desire to help you will diminish. You will suffer, and so will your team.

THANK THE PASSER

Americans love clear-cut, definitive resolutions. We don't like ties or even split decisions. One team wins; one loses. That's easy enough. A politician wins by less than one percentage point of the popular vote and declares that the voters gave him or her a mandate. A salesman made the sale or he didn't. Keep things simple.

In basketball, it's not unusual to praise the leading scorer and call him the game's most important player. It's easy for anyone to look at the box score and say, "Wow, John scored twenty-eight points. He was great." Well, somebody had to throw John the ball, set screens for him to get open, play defense so he could get the ball back, throw the ball inbounds for him. John gets great credit for points scored, but how about the others who made it possible?

Early in my career as head coach I wanted tangible evidence that North Carolina's players and coaches recognized and appreciated a good pass that led to a basket. UCLA's coaching great John Wooden and I talked about it as far back as the mid-1960s, when he said he wanted the recipient of a pass that led to a basket to say thank you to the passer or wink at him.

That was a good idea, but I wanted a stronger, more visible signal of thanks. I preferred a gesture that the fans could see. The media too. So we asked the player who scored to point to the man who gave him the pass that resulted in the basket, to show appreciation for an unselfish act that helps the team.

It was a rule in my early years as head coach: Thank the passer by pointing to him. We insisted on it in practice and games. It became contagious. Soon my assistants and I were pointing to the passer; next the substitutes on our bench picked up on it; then the fans at our home games were standing at their seats, pointing to the passer. The public address announcer at our home games began saying, "Assist to Karl, basket by Jones." It went just as I hoped: a show of appreciation for the passer; applause for his unselfishness; recognition of his good play. As the seasons went by, I seldom had to mention it to our players. The North Carolina tradition was set in stone: Thank the passer. Players picked up on it automatically. If they failed to do so, I didn't hesitate to remind them.

The gesture took on a broader definition in 1972. Bobby Jones, a great, unselfish player for us, ran on the break, took a pass from a teammate, and missed a layup. Still, he pointed to the passer, birthing the Bobby Jones Rule: Even if you miss an easy shot after a good pass, thank the passer. The ritual expanded shortly thereafter when we thanked the passer if the shooter was fouled and sent to the foul line. The passer had still done his job and committed an unselfish act. Now we see players at all levels of basketball, from church leagues to the NBA, pointing to the passer.

It makes for a stronger team because everyone likes to feel appreciated.

Bobby Jones,
class of 1974, former NBA all-star

Coach Smith wanted a visible way to thank the player who passed the ball that led to a basket, so he asked the player who scored to point to the passer to show his appreciation.

In one game I received a good pass but missed an easy shot. However, I still thanked the passer by pointing to him. He had done his job; it wasn't his fault that I missed a shot that I should have made. We had been trained to thank someone for the pass when we scored, so I just extended it to include passes that I should have converted to baskets. I think it was just an extension of the habits Coach Smith instilled in us as we developed under his direction.

It is crucial for the leader to praise his or her people personally. I know a CEO who doesn't leave work each day until he has thanked at least one person, either in a handwritten note or by personal telephone call: "Thank you for your work on this project. Job well done." It's amazing what it means to the employee on the receiving end.

Historically, many male leaders have been trained not to show their feelings. It's unfortunate because it makes them reluctant to express praise or appreciation. They need training and encouragement on how to do so.

EXAMPLE

A large international company held a meeting for its senior managers at the London School of Business. People from twenty-five or thirty countries were present.

Since the people at the meeting didn't know one another very well, it was a little stiff and formal. During the discussion of one Harvard Business School case on leadership, I noticed one of the participants searching through his briefcase. He then sat there for a long time with a sheet of paper in his hand as the case discussion continued. Hesitantly he raised one hand and shared his message with the class: "I carry a letter with me that I got ten years ago from the CEO of our company where I worked. It's a simple thank-you letter for the good work I did on a project. It's the only letter of appreciation I ever received from any manager. I carry it with me every day to remind me to thank people for their positive behavior on our company's behalf."

The man's voice was filled with emotion as he shared his story. The room was very quiet during his short talk; the class was struck by the power of appreciation. Class members then talked about how the business version of pointing to the passer is a small but significant action of good leadership, one that takes just a minute to do and costs pennies.

TIP FOR PARENTS

Go find your children, and tell them how much you care about them. If they are not at home or if it feels uncomfortable to do in person, tell them in a handwritten letter. It might be the most treasured inheritance they'll ever receive. As Ken Blanchard wisely advised, "Catch people doing things right."

STAND UP FOR A TEAMMATE

Another of our rituals required the players on our bench to stand and applaud a teammate as he came out of the game. We were serious about this. I didn't require players to applaud for made baskets, but when one of their teammates came off the court, the entire bench, including coaches, stood to greet him.

The player had been on the court helping his teammates succeed. His effort was on behalf of all of us, and he had earned the thanks of his teammates on the bench. The greeting made the player leaving the game feel appreciated. I told our team that if the president of the United States entered the room, we would stand and applaud out of respect for the office. In basketball, a team game, no one is more important than a player's teammates. No one is more deserving of his respect. It's a long season, and the players depend on one another. Part of being a strong team includes saying thank you. Our coaches and players all said thank you to a manager who wiped the floor after someone fell in practice. It pays to show gratitude.

We wanted our players to enjoy the game and have fun playing it. We also wanted them to feel appreciated. The more they liked it, the more appreciated they felt, the better they'd perform. That was almost always true. Knowing that your teammates and coaches recognize your effort, and appreciate it, makes the hard work more enjoyable.

Once a player took a seat on the bench near me and the crowd's attention was back on the game, I might chastise him for a careless mistake or lack of effort. The fans in the building and those watching on television wouldn't know it. It's better for the team and the player than to berate him as he comes off the court.

Early in my coaching career I saw Coach Chuck Noe's South Carolina team stand and applaud a player as he came off the court. They didn't do it consistently, but seeing it planted a seed in my mind that it would be a terrific way to create enthusiasm and camaraderie. It became one of our rituals and was ingrained as a part of our tradition. I rarely had to mention it to players on teams that came later. They took it upon themselves to stand and applaud for a teammate. It was particularly helpful on the road when it was North Carolina versus the other team and most of the spectators in the building.

When a player knew that he was playing for his four teammates on the court and for all of them on the bench, it inspired him not to let them down. He put team play in front of individual glory and made the team stronger in the process. It's amazing how positively we react when we know that those close to us recognize and appreciate our work and thank us for it. Another friend, Dr. Dean Martin, a Methodist minister in Florida, once said, "You can act yourself into a new way of thinking more easily than you can think yourself into a new way of acting."

PLAYER PERSPECTIVES

Pat Sullivan,

*class of 1995, member of the 1993 NCAA
championship team at UNC, player in three
Final Fours, now assistant NBA coach*

Standing for a teammate was Coach Smith's way of showing a player that his work was appreciated. It made the player feel important and appreciated.

I was a role player at North Carolina. Sports Center didn't make players like me feel good, but Coach Smith did. We didn't make ESPN's highlight reel, but in our team meetings Coach Smith went out of his way to praise us for setting good screens, making good passes to the post, or helping teammates on defense. He recognized the little things we did to help the team.

Standing for a teammate was just one of the things he did to make us feel important and good about ourselves. Believe me, all the players tried to return the favor by giving him everything we had.

Brad Frederick,
class of 1999, assistant basketball coach,
Vanderbilt University

Coach Smith had a very specific way he wanted the bench to conduct itself during a game. The players, coaches, and managers were expected to stand and applaud for a player who came out of the game.

The bench was also responsible for being into the game, cheering, talking to the players, helping our players on the court realize how much time was on the shot clock, and things of that sort. Several times during the year Coach Smith showed us video clips of the bench's actions to make sure we all stood to applaud a player as he left the court.

You often see teams that get no emotion or encouragement from their bench; we were the opposite. We got so excited that sometimes the referees had to tell us to sit down. This went both ways too because when we blue team (second-string) members got our minutes at the end of games, the starters were just as excited and supportive of us as we had been of them. They knew we worked hard in practice to help them and the team improve, and they expressed their appreciation. As a career blue team player I can say we always took pride in giving everything we had in practice to help the team.

Coach Smith and his assistants often told us how valuable our efforts were in helping the team prepare for a game. We had the attitude that we would fight the white team (starters) every day in practice to help make the team better.

BUSINESS PERSPECTIVE

Businesspeople ought to stand and applaud for their teammates too.

There's a grocery store chain located in the Southeast, a family business, made up of twenty-four stores. It's an extraordinary company, a world-class company, in fact. When I first talked to the owners and managers about its becoming world class, they doubted that such a small company could ever qualify for that distinction.

"You'll be world class," I told them, "when you are in the top ten in your industry in the entire world and when people from around the world come to visit with you to see how you run the business." The chain qualifies on both counts. It has so many visitors from around the world that it had to set up a separate department to take care of them.

This particular company starts every meeting of any substance by taking the first ten minutes for employees to relate instances of another worker's going well beyond the call of duty to do a good job for the team and the company.

At a recent meeting an employee said he had seen his store manager go into the parking lot to help a shopper with two young children in tow get her grocery bags into her car. It was raining heavily, and when they got to the car, they discovered it had a flat tire. The manager helped the woman and her children into the dry car, and he changed the tire in the rain. The recitation of his ten-minute exploits drew a standing ovation from his colleagues. He stood up for them, and they in turn stood up and applauded him. After all, his performance had made the entire team stronger.

Do you think this particular young mother would even consider shopping at another grocery store?

I encourage all managers to have their employees publicize stories of fellow workers who did good and unsung deeds. What does it do? It builds company pride and encourages everyone to act in a way that doesn't let his or her colleagues down.

SENIORS AS LEADERS

An emphasis on senior leadership was a vital part of the way we built our North Carolina teams. The seniors had been through our program for three years. They knew what was expected of them in the classroom and on the court, and they could impart that information to the freshmen. If a freshman slacked off in practice, he definitely heard about it from the coaches and it was probably reinforced in the locker room by the seniors.

Off the court, we honored the seniors; on the court, if a freshman played better, he won the job. If it was even between the two, the nod went to the senior. I respected seniority.

We honored the seniors in many different ways. Among them:

- On the court, I made the rules, but we allowed the seniors to make the off-court team rules. They'd make them, and I'd enforce them. It was my classroom.
- Their photographs and biographical sketches appeared first in our media guide, which was published before every season. Most schools put the president or chancellor first, followed by the athletic director and the head coach and then the players. In ours, the players went first, led by the seniors. The seniors were also pictured on the front of the guide, on schedule cards, and in other materials.
- The seniors were the speakers at the annual basketball banquet, held shortly after the end of the season. The decision to allow the seniors to speak came one year when our guest speaker became ill and couldn't make it. We turned to the seniors that night and

asked each of them to make a short speech. From that point on the seniors did it, and they looked forward to it. When Michael Jordan went to the NBA after his junior season at Carolina, his mother told me that he was extremely disappointed to miss out on making his senior speech. Some players stood before the banquet audience anxiously and apprehensively. Others went to the podium with the confidence and aplomb of David Letterman. Some were serious; other were humorous; most were sentimental.

- The seniors started their last home game and played for at least two minutes. That was true even if they were walk-ons who had played sparingly. They were introduced before the game along with members of their families.

- During recruiting, we told each player who lived a long distance from Chapel Hill that he could pick a game near his home and we would try to schedule it during his career at Carolina. When I was a player at the University of Kansas, we had returned to Topeka High School, where I played my junior and senior high school seasons, to play an intrasquad exhibition game, and I had enjoyed the experience greatly. As a coach I tried to put myself into the minds of the players to understand what would make the college experience more enjoyable for them. Many times these "home" games for the players came during their senior season, and the player always was in the starting lineup for that game, no matter what his status was on the team. Eric Montross chose to go back to Butler, where his high school team had won the Indiana state championship. Rick Fox chose Purdue. Dave Colescott chose Indiana. Tom LaGarde and Tom Zaliagiris decided to return to their hometown to play the University of Detroit when Dick Vitale was head coach there. Sometimes the player was tight for his "homecoming" game, but his teammates usually pulled through for him. We seldom lost one of these games or the last home game for our seniors.

- We had four great seniors in 1974 in Bobby Jones, Darrell Elston, Ray Hite, and John O'Donnell. They requested a meeting with me, leading me to believe that we might have a major team problem. They came to my office and sat down. I waited. They said that some of the young players were drinking extra water at the water breaks during practice and using up all the cups. I was thrilled to learn there was no more to it than that. The next day in practice, we had a pecking order at water breaks: seniors first, next juniors, then sophomores, freshmen last.

PLAYER PERSPECTIVES

Bob Bennett,
class of 1966, attorney, Los Angeles

———

The moment I arrived on campus as a freshman, I understood that the seniors on the team were the leaders. If any of the rest of us misbehaved, the seniors would look into it and report back to Coach Smith.

The underclassmen had tremendous respect for the seniors. We worshiped them and listened to everything they said. There was no meanness or arrogance in the way they led, but if I ever got out of line, Billy Cunningham was there to knock some sense into me, as if to remind me: "Hey, you have to earn your spurs here." In those days the NCAA allowed schools to buy travel blazers for their basketball players. Ours had a North Carolina basketball emblem on the front pocket, and we wore them proudly. The seniors reinforced what it meant to wear the jacket and be a part of the Carolina basketball program. "It is a privilege," they told us, "not a right." We were taught to treat everyone with respect. There was no breaking into lines on campus or anywhere else, no feeling of superiority because of our status as basketball players. We were students who also played basketball. As corny as it may sound, the seniors taught us to be Carolina gentlemen. This conduct carried beyond basketball to the campus. We were expected to represent ourselves well wherever we were.

When my class rose to senior status, the freshmen were deferential to us, even though they were much more talented as basketball players than we were. We took our role as senior leaders seriously and enjoyed helping the younger players, just as the seniors had helped us for three years.

Jim Hudock,
class of 1962, retired dentist,
Kinston, North Carolina

Senior leadership evolved out of Coach Smith's respect for his players. He wanted the best for each of us, and he honored his seniors by putting them in a position of leadership. Freshman players learned about this the minute they stepped foot on campus. They learned from the seniors, who set good examples by busting their butts every day in practice to improve. The seniors led; underclassmen followed. It was part of Carolina basketball.

Like all team members, the seniors did not want to disappoint Coach Smith. The seniors felt this most strongly because they had been in the program and knew what it stood for. Coach was not a yeller or a screamer but a teacher. He didn't humiliate his players. He was always positive and took the blame for the losses and gave us the credit for the wins.

More than anyone else, the seniors knew how hard Coach Smith worked. He set the example, and the seniors made sure everyone honored and respected it.

BUSINESS PERSPECTIVE

Generally American business lags far behind the rest of the world in the way it treats its senior employees. Companies often discard these people, ignore them, or take them for granted. It's a waste of a valuable resource. Businesses ought to take more advantage of these senior employees on the payroll by giving them a chance to teach and train others. They have the intellectual capacity to do it but usually don't get the chance. No wonder many of them feel disenfranchised.

A vice president of sales in a pharmaceutical company with a large sales force said he had problems with about twenty-five veteran salespeople who sat together at the back of the room during meetings. They were intelligent people, but their work attitudes left much to be desired. They believed that they already knew all they needed to know. They had become somewhat cynical, tired, and ignored. In their own way they were disruptive.

"What can I do?" the sales manager asked.

I met with the twenty-five senior people involved, plus the top sales management. I asked them to tell me about the history of the company. They were cynical and laughing and joking during the early stages of the meeting, but then they got involved and excited about the process.

I had them do a little exercise and answer questions such as these: What are the four turning points that changed your company? Who are the three best salespeople you've known, and what are the ten characteristics they had that made them successful? Who are the three worst salespeople and the ten characteristics that made them failures? What are the five major missed opportunities the company is experiencing now? What are the five biggest goofs you've made so far? What are the five best things you've done in your job over your entire career? What are the four things most of our new sales reps need to learn to be more effective?

The group took ninety minutes to complete the exercise, and then I led a discussion reviewing their answers. The sales manager couldn't believe what a great meeting we had. He'd never seen these people participate in such a positive, interested way. They wouldn't let the meeting end. We went until 10:30 P.M., when I finally had to leave.

The next day all the sales officers were asked to report back to the group on what they'd heard in the meeting. We divided these twenty-five senior salespeople along with the senior management team into six-member teams and asked them to prepare for us five ways the company could improve on the basis of what they'd heard from the veteran group the previous day. Some great ideas were developed. Plans for execution were drawn up. The veterans contributed and felt more as if they belonged and had something to learn than before.

Excited that they could contribute, the senior salespeople agreed to our request and picked out three salespeople whom they would mentor and coach. "Pick out three people you like, believe in, and believe have the potential to grow," we advised them.

They met with these junior reps once a month during the first year and once a quarter the next year. The senior reps asked their "students" to bring in the ten major problems they were facing on the job so they could work through them together. Without being promoted, the seniors were fired up and involved because they were asked to contribute and were respected.

The work of the sales managers grew much easier because about twenty of the twenty-five veterans became capable assistants—without adding a penny to the payroll. It was all about showing respect and gratitude to those who had been with the company a long time yet not advanced up the corporate ladder. Five of the senior salespeople did not join the team at first, but group pressure brought two of those on board. The other three were not able to resurrect their careers, and their responsibilities and acceptance further eroded.

Senior leaders, when they are given opportunity to grow and the responsibility to mentor, can exert a powerful force for education and loyalty in an organization.

COACHES' HONOR ROLL

The official statistics kept at college basketball games don't serve as a very accurate guide for someone trying to learn what decided the outcome. The statistical sheets that are handed out to the news media after the game and later reported on television and in newspapers tell how many field goals a player attempted and made, how many free throws he shot and made, how many rebounds he got, how many assists he contributed, how many turnovers he made, how many steals he had, how many minutes he played, and how many points he scored.

I didn't want those statistics given to our players after games. At home games I didn't allow them in our locker room. I knew the players would look at them, but I wanted to impress upon them that I thought statistics were unimportant.

We would give them the significant statistics the next day at practice. It came in the form of our coaches' honor roll, which we posted on the bulletin board in the locker room. Unlike the official game statistics, unselfish acts brought our players honors. We didn't give awards for points scored, defensive rebounds, or steals because those could have been selfish acts. We didn't award points for forced shots or defensive rebounding, which could have resulted from not boxing out or steals, which could be because of gambling on defense.

Our coaches spent more than five hours looking at tapes of every game we played and graded what each player did on each possession. It was painstaking work, but we felt it was important enough for us to invest the time and effort to get it right. We handed out awards for the players who performed best in the unselfish categories that helped us succeed, such as defense, offensive rebounding, assist/error ratio, deflections, charges drawn, screens set, blocked shots, and a category we called good plays (basketball savvy).

We wanted our players to wait for this report before deciding who played the best for North Carolina in a game. This was also a way to tell our players that we appreciated the little things they did to help the team win.

PLAYER PERSPECTIVE

Dr. Eric Kenny,
class of 1981, rheumatologist, Lynchburg, Virginia

With the advantage of hindsight, I appreciate the honor roll as a form of positive reinforcement for team-oriented accomplishments that might have otherwise gone unrecognized. The coaching staff emphasized the importance of unselfish play and doing the little things that resulted in success.

The honor roll recognized unselfish acts that helped the team, like pass deflections, offensive rebounds, diving for loose balls, defense, setting screens, assists, and smart plays. The honor roll was displayed prominently in our locker room and every player was well aware of it. The defensive award was the most coveted, and I recall seeing Dudley Bradley's name posted beside it frequently during my sophomore year.

BUSINESS PERSPECTIVE

Businesses would be smart to devise their own honor rolls, whereby teamwork and unselfishness were rewarded, and selfishness and hurtful behavior punished.

Businesses know that it's important to make the effort and then make the results visible for all employees to see. Many companies use a custom-tailored employee satisfaction survey. After the results are tallied, they can be printed in book form and given to the CEO and distributed to each manager, who in turn makes it available to all employees.

Every person in the company can see how each department grades out. A grading system that rewards and recognizes selfless behavior that might otherwise go unnoticed is a powerful ally for business. Those who do well are placed on an informal honor roll because they set the standard for others to use as benchmarks, and they are sought after to share their keys to success. Those who grade out poorly know it and are helped to develop solutions to improve their teamwork.

THE TIRED SIGNAL

When I played basketball for the University of Kansas, I recall a game in which I played more than I usually did. I asked Coach Phog Allen to remove me so I could catch my breath. I expected to return to the court after a few minutes, but Coach Allen forgot about me and never put me back in the game.

Lesson learned, one that I filed away for future reference. When I became North Carolina's head coach in 1961, I instituted the tired signal, whereby a player could remove himself from the game by holding up a fist. We played at a very fast pace, with pressured defense, and no matter how well conditioned a player was, he couldn't play our style for forty minutes without getting tired. Remember, there were no long television time-outs four times a half in 1962. Tired players end up hurting the team, mostly on defense, where they might be more inclined to grab some rest.

These were competitive young men who wanted to play. If they told me they needed a rest and I failed to put them back in, they wouldn't tell me the next time. The key was to devise a system that would encourage them to remove themselves when tired. It was an unselfish act for them to recognize that a rested substitute would help the team more than a tired starter.

Once the player who had given the tired signal was rested and ready to return, I allowed him to put himself back in. I decided who would come out. In 1973, Ed Stahl, one of our big men, gave the tired signal, and I replaced him with freshman Mitch Kupchak. About four minutes passed, and Ed was still on the bench. "Aren't you ready yet?" I asked. He replied that Mitch was playing so well that he didn't think he should replace him. "I wasn't going to put you in for Mitch," I replied, although I was impressed with Ed for putting the team first.

Some writers used to allege that Carolina basketball was so organized that we had seating assignments for the players on the bench. We didn't, of course. Most of that stuff was overcooked. However, I asked any player who came out of the game to sit next to one of my assistant coaches, one seat removed from me. He could tell me when he was rested and ready to go, and I would send him back into the game. Also, by having the player sit just one chair removed from me, I could lean over and talk to him if I needed to.

Our players were further encouraged to use the tired signal because they knew if the coaches saw them playing with less than full effort, we'd pull them from the game and let them sit for extended periods. I didn't make very many substitutions; the players took themselves out of the game at North Carolina.

Sure, there were times when I didn't want to see the tired signal from some of our players. But if we asked them to shoot straight with us, we had to honor our end of the deal. That was true even if it was the national championship game, as turned out to be the case in our 1993 game against Michigan. With 6:50 to play, Michigan was leading, 62–61, when four of our players gave the tired signal. We substituted four players and were criticized strongly for it during the game's telecast, which I can understand. I didn't hesitate to make the substitutions. But was I supposed to tell the players that we abandoned our rules and rituals for the national championship game? A rested North Carolina team outscored Michigan, 14–4, over the last 4:12 of the game, as we won the championship, 77–71.

Putting the responsibility on the players to tell us when they were tired enhanced team togetherness and fostered honesty. It also made the players on the bench feel they were a part of the team when a starter in effect said, "Go in for me while I rest."

We trusted our players to make wise, unselfish decisions for the good of the team.

PLAYER PERSPECTIVES

Phil Ford,
class of 1977, former college Player of the
Year and NBA Rookie of the Year

Coach Smith and I laugh about the tired signal to this day. When he explained it to me when I arrived as a freshman, I knew I'd never give it. I don't know why exactly, but I could play seemingly forever and not get tired.

Still, the thinking behind the tired signal is brilliant. Coach knew we couldn't play the Carolina Way if we were tired because tired players usually try to catch their breath on defense, and that would have hurt our team defense. Still, players hesitate to take themselves out of games because they are afraid they won't get back in. Coach Smith's tired signal policy removed that fear because he allowed players to put themselves back in once they were rested. It encouraged fatigued players to come out of the game for the good of the team, an unselfish act.

However, if Coach noticed a player was letting up because he was tired and hadn't taken himself out of the game, Coach would take him out and let him sit a good while.

Mike Cooke,
Class of 1964, businessman,
Myrtle Beach, South Carolina

Sprints, sprints, sprints! Coach believed in getting us in good shape, and it seemed we ran sprints forever. After forty years I can reveal our own secret tired signal. Bryan McSweeney, six-four, two-hundred-pound forward, was a track star who was in great shape. He was Coach Smith's barometer on when we had run enough. Our secret is that Mac could make himself throw up on command.

After running a series of demanding sprints, the players would beg Bryan "to do his thing." He teased us along for several more minutes because he could run all day without its bothering him. Finally he would dash over to the trash can and throw up. When it appeared that McSweeney had had enough, it was Coach Smith's signal to call it a day.

BUSINESS PERSPECTIVE

How business could use the tired signal! One of the major problems business leaders and employees face today is working themselves into a state of fatigue. Managers refuse to take themselves out. They don't want to be thought of as slackers, nor do they want the bosses to think they can't keep up with the pace because it could cost them promotions. A prevailing myth in business today is "The more hours I work, the more valuable I am." It shows up in most businesses and is emphasized in schools of medicine and in investment banking. Some investment bankers and other managers log fourteen- to sixteen-hour days, but only do ten hours of work. People pace themselves by working more slowly, taking diversionary breaks, and coasting in lower-priority assignments or meetings.

One senior manager led a business that was owned by his father-in-law, who wanted his manager in the office all day Saturday. The manager was there on Saturdays for several years, but when he had children, he wanted and needed Saturdays off. He was forced to create his own way to rest. The father-in-law used to ride by the plant on Saturday afternoons to make sure his son-in-law's station wagon was there. The son-in-law bought another identical station wagon, which he drove to work on Saturday mornings and left in his parking space. His wife picked him up and drove him home for the day. This is hardly the ethical stuff of which leaders should be made, but sometimes the pressure to work can be so severe that a balanced person has to be somewhat wily to save his or her health.

A Spartan attitude like this owner's results in poor performance and a high rate of burnout. Major and costly mistakes occur much more frequently because of fatigue. Business leaders and employees need to give the tired signal in order to sustain peak levels of performance year after year. To overwork is to underperform.

Companies should require it in their training programs. They should make their managers and employees have tired signals. Studies show that the maximum most people can work and be consistently effective is ten hours a day, five days a week. The key to staying at your peak all day long is to work intensely for about fifty minutes and then take a ten-minute break, starting with the first hour of work.

On weekends, people should allow themselves to work a maximum of two to three hours on either Saturday or Sunday. On one of those days they should do absolutely nothing that is work-related. There should be no guilt involved either. The time off is a must. In fact they should be out of touch for one day of the weekend, not to be reached by telephone, fax, E-mail, pony express, or carrier pigeon. No work allowed.

A woman started a banking and mortgage business from scratch and built it into a thriving hundred-million-dollar business. But in the process of achieving this success, she neglected herself and her family. For sixteen years she worked without giving the tired signal. She became wealthy, but at a steep price. Her marriage almost ended in divorce, she seldom saw her children, and her health declined. She was a workaholic, nothing else. Usually when someone lives that way, sooner or later the body is going to make him or her give the tired signal. She or he burns out, becomes sick or injured, makes major mistakes, alienates family and friends, and loses her or his life.

This woman thought the solution was to hire a professional manager. The new manager's role was not to set strategies or lead the company but to *maintain* it. The owner was to continue in her role as the leader and strategy setter.

The owner, however, was so exhausted from her years of relentless work that she could no longer push herself to strategize. She began to go on pleasure trips for six weeks at a time. She went from being at her desk all the time to not paying enough attention to what was happening to her own company. In three years the company went from a hundred-million-dollar business to one that was doing forty million dollars' worth.

She awoke in a state of shock one morning to discover this steep decline in the business that she had started and nurtured to a powerful position in the industry. "I have to go back to work," she said. Fortunately she had recovered from her fatigue, and she realized that she could rebuild her business only if she balanced her life and her work.

The owner had made two crucial mistakes. First, professional managers are not professional leaders. They focus on maintaining the status quo, which is a sure way to fail. Instead a business leader should have been hired to build the company, with the goal of making it excel. He or she should have been the day-to-day leader in the owner's absence. The owner should have turned over the reins and major decision making to her replacement until she was ready to lead again. Merely trying to maintain a business rather than growing it is an invitation to disaster.

Second, the owner should have given the tired signal at the end of each day. She needed to go home, get refreshed, and return to work the next day ready to go. If managers see their employees working unusually long hours, they should make them go home. Rest will pay off in the long run.

Accounting firms have been known to adopt the policy of churn and burn. They hire talented young recruits, work them sixty-plus hours a week, select a few to be partners, then ask the workhorses to leave, at which time they start over with a new class of ambitious chargers. The productivity and profitability they think they gain by working their people sixty hours a week are almost always lost because of major mistakes, turnover, and loss of legitimacy of the firm. Arthur Andersen, Enron, and WorldCom are examples. Even if this weren't the case, what's the point of working if it's not enjoyable or it ruins other key parts of one's life? Learn to give the tired signal.

· PART FOUR ·

PLAYING
SMART

15

EVERY MAN ON THE
TEAM IS IMPORTANT

Every person on the team was important. There were no exceptions. This included not only the last man on the team but also the student managers, who worked hard on our behalf. They picked up towels, washed uniforms on road trips, made sure equipment got to where it was supposed to be, set the gym up for practice. They came early and stayed late. I told many business friends that if they wanted to hire a great employee, then choose one of our student managers. They would find a hardworking, self-starting, highly organized, dependable individual.

Our players respected the student managers and didn't boss them around. Nor did they expect them to wait on them hand and foot. The players had a role; the managers had a role. They all were important to the team. One season I had to discipline a few players for behaving poorly toward the managers. I told them I wouldn't tolerate its happening again, and it didn't.

As for the players, one through thirteen, each was important. Otherwise he wouldn't have been on the team. A coach couldn't begin to have a basketball team with only five players. Whom would they practice against? Who would substitute for them if they fouled out, got tired, or became injured? Good substitutes contributed greatly to team chemistry. If they practiced hard and supported the starters in games, they made a valuable contribution to our team.

It could be that I felt strongly about this as a coach from my experience of playing college basketball at Kansas. Although I was one of eleven lettermen on our national championship team of 1952, I didn't play much. Dick Harp, the assistant coach on that team, constantly told the reserves how important we were to the team's overall success. He told us on a regular basis that our hard work in practice was appreciated. That was a valuable lesson I took with me into coaching.

We made it clear to the starters and the first substitutes that they should be supportive of their teammates on the bench. We were careful in team meetings to point out the contributions made by the substitutes, in practice and games. In many ways it was more impressive for the substitutes to have and maintain good attitudes than it was for the starters. I was thrilled with the way our starters supported their teammates on the bench. Pull out an old North Carolina basketball tape in which the reserves played the last few minutes, and observe the way the starters stood and cheered the play of the reserves. I recall the last home game for senior walk-on Travis Stephenson against Duke in 1993. We were well ahead when Travis scored a field goal at the final buzzer. Although the points really didn't matter, the starters were so happy for Travis that they piled on him on the court. You'd have thought we'd just won the national championship.

We divided the team members once a week in practice and held a scrimmage. We split up the starters so that each side had starters and substitutes, a good idea because they played together in games. It produced very competitive basketball. Our assistant coaches officiated at these scrimmages. I told them, when in doubt, make the call in favor of the reserves. It served a dual purpose: The substitutes appreciated the boost, and it conditioned the starters to deal with bad officiating calls that they might be victimized with in games.

Maybe the best way we ever had of showing each man on the team that he was important was the utilization of our blue team concept, which lasted from 1968 until 1981. The group usually comprised team members eight through twelve or nine through thirteen, depending on how many players we carried on the roster. It took a careful blend of talent and personalities to make it work: a couple of seniors who hadn't played much but were good leaders, along with sophomores and freshmen, including walkons. The last thing I wanted was for that group to try to impress me with their individual play. They weren't out there to win individual playing time but to give a true team effort.

These reserves knew at the pregame meal that they were going to be in the game for two minutes in the first half. They built their own team chemistry. It was terrific for our team. It didn't matter if the blues won those two minutes or lost them; they were coming out. They knew it was their role. Our fans loved it. I wanted the tempo of the game to change when the blues went in. Their mission was to move the ball, play good defense, take good shots, and make the other team work. An additional advantage for us came because our opponents spent practice time deciding how they'd play when our blues were in the game. One coach always tried to press the blues, and if he wasn't able to gain some ground, as was usually the case, it frustrated him. It was like an ice hockey team's failing to take advantage of a power play, a real letdown. Meanwhile our starters got a good rest and were able to watch what the opponent was trying to do against us.

Having the blue team did wonders for team morale. It encouraged the blues to practice better, to focus and pay attention. They felt like an integral part of the team, which they were. They usually won or tied their two minutes. They certainly knew how they did, because most of them kept records and told me about it at the end of the season.

After those games in which the blues lost, 8–0 and 10–0, in their two-minute stints, I made the decision to discontinue the practice. It took a perfect blend of talent and personalities to make it work. Still, we had a great thirteen-year run with our blue team, and it is one of the things basketball people remember about North Carolina basketball.

Charles Lisenbee,

*class of 1995, UNC team manager for four years,
now regional security officer, American Consulate,
Guangzhou, People's Republic of China*

I often wondered why Coach Smith chose Matthew 25:40 as a perennial Thought for the Day. It wasn't unusual for Coach to select quotes from Martin Luther King, Jr., or Mother Teresa that had nothing to do with basketball, but it wasn't until after I graduated from UNC that the passage from Matthew, "Whatever you did for one of these least brothers of mine, you did for me," became such an important benchmark for my own life.

It was so important to Coach Smith that he usually took time to explain what the Scripture meant, further illustrating the Golden Rule and why we should treat others as we'd like to be treated. In the hierarchy of the Carolina basketball family—player, coach, manager—I was fortunate to be selected by Coach Bill Guthridge to be a student manager. Sure, my job included some menial tasks such as wiping up wet spots on the court, lugging equipment bags, and laundering uniforms, but my loyalty to Coach Smith and Coach Guthridge was cultivated by witnessing their daily commitment to treating everyone the same. Star player, substitute, manager: We all received equal good treatment and respect.

As a manager I was allowed to join the players and coaches in cutting down a piece of the net after we won the 1993 national championship. I received a scholarship, a championship ring, and everything afforded a player, down to the gear and meal money. In the eleven years that have passed since Carolina beat Michigan for the national championship, Coach Smith remains as committed to equal treatment for all as he did when winning was on the line. He continues to spend much time, maybe even more time, helping members of the blue team and student managers as he does his star players.

Since college I've lived and worked in Africa and Asia, for which I'm grateful. I've visited with AIDS patients at clinics in Uganda, delivered toys to orphanages in mainland China, and contributed to grassroot self-help projects in Tanzania. Although none of us does enough to give back to the community, I'm grateful to have learned firsthand from Coach Smith why it is so important in all aspects of our lives. Whether it was when he took his team to visit inmates on death row at Central Prison or to pediatric wards to talk with and sign autographs for sick children, he taught us all that there are many things more important than winning basketball games. I will never forget the lessons he taught, or the way I was treated when I was under his guidance.

Randy Wiel,
class of 1979, former head coach at
UNC-Asheville and Middle Tennessee State

I had served in the military police before I was recruited to North Carolina, so I was twenty-four years old when I came as a freshman. I was the oldest player on our team by at least two years. Mitch Kupchak, a senior, was only twenty-two.

When our team played in Charlotte over one weekend, my brother drove down from New York to watch the games. He traveled by himself and wasn't familiar with the area. He was going to Chapel Hill after the game, a 130-mile drive from Charlotte, and he wanted some company, so he asked me if I'd ride in the car with him. The team was traveling by bus, and it was important for the team to be together. I told my brother I would ask Coach Smith for permission to ride with him in the car, but I didn't hold out much hope that he'd allow it.

I approached Coach Smith and said, "My brother is here from New York and would like me to ride in the car with him to Chapel Hill. Would you allow it?"

Coach thought for a minute and said, "That's a tough one. Get on the bus, and let me think about it for a few minutes."

I was seated on the bus with the rest of my teammates, not knowing how Coach Smith would handle my request, when he came aboard and announced, "If any man on the team is twenty-four years old or older and has family here for the game, he's free to leave the bus and ride to Chapel Hill with them."

Although this incident occurred twenty-six or twenty-seven years ago, it had such a profound impact on me that I remember it like it happened yesterday.

BUSINESS PERSPECTIVE

If people don't believe they will matter to your team, they won't join it. If they don't believe they can succeed personally on your team, they won't work hard, certainly will have no motivation to work together, and won't work smart. Leaders must make sure that each person on their teams plays a valuable role, or they should help the person leave and find another job.

When a leader—for whatever reason—overlooks or too readily forgives a team member who is not performing effectively or is not up to standards, team members will reject that individual if the leader doesn't. They will exclude them from meetings, ignore their input, and ostracize them from the group. Each team member pays a price when a leader allows a weak link to remain and damage the team's performance. When it happens in business, each team member suffers, as do the customers and the entire organization. In fact the mission of the organization is damaged. Making each team member count (and be accountable) should be a foundation of an organization's work-smart efforts.

In a medium-size Mexican company the CEO promoted a veteran employee to vice president of sales. Unfortunately this individual was cautious, quiet, shy, and too concerned with minutiae. He wasn't a salesperson or an effective business builder. We all make mistakes, and the CEO certainly did with this particular appointment, as I learned during one of my seminars. While there, the CEO got a call that left him fuming and frustrated.

He explained that he'd been having major problems with his sales division. The caller had informed him that one of the company's most important customers was complaining about the sales vice president, to wit: "He doesn't take initiative to return phone calls. He doesn't follow through on projects. He doesn't offer any new ideas or alternatives, and he's made several major mistakes for us." The customer informed the company that it was taking its business elsewhere. The company lost four hundred thousand dollars that morning.

It was clear to me after talking with the CEO that the vice president of sales had been put into a job he wasn't qualified to handle. He was destined to fail. The salespeople, other company vice presidents, and customers rejected him. He failed in his job, and the team suffered. Finally, the CEO removed the man from his position as head of sales and found him another role in which he could succeed.

Leaders need to treat each team member fairly, playing no favorites and exhibiting no biases. This includes the stars and the folks who are not the stars. I know a senior officer of a large construction company who treated his top three experienced and effective senior managers favorably but treated horribly the six others who reported directly to him, who had less prestige, experience, and power. He ignored their ideas, yelled at them, and embarrassed them in front of others. Even though they had meaningful roles and were contributing in an effective manner, he treated them as fourth-class citizens. As a result, they didn't work smart, nor were they inspired to work as hard or together as a team. It was a waste of talent and ideas. They felt like they were losers on the team.

I know still another leader, a regional manager for a medical instruments company, who treated each person on his team as important. He was skilled at finding a person's strengths and building upon them. He accepted people's weaknesses and worked around them. Each member contributed to the team in powerful ways and succeeded personally in a team environment. Sales for this manager's region were always number one or number two in the company. All the new company sales reps sought the opportunity to work for him.

At a recent annual sales meeting this manager received a note from one of his employees saying that the team was going to meet in a ballroom to celebrate the end of the year. The manager arrived to find all twelve of his team members present. They formed a circle around him and one by one told him how much they respected him, cared for him, and appreciated what he did for them. They also showed their gratitude all year long by their outstanding job performances.

The manager said he was deeply touched by his people's affection and feedback, which he called one of the most satisfying experiences of his life. Just as teams reject those who don't contribute, so they embrace those who do.

16

TAKING CARE
OF THE LITTLE THINGS

A steady focus on taking care of the little things, attending diligently to the many details involved with building a team, helped us produce a mind-set that enhanced our ability to handle the big things. Handling details haphazardly often leads to treating the bigger things carelessly, and those things determine the outcome of games.

But while it was important for us to take care of details, we did not immerse ourselves in minutiae. For instance, after showing a player how to align his feet properly in taking his defensive stance and explaining why we did it that way, we weren't going to spend so much time on it that it would take practice time away from something more important to the team. My college coach, Phog Allen, used to have us spend ten or fifteen minutes a day on the simple act of pivoting. We were very good at it, but it seemed to me that we overdid that particular detail fundamental.

When I became head coach at North Carolina, I tried to put myself in the shoes of the players. How did they want to be treated? How could I help them reach their potential? How could I make the game fun and enjoyable and still work them hard? We worked hard in practice, but was there a point at which it could be counterproductive, or hurtful to the team, to stay on the court too long?

I got my ideas about many of these questions from recalling what many of my college teammates and I liked and didn't like about practice and games. For example, Doc Allen routinely had three-hour practices, which sometimes went longer if we weren't getting the job done. Our North Carolina practices usually were two hours or less, but there was very little wasted motion or downtime. Except for occasional two-minute water breaks, we worked every minute we were on the court.

Here are some other so-called little things that we integrated into our program:

- PUNCTUALITY

Our former players still talk about how serious we were about this. Players knew I used to arrive early for meetings and practices, and I expected everyone to be there and ready to go. Phil Ford still sets his watch ten minutes ahead to what he refers to as CST, Coach Smith Time. Being late to a meeting, a practice, a pregame meal, or the bus that took us to the airport was unacceptable. Tardiness is the height of arrogance. In effect, you're saying, "My time is more important than yours." Being on time is being considerate of others. We disciplined our players for being late. This went back to our philosophy of not having many rules but enforcing the ones we had. Being on time was one of them. It's a life lesson. Consider the impression someone makes by showing up late for a job interview.

- THE UNIVERSITY'S FRONT PORCH

The players represented themselves, their families, and their teammates, plus the entire constituency of the University of North Carolina. Our basketball team was on television constantly, and millions of people got their first impression of UNC from the appearance and behavior of our basketball team. Therefore I wanted our players in coats and ties for road trips, and they also dressed and acted accordingly when we stayed at fine hotels, which, as I said, we often did.

Ferebee Taylor, who served as UNC chancellor from 1972 to 1980, once explained that the basketball program was the university's front porch. Chancellor Taylor was a Carolina graduate and had been a Rhodes scholar and a corporate lawyer in New York before he returned to Chapel Hill. He said the most important part of the "house" was the education of the students, but he understood the value of athletics in their rightful place. Often our basketball team, cheerleaders, and band were the most visible part of the university. First impressions are powerful. We took seriously our responsibility of representing the university.

- SWEARING

We discouraged it in our program. When a player cursed in practice, the entire team ran for him. Growing up, I never heard profanity in our Kansas home. My father even denied my wishes to caddie at the Emporia Country Club because he knew I'd hear some swearing from frustrated golfers. This is not an easy subject to talk about because it can sound pious. I'm not offended when other people use profanity, and I'm certainly not suggesting that not swearing makes me better than anyone else. However, I believe to this day that anger can be expressed without using profanity.

- UNIFORMS

I wanted our players to be dressed the same. I made a mistake in 1970 by allowing our players to wear any style and type of shoe that they chose. We didn't quite look as if we were in uniform; it didn't look good. For the same reason I didn't like one or two players wearing T-shirts under their jerseys. When facial hair became stylish, I told inquiring players that all of us would grow beards, including the coaches, or none of us would. The only exception was for medical reasons.

- THROWING AN INBOUNDS PASS

Unless a player could show me that he could hold the basketball in one hand and pull it back once the arm and shoulder moved forward in the throwing motion (none could), I insisted he use two hands to throw the ball inbounds. If a defender surprised the player by jumping in the path of the intended pass, the passer could redirect the ball if he used two hands, but not if he passed with one hand. A violation of this detail cost us a game at Georgia Tech in the late 1980s.

- SCOREBOARD GAZING

Although I don't think many of our players listened to me on this one because it was so hard to do, I didn't want our players looking at the scoreboard and worrying about the score until there was five minutes left in the game. At that point managing the clock became an important factor. Otherwise I wanted them to concentrate on each possession and execute well. That was hard to do if they were preoccupied with the score and the outcome of the game. It's important to stay in the present. As coach I seldom looked at the scoreboard until the second half.

- ENDGAME

We spent much practice time working on end-of-game situations. Anytime we got the ball late in the game with the shot clock off and the score tied, we were going to win it at the buzzer or at the worst go to overtime. We would start our offensive move with eight seconds left on the clock; that left a couple of seconds for an offensive rebound if our shot missed. Obviously, if we had an uncontested layup while holding for the last shot, we'd take it at any time and go play defense.

In most instances I didn't want to take a time-out in these late-game situations. After all, we had worked on these things in practice and knew what to do. Calling time-out allowed the opposing coach to set his defense and make some defensive substitutions. We weren't in the business of handing the advantage over to the other team. We wanted our opponents to have to react to us.

If we were down one with, say, twenty seconds to play, we'd take the first great shot that surfaced. Michael Jordan's shot against Georgetown in the 1982 national championship game, taken with seventeen seconds left, is a good example. He was the second option on the play and was wide open, and it was a good shot.

Now, if I coached a team that was a huge underdog and trailed by one with twenty seconds to play, I might decide to hold for the last shot and take my chances of winning by one or losing by one. We used this strategy at the Air Force Academy to upset a heavily favored opponent.

Paying so much attention to late-game situations paid off handsomely for us over the years. Our teams won a lot of close games. A bonus was that players enjoyed ending practice with an overtime scrimmage. It was competitive and fun.

- OPPONENT'S LAST SHOT

If the opponent had the ball in a tie game with the shot clock off, we weren't about to back off defensively and let it hold the ball without a problem. Instead we pressured it, tried to trap out of our double teams, tried to make it uncomfortable and force a turnover. We weren't content with letting the opponent dictate action. That followed our philosophy of being the aggressor, not the reactor. However, at ten seconds remaining, we would back off with our defense, pay special attention to the opponent's best shooters, and hope for overtime.

- TV CHANGED EVERYTHING

I laugh when I read reports from groups studying intercollegiate athletics that say college basketball "is getting too commercial." Well, when the NCAA accepted CBS's eleven-year, six-billion-dollar contract to show regular-season and NCAA tournament games, it should have expected commercialism. The tremendous interest that exists in college basketball today can be traced to television's encroachment on the game. With due respect to all the study groups, television wasn't about to pay this kind of money without getting a whole lot in return. Basketball is the perfect game for television: big ball that's easy to follow, cameras close to the action to catch the emotions on the faces of players, coaches, and cheerleaders (although I wish they'd keep the camera on the players and quit showing the coaches), bands playing, crowds cheering. It's a festive, suspenseful setting, a ready-made television spectacle. To recoup its six billion dollars, television is going to continue to commercialize it.

Looking at the broad picture of college basketball's relationship with television, I'd say television has been more helpful than hurtful. I can't begin to tell you how many letters I received over the years telling me stories of how families got together to watch our teams play basketball on TV. One young man, mourning the death of his grandfather, wrote to tell me how the two of them had always made it a point to watch Carolina games on television. Carolina basketball became a family outing because of television. It brought together families when nothing else could in some cases. It was also great for people who could not travel for whatever reason and for those who weren't lucky enough to see us play in person. Having our games on television was also a huge asset for the university. Our alumni around the nation would meet in groups to watch our games. When we won national championships, it was common for student applications, as well as fundraising, to rise. In addition, television brought us many fans nationwide, and the money they spent on Carolina hats, sweatshirts, and other paraphernalia went to the university's general fund. Television has created thousands and thousands of new fans for college basketball.

Our UNC teams were on TV so much that our opponents always had us well scouted. To combat it, we changed some of our signals frequently and put in some new wrinkles in 1979. Some opposing players told the press that they'd seen North Carolina on television so much that they thought we were a running network series. Make no mistake about this either: It inspired players from teams that seldom appeared on television to show us what they could do. They were fired up to play us.

• CHERRY PICKING

I didn't want our players surprised by anything, so we tried to cover all eventualities in practice. This included working against a strategy that we referred to as cherry picking. That would occur if a team chose to leave one man under its basket and defend us with four players, to see how we would respond. Its goal would be to throw long passes to the cherry picker so he could shoot layups before we got back on defense. Leaving a defender back to guard the cherry picker and playing offense with only four players would have been playing into the opponent's hand or letting it dictate how the game was going to be played. That was never our policy. While we could have said we were taking what they gave us, we preferred to be stubborn and took what we wanted.

Thus we practiced playing five offensive players against the other team's four defenders and taking only great shots. Once the shot was in the air, we released one of our players to sprint back on defense to cover the cherry picker. No team ever used this strategy against us, but we were nonetheless prepared for it.

• ARCHIE

If we were down two points with one second to play and were on the foul line to shoot one shot, we called for a play we named archie. We asked the shooter to miss on purpose with a high-arching shot (thus archie). We practiced screening actions along the foul lane that were designed to free one of our players so he could rebound the shot and have a layup to tie the game.

• MORE ON TIME-OUTS

I didn't hoard time-outs the way some critics suggested, but neither did I burn them needlessly. I wanted to save them in case they were needed in our catch-up offense late in the game. For example, if we fell behind 10–0 to start the game, the TV announcers and the fans would be screaming for me to take a time-out. Well, if we had taken five good shots and missed them while the opponent had taken five tough shots and made them, I wasn't going to waste a time-out to tell our players, "Keep doing what you're doing. Our shots will start to fall, and theirs will begin to miss." I'm also not a big fan of players' burning time-outs early in the game to avoid being tied up or going out of bounds. Of course situations can change late in the game, when possession of the ball is crucial. That's another reason to save time-outs for real emergencies. Also, with TV taking four long time-outs each half, how many more time-outs are needed? The television time-outs took so long that I sometimes ran out of things to say to my players. We were often back on the court and ready to play a full thirty seconds or longer before the buzzer sounded to end the TV break. Hey, those long commercial breaks were part of the six-billion-dollar deal. CBS has to sell a lot of ads to get that money back.

- HITTING THE WALL

To improve shooting mechanics, we'd have our players stand fifteen feet from the wall and shoot the ball at it. We wanted them to work on spinning the ball correctly, getting the proper arch on it, releasing it properly, and keeping their eyes on the target. Shooting at the wall instead of at the basket allowed the players to focus entirely on fundamentals instead of on making the shot. Had they used the basket in this drill, their competitiveness would have intruded, and their concentration would have been on making shots, not on fundamentals. I started this drill because my practice swing in golf is smoother than when I'm actually hitting the ball. Too bad I can't groove my practice swing as our players did to perfect their shooting form.

- MORE SHOOTING

The hardest shot for most players is the six- to ten-foot shot off the baseline. Many players "short-arm" the shot as they attempt to guide the ball into the basket. Walter Davis, one of our great players, was sensational at this shot because even though it was a short distance, he employed full extension coupled with perfect form. Each day during the shooting period we had our players practice the technique that was perfected by Walter, and for generations of Carolina players the drill was known as the Walter Davis Rule.

- WATER BREAK

In the old days (not all that long ago, really), coaches didn't allow their players to have water during practice. Coaches thought it was bad for players and slowed their physical conditioning. We learned better. We had water breaks during our practices, and they were timed on the clock—exactly two minutes. Seniors drank first, then juniors, then sophomores, then freshmen. I've been asked why the water break was for two minutes. It was because players ought to be able to get a drink of water and be ready to resume practice in two minutes. That seems reasonable to me.

- YOUR SHIRT, SIR

After our program began making enough money to afford it, many of our players changed at halftime to clean, dry jerseys. It made them feel fresh. During practice they were allowed to change jerseys at the water break.

- SPRINT TO THE BENCH

When the horn sounded for a time-out, we expected our players to sprint to the bench. The same held when they were taken out of the game for substitutes as well as when they left the court at halftime. If we were fouled at our defensive end of the court, I wanted our players to sprint to the other end to take the foul shot. There were a couple of reasons for this. One, it looks bad for players to shuffle over to the bench during time-outs or when they're being replaced. More important, we wanted the opponent to see us running and running. Maybe a seed would be planted: "Don't those North Carolina players ever get tired?"

• DONALD, MEET DANTE

We switched the personnel in practice drill groups (when grouping by size wasn't a factor) every two weeks throughout the season to avoid cliques from forming.

• TAKING GOOD SHOTS

To encourage the taking of good shots, we sometimes scrimmaged without keeping score on the board. I secretly gave the score to a manager, and all the scoring was based on shot selection. A great shot (layup), even if it didn't go in, was worth three points; a good shot, even if it didn't fall, was two points; for a shot that was merely acceptable because of the shot clock winding down, one point. If a player made a tough three-point shot that shouldn't have been taken, zero points. Loss of ball without getting a shot was minus two points. I announced the winning score at the end of practice. We defined a good shot as one the shooter could make most of the time that was taken with our rebounders in position, unless it was an open layup. We'd shoot that anytime. Part of playing smart involves taking good shots.

• HITTING THE ROAD

Bill Guthridge, one of my assistants, who succeeded me as Carolina's head coach, was in charge of our team travel plans. We gave the players an itinerary that told them when we'd be leaving, where we'd be staying, what time we would be eating, the time they should be in their rooms, what time we'd leave the hotel for the arena, and that sort of information. We did not include plans about the return trip. We wanted the players to focus on the reason for going on the trip in the first place and not worry about what time we would get home. They received the return trip information in the dressing room after the game.

- QUESTIONS, QUESTIONS

One of our young players asked to see me to discuss a problem he was having. "Coach, I want to break up with my girlfriend. How should I go about it?" That was *not* part of the practice plan.

- COME TO WORK

Practice was the foundation for everything we did in our program. Therefore I told our players, "Practice is a privilege. If you're not here to work, then leave."

- FALLEN TEAMMATE

If one of our players took a charge, or dived for a loose ball, or hit the floor fighting for a rebound, his teammates ran to help him get on his feet. If it happened in practice, the coaches also assisted him. The player took the fall for all of us, so we should show our appreciation.

- THE TOP PRIORITY

We checked on the class attendance of our players, as well as their grades and academic progress. They knew we were serious about it. We owed it to their parents to make sure they were in class and doing as well academically as possible. After all, we had recruited them, so it was our duty to make sure academics came first. Their basketball-playing days wouldn't last forever.

Brad Frederick,

class of 1999, assistant basketball coach,
Vanderbilt University

———

Our student managers kept statistics on everything we did in practice: how many shots we took and from where, how many we made, our shooting percentage on three-point shots and free throws, how our playing weight fluctuated. They recorded all our missed layups during pregame warm-ups, and those misses meant extra running in practice the next day.

He didn't want us to practice crazy shots or fail to take practice or pregame warm-ups seriously. He admonished us to practice and prepare with a purpose. One day a player took a wild shot, and Coach Smith asked him, "Do you think Tiger Woods practices golf shots that he'll never use in competition?"

I recall having daily shooting contests before practice with one of our leading players, Ed Cota. We were arguing one day about who had won the most often when Assistant Coach Dave Hanners overheard us. He settled the matter by giving us the exact number of shots both of us had made and missed for the entire year. Our team travel itineraries were carefully planned, and our arrival back to the Smith Center, even from long trips, was usually accurate within five or ten minutes.

Coach Smith believed in taking care of details. Our practices and pregame warm-ups were timed to the precise minute. In practice our individual water cups were arranged in the same order on the table each day. We were so well drilled in practice for all eventualities that it usually was unnecessary for Coach Smith to call time-out to cover something with us at the end of games. For the same reason, he didn't have to call every offensive or defensive set that we ran during a game. He had prepared us and could therefore trust us to do what we'd been taught.

Business Perspective

Perfectionist leaders can get mired down in minutiae and spend a lot of time on unimportant details. There is a major difference between fine points that count and those that don't. How can you tell the difference? Being able to differentiate between the two can be the deciding factor that results in a big victory or a crucial loss.

So, how *do* you distinguish between what's trivial and what's important? Start by asking the question, Do these details count and really make a difference? In such areas as customer service, for example, little things count greatly. The difference between customers who answer that they are "very satisfied" with service and product compared with those who answer that they are merely "satisfied" is massive. Those who are "very satisfied" will buy again almost 50 percent more frequently than those who are just "satisfied." The relevant fine points that help some individuals and organizations excel over others are what I call the Significant Details of Success (SDS).

Great leaders are adept at identifying and tending to the crucial details. A CEO I know who rose from poverty to become a world-class leader has learned over his career that when he is ready to start a new project, the smartest use of his time, effort, and money is to spend far more of them in the planning stages than he used to think necessary. He found that there are big payoffs when he spends several hours a day for ten weeks simply thinking through every question: things that might go wrong; tasks that need to be done; possible pitfalls of the project. Then he asks all the key experts for help to refine the significant details of his project. One of his favorite truisms is "The devil is in the details."

I know also of a great real estate developer, Harry Frampton, who has learned through experience that one of the keys to success in getting zoning approved for his projects and gaining the support of neighborhood groups, the general public, architects, contractors, and financiers is to meet with each of these constituencies a total of ten to fifteen times in town hall types of hearings in order to get their ideas and input and to encourage their involvement. Each of these meetings usually focuses on the fine points, and even though the meetings often are hostile and repetitive, he maintains that he and his staff always get good ideas that make their projects better. They also learn the objections of their opponents and are consequently better able to perfect the SDS. In addition, former opponents frequently turn into supporters, improving the project's chances of succeeding. Taking care of all these little things can lead to big victories.

EXAMPLE

I once worked for a CEO who, in preparation for forthcoming appointments, meetings, or conference calls, called me at least a week in advance to review the major goals we would be discussing. Giving me time to think about each goal and the issues surrounding it helped our meetings be more productive. This is a sound way to work on the details.

However, there are details and details. When leaders focus on the fine points of expense control or safety management, for example, they help their companies succeed, but micromanagers who get engrossed in insignificant details and in making sure their subordinates follow them can be in big trouble.

One such manager was so focused on minor issues that she didn't realize she had lost touch with the major ones. She actually spent an enormous amount of time figuring out what size and color of paper clips should be used on which types of reports and then making certain her subordinates complied with her conclusions. If someone didn't follow her "paper clip plan," he or she was brought in, lectured on how to do it right, and severely reprimanded.

This manager also designed a plan for how each employee's desk should be arranged before the lunch break or at the end of the day. It wasn't a question of whether or not the desks were clean, as they always were, or if things had been put away properly. It was more about having things on the desks arranged the way *she* liked. She even prepared a book with instructions, diagrams, and rules for desk arrangements that outlined where folders, paper, staplers, and telephones were to be placed. She was very organized—and quite ineffective. You can imagine how the morale of busy employees was affected by this tomfoolery.

Another leader, a senior sales manager in a consumer products company, was so focused on minutiae that his salespeople became so frustrated that most quit even trying to "sell smart." The manager spent months preparing a single-spaced, six-hundred-page, multi-volume "sales bible" that detailed the rules and procedures of every sales activity the company encountered. He required each of his eight hundred sales reps and managers to carry the volumes with them on every sales call. He wanted to make sure they could find any answer they needed in any situation.

The salespeople found it impossible to find the answers they needed in these unwieldy volumes. The binders were useless to them when they were in the middle of sales calls, so they referred to them maybe one time in a hundred. The manager's penchant for sales minutiae was expensive and debilitating. The by-product of this poor decision was that the sales force was stymied and frustrated and performed poorly because they spent so much time on minutiae they couldn't focus on the significant factors for success.

Another sales manager required her reps to carry with them and use identical sets of colored pens to take notes, write reports, and store specific information. If they attended a meeting and didn't have a "correct" pen, they were asked to leave the meeting and go to a nearby office supply store to buy one. It was a form of punishment and discipline for breaking the "colored pen code." This manager got confused between excelling in the details and drowning in trivia. A key question to ask is, Is this detail a substantive one that will help us succeed, or is it simply a matter of form?

· 17 ·

ONE-ON-ONE MEETINGS

I believed strongly in scheduled one-on-one meetings with our players. It was a good way to keep communications open as well as to learn what was going on with them. They also learned in greater detail what I was thinking about their overall college and basketball performance.

When I had a player come to my office for a talk, the first topic on the agenda was his academic performance. We had our way of knowing about his attendance and performance in each class. We had recruited these young men to come to North Carolina, so we believed we owed it to their parents to make sure they put academics first and did as well as possible in school. They knew from the day we began recruiting them that their academics had to come first if they chose North Carolina. My staff and I tried to assure that they maintained that focus.

One-on-one meetings with the players helped keep this in mind. People seem to take more care and respond more effectively when they know the results of their efforts will be scrutinized on a regular basis.

I had a one-on-one meeting with each player when he arrived on cam-

pus to begin the fall semester. A second one came before the start of practice on October 15, and the third after our annual blue-white scrimmage,
usually held about the first week of November. A fourth series of individual meetings was held in mid-December because by then I had enough
game tapes to show them some really good plays they had made as well as
some bad ones. Videotape served as a great teaching tool for me and a superb way for them to learn. We had a fifth set of one-on-ones midway
through the ACC season (early in February) to review the season and talk
about what was in front of us and what was expected of them in basketball
the remainder of the season, including the NCAA tournament. At the
conclusion of the season I had another series of meetings with each player,
beginning with the seniors. We talked at length in those final meetings, especially with the seniors. I was extremely interested in knowing how they
felt about their North Carolina careers. I learned a great deal from all the
players in those exit interviews. It would have disappointed me deeply if
one had told me that he hadn't enjoyed his Carolina experience. I never received a response like that, thank goodness. We talked to the seniors about
their schoolwork and what they had planned for themselves after graduation and offered to help them with their job searches, whether it was for
pro basketball contracts in Europe or jobs during graduate school. In the
final meetings with the underclassmen, in addition to going over their academic pictures and reviewing the season, we gave them detailed plans for
what basketball-related things they should work on over the summer to
improve their games. We gave them specific goals, which I'll discuss in the
following chapter.

In addition to these scheduled one-on-one meetings, others popped up
from time to time on an as-needed basis. For instance, if I threw a player
out of practice, as happened on occasion but not often, he was temporarily
off the team until he came to my office to see me the next day. I did all the
talking in those particular meetings. I made sure the player understood
why I had been upset enough to throw him out of practice, told him how
it hurt him and the team, and made it clear that such conduct would not

be tolerated. I didn't have a three-strikes-and-you're-gone policy, but the players knew I was serious. I threw one player out after he really whacked a nonscholarship player who was much smaller than he was. "Is that supposed to show me how tough you are?" I asked him. "Pick on somebody your own size." Once the players understood the problem and apologized for their actions, I'd say, "Okay, you're back, but I don't expect to see this again."

Also, if a player had a problem he needed to discuss, he could come see me immediately. We made that clear to them. The players came first. I had a rule from day one in my head coaching tenure, that if a player needed to see me, it took priority over *everything* else, even if it meant asking the governor of North Carolina to leave the office temporarily.

Furthermore, if a player was really struggling with his academics, basketball, or something else, I might call him in at any time to talk. The players knew and honored this rule about our one-on-one meetings: What was said stayed behind closed doors.

I was honest and forthright with the players. I never made any promises of playing time to anyone. I never conducted the talks in a way that pitted a player against one of his teammates, such as "To beat out Jerry, you must . . ." That would have been counterproductive to building team goals. If playing time was a concern (and it was with most competitive young men who weren't playing as much as they wanted), I told the player to work hard for improvement each day in practice. Also, he could help the team by providing good competition in practice for those who were playing more regularly. I wanted the players to maintain a hope and belief that they could improve and earn time, but I wanted them to be realistic. Sometimes they needed too much improvement for it to come during the season, when the emphasis was on team goals. Players usually learned their roles through what transpired in practice, but if a player was confused about his role on the team, we'd talk about that in the one-on-ones.

Some players were slower than others to open up and share their thoughts. Freshmen were often subdued and hesitant to talk, but that changed as they grew more sure of themselves and felt more at home in our program. One young man, who wanted me to know that he thought he should be playing more, had a difficult time articulating his thoughts. I asked him to change chairs with me. He became the head coach, and I became the player in this role-playing session. "Where would you play me?" I asked him. He thought for a minute and said, "I'm not sure, but I'd play you."

There's such a discussion among the media and fans about basketball players' leaving college early to sign professional basketball contracts. Ironically, it doesn't seem to bother anyone when golfers, tennis players, baseball players, and ice skaters do it, but when a leading basketball player forfeits his college eligibility to enter the draft of the National Basketball Association, there's a shrill response.

We had nine North Carolina players leave early for the NBA when I was coach. They didn't leave *college;* they left *college basketball* and, in the process, made themselves and their families financially secure for life. Six returned in the summer to earn their degrees, and two others are working on it. I had no problem with their choosing to make their livings in professional basketball, none whatsoever, provided I knew they would be a top five draft pick. We lost eleven years of eligibility from the nine excellent players who left early, but it worked out well for them. Our teams certainly did miss them, but we nevertheless continued with very good teams.

Sure, there are some horror stories concerning college basketball players who left early for the pros and didn't make it. But before our players left, they had an excellent idea of where they'd be picked in the draft. We made sure of that by talking to coaching friends and front-office friends in the NBA. Over a thirty-six-year period, 96 percent of our players earned their degrees, and more than a third went to graduate and professional school. Our emphasis was in the right place, and I wasn't going to send a player early to the NBA unless I thought the conditions were right and it was to his benefit. So some of my most important meetings with our players dealt with this subject.

The Tuesday afternoon after we won the 1982 national championship a crowd estimated at twenty-five thousand was in our football stadium to welcome the team home. The fans chanted to James Worthy, a junior on our team and the MVP of the Final Four, "One more year! One more year!" There had been widespread speculation in the newspaper that James would enter the NBA draft after the season. Neither James nor I would discuss it with the media during our season, other than my saying, "I will meet with James and his family after the season to discuss what's best for him." Out of season, what was best for the individual; in season, what was best for North Carolina.

The first pick in the 1982 NBA draft, to be determined by a coin toss, would belong to the Los Angeles Lakers or the San Diego Clippers. Both teams told me James would be their pick if they won the coin toss. His pay would be at least five hundred thousand dollars a year for five years, guaranteed. While that might not sound like much today, it was a huge contract in 1982.

Shortly after the season James, his parents and I met to talk about his choices. Adding perspective to this discussion was the fact that James had suffered a serious foot injury during his freshman season, one that required surgery and the insertion of a screw into his foot to hasten recovery. It had sidelined him for the last half of the season. I told the Worthys what I'd learned about his draft status: He would be the top pick and make a lot of money.

Certainly I wanted him back at Carolina. He was a great player and a delight to coach. With James back, along with Sam Perkins, Michael Jordan, and Matt Doherty, and with Jimmy Braddock taking over for Jimmy Black at point guard, we could win another national title. But as I said, there was no disability insurance on James's ankle. If an undergraduate is sure to go in the top five of the draft, and it is his goal to play in the NBA, I believe he should go. James's father agreed with me, and the decision was made for him to go. It worked out well. James got his big contract with the Los Angeles Lakers, played on numerous NBA championship teams, became one of the league's great players—and still earned his degree.

Michael Jordan never brought up the subject of going pro before graduating from Carolina. One of our former players with NBA experience as both a great player and coach, Billy Cunningham, told me Michael would go no lower than third in the 1984 draft if he decided to leave early.

My research also indicated that Michael would go no lower than third and maybe second. The money would be less than but similar to that which James had received, all guaranteed. I asked the Jordans to meet with me in my office. In the meeting with Michael and his parents, it was obvious that Deloris Jordan wanted him to stay in school and get his degree before going pro. Mr. Jordan wanted him to go pro. I was neutral, and Michael was undecided. My assistant coaches wanted him to stay and wrote down the reasons they thought the way they did.

I told Michael and his parents to discuss it overnight, then come back to my office the next day, and we would make public their intentions, since media speculation was heating up. They met with me for thirty minutes the next morning, and we concluded that Michael should go pro. I told them it was a wise decision. Some of our fans reminded me the next year that having had Michael on our team as a senior leader might well have resulted in another national championship. Still, without him, we made it to the Elite Eight before losing to eventual national champion, Villanova, and we did that with one of our most valuable players, Steve Hale, out with a dislocated shoulder suffered in the first NCAA tournament game of that season. It was fun to imagine what we would have done with Michael back, but that wasn't important. What was important was what was best for him at that particular time in his life. He won six NBA championships with the Chicago Bulls, and many consider him the best professional player of all time. And yes, he received his degree from Carolina.

When the players made decisions to go pro early, I brought in the dean of the Business School and the dean of the Law School along with my accountant and friend Bill Miller, as well as a financial expert such as Bob Eubanks to advise the players about choosing attorneys and financial advisers. These meetings were also set up for our players who were hoping to play pro after their senior seasons.

I had a one-on-one with one such player, Sam Perkins, after his junior season and said, "Sam, I've done the research, and the best I have guaranteed is that Detroit, with Jack McClosky as general manager, will take you with its pick at number eight in the first round. Therefore I don't think it would be wise for you to go pro this year. I believe you should return for your senior season, graduate, and then turn professional. But I'll support whatever decision you make." Sam smiled and said, "Coach, I haven't given one minute's thought about going pro early. I plan to be back next year." He had a great senior year, earned his degree, was drafted in the top four that spring, and went on to have one of the most successful NBA careers of all time.

So one-on-one meetings were very much part of our Carolina program. The discussions were direct, honest, and often revealing. We used them to teach, to mentor, to explain disciplinary decisions, and to keep the lines of communications open. I also received some valuable feedback from our players in these meetings, especially from the veteran players who had been in our program for several years.

PLAYER PERSPECTIVE

Mike Cooke,
class of 1964, businessman,
Myrtle Beach, South Carolina

In the early fall Coach Smith would mail a postcard to the players at their dormitory rooms, stating that we were to meet individually with him on a certain date and time. We usually received the cards about two weeks prior to the scheduled meetings, and it was up to us to remember the date and time and be there. There wasn't going to be a follow-up card or call to remind us.

The one-on-one meetings were informal, as Coach tried to put us at ease. We talked about career interests, how we felt about different things, how things were going at home, our academic progress, life in general. Except for one thing: basketball. We did not talk about basketball.

I believe Coach called these one-on-one meetings for several reasons:

1. He wanted to make sure we recalled the meeting date and arrived on time. Punctuality was very important to him, as was living up to one's responsibilities. He knew we would face these kinds of things, meetings and obligations, in the future, and he wanted to get us ready for life after basketball.
2. He wanted to learn as much as he possibly could about each player on his team in an individual setting. He truly wanted to hear about our problems, our successes, our dreams and desires. It was another way in which he showed us how much he cared.
3. The more he knew about our future ambitions, the better he would be able to help us face life after Carolina and life after basketball.

These one-on-one meetings revealed much about Coach Smith as a man, coach, teacher, and friend. Over the years I have talked to many ex-players from other universities, and they agree when I say, "Coach Smith is unique."

BUSINESS PERSPECTIVE

Most people's jobs today are more complex, fast-paced, and highly interdependent than ever. As a result, attempts to formalize communications between people can seem futile or worse. Most employees are so rushed because of their workloads and deadlines that their communications tend to be cryptic, hurried, and superficial and are often delivered by E-mail, a technology that can create as much hostility as clarity. The more complex the job, the more difficult it is to communicate.

There is a practical solution to the dilemma: People should get together regularly in informal, unstructured meetings to discuss everything they're doing and thinking about. The key is to get people together and encourage them to discuss openly and listen to one another's problems, needs, expectations, hunches, and hypotheses. In other words, get them to think out loud. They should be allowed enough time to think of questions, problems, and opportunities they didn't even know were in play.

Informal, unrushed meetings that are not agenda packed or overly focused on the short-term tasks are missing in most businesses. That means people are missing terrific opportunities to communicate better. I suggest establishing one-on-one meetings with each member of your team at least once a month. The meetings should last from one to three hours. Employees should be prepared to discuss everything they are thinking about. You should prepare your own list of things you think important to discuss and set aside more time than you typically need. If you get the work done, then you can finish the meeting early, but often the best ideas come from having ample time to think more deeply about the work. I strongly urge you to consider trying this for at least a year to test if it works for you.

In addition, it is wise to establish a series of informal meetings between your team and other departments within your organization. Allow mingling and creative communications so people can discover problems and opportunities and solve the interdependent problems they all face.

One of the major dilemmas of leadership today is that leaders spend more time doing than they do teaching. The higher your position, the more time you should devote to teaching. The key is to teach your methods and principles so they can apply them.

MENTORING

One of the best ways to teach is for all leaders and workers to mentor younger associates. Interestingly, most managers at the end of their careers fantasize that when they retire, they would like to teach. Few ever do. There's a way to solve this yearning: Do your teaching now, on the job. Young people have a serious need for effective tutoring concerning their careers and their professional growth.

In my opinion, here's the best way for a leader to go about it:

1. You should pick out two individuals a year to mentor. They should be individuals you like personally. They should not be people that you pick because you are assigned them, because your position suggests you should choose them, or because human resources picks out the "stars" and assigns them. Mentoring usually doesn't work unless the mentor likes the people he or she is working with, believes in them and their futures, and wants to help them. When this is the case, the mentor also learns from the student.

   If you don't like and believe in the people you're mentoring, you won't give up the time to carry out effective mentoring. Moreover, two employees a year are the most you can effectively mentor. They can come from any department within the organization and from any level, as long as you clear your selections with the appropriate hierarchy.

2. You should meet quarterly with your students. It can be over breakfast, at lunch, or in the evening, whichever you prefer.

3. You should ask your students to prepare for the meetings by making an outline of the ten biggest problems they are working on as well as the ten biggest job decisions they will need to make in the near future. You can discuss their ten problems and help them think about them more effectively, as well as give your advice on how you would approach solving them.

4. You should prepare five questions to ask your students, concerning their jobs, views of the company, or any other work-related topic that interests you. If you benefit personally from spending time with a young associate, you will feel rewarded. Effective mentoring ends up being a two-way street.

5. At the completion of one full year with your students, you should ask them to prepare lists of the twenty major lessons they learned during their time with you about leadership, business, and personal effectiveness. This will ensure that they articulate and reinforce what they learned and are held accountable for their time with you. In the process they most likely will provide you with some new ideas about coaching and teaching.

6. You should select new employees to mentor each year. It will allow you to spread your wisdom among more people, have more fun, and help your organization prosper. Also, the employees you mentor will probably be dedicated to you for the rest of their careers.

GOALS AND EXPECTATIONS

We didn't start the year with a long list of goals because so many variables in basketball cropped up over the course of a long season. Many of them, such as injuries to players, poor calls by officials, or just superhuman efforts by opponents, were out of our control. It's possible for a team to do its very best in all areas and still lose. In such situations, say congratulations and move on.

I wasn't a Pollyanna who advised our players, "Shoot for the moon, and if we miss, we might hit a star." As I've said, I was more inclined to give our players goals and objectives they could control. They could make sure that no team played harder than they did. No opponent could stop them from playing together as a team, unselfishly. No opponent could keep them from playing smart.

Instead of writing down a smorgasbord of goals, I was more specific. I wanted us to have as a goal improving ourselves each day and treating each opportunity to practice as a privilege. I wanted the players to stay in the present and not look so far into the future that they lost focus of what was important to accomplish that day. Our ultimate goal was to have a great season, and we believed if we stayed with our process, there would be some honors waiting for us at season's end.

The team and coaches held a tip-off dinner the night before we started preseason practice. We talked about the kind of season we wanted to have and the work we'd need to do to get there. We advised the players not to allow the media, fans, or fellow students to set expectations or goals for them or get them looking past the regular season to the NCAA tournament. We had to *make* the NCAA tournament before we would have a chance to win it. It wasn't a given.

Goals and objectives changed for me and our teams during my coaching tenure. In my first fourteen years of being Carolina's head coach, only the ACC tournament champion was allowed to represent the league in the NCAA tournament. Our ultimate goal during that time was to win the conference tournament. It was so important that we sometimes held back things in the regular season so we could surprise opponents in the conference tournament. Sending the tournament champion to the NCAA tournament wasn't the fairest way to determine the league champion, but it was the rule. I didn't make a big deal about the unfairness of it because I didn't want our players to have a psychological block concerning the tournament. I wanted them to look forward to it and, as much as possible, enjoy it. We were pretty good at it. We won seventeen regular-season and thirteen tournament ACC championships, far more than any other ACC school. Our 1967–69 teams won three consecutive ACC regular-season championships and then had to do it all over again in the tournament to keep our season going, as they did. Those players were remarkable in the way they responded to the pressure. Everything we did in those days was designed to help us win the ACC tournament. It was the key to our season.

That changed when the NCAA voted in 1975 to allow more than one team from a conference to go to the tournament. Our long-range goal was to win the ACC regular season; then we'd think about the ACC tournament and the NCAA tournament. Our short-range goals of course were to play hard, together, and smart and to improve each day. Our players were very good at staying focused and improving on a daily basis. I can't think of one of our thirty-six teams that didn't improve as the season went along unless we had late-season injuries to key players.

Once our program was established and we became a national contender each year, there were many fans and media representatives who were more than prepared to set our goals and expectations for us. We certainly didn't need to fuel their expectations because they were usually sky-high and often unrealistic. Our players and coaches heard it all the time: "Are you guys going to win it all this year?" That bugged me because I was concerned about our first game and they had already jumped ahead to the national championship. Of course high expectations were part of the territory at North Carolina. Some thought it was ordained for Carolina to go to the NCAA tournament each year. That was tremendously unfair to the players, who had to work hard to achieve the goal. Winning is not that easy, and never was. The players and I never took it for granted. It took a lot of hard work on the part of talented, dedicated players.

Before we beat Georgetown in the 1982 NCAA championship game, a popular topic among basketball writers was to speculate if, and when, one of my teams would win a national championship. I wasn't bothered by the talk as much as family and friends were. Our Carolina teams had been to six Final Fours before we won in 1982, and that mattered more to me than going once, winning, and never being heard from again. I knew how good and lucky a team had to be to reach the Final Four. No matter what the pundits said, I also knew our players had won countless "big" games en route to those Final Fours. I am, and was, grateful to our players for winning the NCAA championship in 1982. It kept me from having to deal with that question again. But if I told our players not to allow media and fans to set their expectations, I wasn't going to turn around and let them set mine. Beating Georgetown by one point did not make me a better coach or person. I never felt one of our teams needed to win a national championship to validate my career as a teacher and coach. I wasn't obsessed with it. Nevertheless, American society seems to recognize number one and nothing else. It's an uninformed and unrealistic mind-set. For intercollegiate athletics to be worthwhile, there must be appreciation for teams and players that do their best, even if doing so doesn't result in championships. To say that a college basketball team that came in second, third, or fourth in the nation somehow failed borders on sickness. But it happens, and it's one of the reasons we were determined to set our own goals without outside interference.

Sure, I knew our players would read the newspapers, watch television, and hear from their fellow students. Still, I wanted them to maintain perspective. In the era of massive television coverage of college basketball, the sport has become almost totally a tournament sport. That's unfortunate because if the regular season doesn't matter, why do ESPN, ABC, and FOX pay large sums of money to show all those regular-season games? My friend Dick Vitale's work would be useless, because he and ESPN do regular-season games, while CBS owns the rights to all the NCAA tournament games. The best chance a team has of doing well in the tournament, unless it's outright lucky, is to improve on a daily basis over the course of the season.

The players needed to be realistic and to stay focused. Most teams are going to have some discouraging setbacks during the course of the season. The good ones fight through the adversity and keep their dreams alive by focusing on short-range goals: "Let's get better today."

My alma mater, Kansas, won the national championship in 1988 under Coach Larry Brown, who had been my team captain in 1963 and assistant coach in 1966 and 1967. It began the season 12–8. Many fans and writers gave up on the team. But Larry was encouraged by what he saw from his team in practice. "We're getting better defensively," he told me in early February. "We're going to be pretty good before the season's over." En route to the national championship, Kansas beat several teams in the NCAA tournament that it had lost to in the regular season. Instead of wringing their hands about being 12–8, the Jayhawks stayed with their process, listened to their coach, got better each day. At a time when their season appeared to be in serious trouble, they remained focused on short-term goals. It resulted in a great Horatio Alger story. Larry's NBA teams also improve as the season progresses. He's a great coach and teacher.

We didn't spend an inordinate amount of time talking to our North Carolina teams about goals and expectations during the season, but we certainly did during our last one-on-one meetings with our returning players before they left campus for summer break. We had specific goals for them, things they needed to work on to improve. Instead of saying, "You need to work hard and improve," I was very specific with each player. I gave each of them two or three areas in which I wanted to see improvement when they returned to school in the late summer.

While we were extremely grateful to our former players and the many big victories they had at North Carolina, our chief concern each year was with the current team and players. The tradition our past teams had established helped us in countless ways, but it could also be undermining if the current players dwelled on those accomplishments and said, "We can't be the team that breaks those streaks." There were a few: a national record for twenty-three consecutive appearances in the NCAA tournament, a record thirteen consecutive years of making at least the Sweet 16 of the NCAA tournament, a record number of thirty-three years not finishing lower than third in the ACC, twenty-two seasons of at least twenty-five wins, a record twenty-seven straight seasons of at least twenty-one victories, including thirty of our last thirty-one seasons. There were others, of course. Our tradition in basketball was inspirational and served as a strong bridge between our past and present, and it truly made us a family. But I didn't want our current players to look at those records in a way that stifled or put pressure on them. Our goal for each team was to do the best it could and not to worry about keeping streaks alive.

We tried hard not to worry about the things we couldn't control. Why waste the time and energy? I just told the players not to have their attention to our goals diverted by others. When Dick Vitale said on television prior to our 1987 game in the NCAA Elite Eight against Syracuse that our freshman J. R. Reid would "eat up" Syracuse's star center, Rony Seikaly, there was nothing I could do about it. Yes, it fired Seikaly up, but it was out of my control. Worrying about it would have been counterproductive.

It's also true that players sometimes set short-term goals that the coach doesn't know about. It happened to us in late January 1979, when Notre Dame was ranked number one in the nation and we were number two. Notre Dame lost an afternoon game that day, and we lost at Clemson that night, 66–61. Afterward Mike O'Koren, one of our most outstanding players, said, "There goes our chance to be number one." Moving up to number one in the polls obviously had been a goal for our players, and it could have affected the way we played in that game.

If the media ranked us highly in the national preseason polls, I told the players not to let it cloud our own expectations. "They voted for North Carolina's past success because this team hasn't done anything yet," I told them. On the few occasions they rated us down in the polls, I told them, "It just goes to show how much work we have to do to accomplish what we want to this season."

In talking about goals and expectations with our players, I was not a rah-rah type of coach. I didn't tell them, "Come on, we're going to run those guys out of the gym." I was more cautious. Some of the games that concerned me most were against opponents that we were expected to beat easily. Phil Ford said he knew such a game was coming up when I told the players, "They give basketball scholarships just like we do."

In the summer of 1992 Dr. Jerry Bell gave me a tape of a speaker from the Young President's Organization who said he had pasted a picture of himself on his bathroom mirror. However, he substituted a trim, physically fit body for his own and left the picture of his head on it. He said looking at the picture each morning inspired him in his battle to lose weight.

The New Orleans Superdome was site of the 1993 Final Four. Before the start of preseason practice, we put a picture of the Superdome in the locker of each player. We had won the 1982 national championship in the same building and had saved a picture with these words flashing brightly on the huge scoreboard: "Congratulations to North Carolina, 1982 National Champions." We doctored the picture to make it read, "Congratulations to North Carolina, 1993 National Champions." It was our long-range goal for the season, and we wanted the players to look at the picture every day as a reminder. We didn't dwell on it or allow it to get in the way of our short-term focus, but for that team I thought the perspective would do some good. We won the national championship, so obviously it didn't hurt.

PLAYER PERSPECTIVE

Kim Huband,
*class of 1972, planner for the North Carolina
Division of Parks and Recreation,
Raleigh, North Carolina*

Goals are not an end unto themselves, but utilized properly, they can provide direction. That was Coach Smith's view as he and his teams set high, clearly defined goals each season, such as winning the ACC regular-season and tournament championships.

What set Coach Smith apart, I believe, was his ability to teach his players that success didn't come from simply setting goals and wishing for them to happen; instead it came from working hard and intelligently each day to improve. Success was the by-product of that intelligent, sustained effort.

Coach planned for success. The improvement that his teams and individual players displayed over the course of a season was not left to chance. His precision practice schedule, for example, could have been the work of an industrial engineer because every second was allocated, none wasted.

He emphasized punctuality. Our practices started on time. As players we were expected to be there, warmed up and ready to practice, by the starting time. The sessions were organized to the extent that concurrent drills were held to maximize player participation, thereby eliminating the possibility that anyone would stand around doing nothing. Coach Smith's video sessions with the players seldom lasted longer than fifteen minutes because only those portions of game films that best illustrated what he wanted to cover were shown. Extra practice time was allocated to areas where we most needed to show improvement. Running and conditioning drills were a part of virtually every practice. Late-game situations were practiced thoroughly and then repeated. His goal was to build good habits that would be repeated in times of stress.

It was never a case of Coach Smith's asking more of his players than he himself was willing to give, because he worked at least as hard as any player on our team, and we all knew it. His preparation was unmatched. He knew our game films, plus our opponent's, as well as Steven Spielberg knows his own. If I missed a box out on a rebound or failed to hustle back on defense, I knew that he would likely catch it and comment on it. While he pointed out our shortcomings and mistakes, he was just as quick, or maybe even quicker, to praise good play. Instead of berating us for mistakes, he explained things to us in a manner that allowed us to learn from them so as not repeat them in crucial situations.

Coach Smith was supportive and caring, in regard to both our basketball goals and our everyday lives. He never expected us to put basketball ahead of academics, nor did he want us to make basketball the most important thing in our lives. Sure, basketball was extremely important to us, as it was to him, but he taught perspective as well as Xs and Os. Instead of using his players as pawns, he encouraged, inspired, and challenged us, and he led by example. For example, his expectation that we support and encourage our teammates, on and off the court, became ours as well because he supported and encouraged us. This loyalty to one another became a foundation of the Carolina basketball family, both while we played at UNC and throughout our lives.

I remember Coach's telling us, "The best and most effective discipline is self-discipline." I've often recalled those words as I go about my own life. How true and meaningful they are! Rather than be restrictive, goals and self-discipline free us so that we may become capable of accomplishing what we want to with our lives.

BUSINESS PERSPECTIVE

Setting short-term and long-term goals is vital to success in all walks of life, of course. The real challenge is to choose the right goals. Dean's teams never had goals that distracted from their team focus but rather enhanced it.

A major danger is that some leaders set goals that say more about their own insatiable egos, an ongoing turf war, or some other personal motivation than what is best for the business and the team members. Leaders have to fight the natural emergence of what I call ego goals, which can misdirect the larger organization toward dysfunctional goals.

One of the largest consumer products companies in a mature industry found that its brands were in a slight decline. In response the company developed a strategy to acquire other consumer product companies that were similar to it but in specialized, rapidly growing niches. A problem occurred when senior officers, eager to raise their company's stock price so they could retire with large personal profits, exaggerated the prospects of these companies and overpaid for them. To exacerbate matters, they instituted drastic cost-cutting measures in the acquired companies, again with the short-term goal of inflating stock prices.

A by-product of this selfish management decision was that when many of the young, talented, hard-driving leaders and MBAs within the company found their careers stalled by the lack of growth in the main business, they pushed to make further acquisitions as vehicles for them to advance their own careers, hoping they could leave the parent company in favor of jobs running the smaller ones. They helped pump up the offering price the parent company paid for several acquistions by inflating their estimates of those companies' prospects.

The parent company ended up paying 30 percent to 40 percent too much for these so-called growth companies. Then it had to face the reality that the expectations, budgets, and pro formas of the acquired companies were unrealistic. The company suffered several hundred million dollars in losses over the next several years. So beware of runaway egos, greed, and poor motives all acting in concert to destroy an organization's goals.

HOW TO SET GOALS

What to do? At the beginning of the year business leaders should meet with each of the people who report to them and ask him or her to write down the ten most important job-related things he or she would like to accomplish during the next year. Even though a goal-setting and performance system of some form might be in place, this is still a valuable exercise to conduct. The goal is to get employees to focus on what they believe, on the basis of their experience, needs, values, and insights, are the ten most important things they can do in their jobs for the next year. This should result in the most important goals for them to work on, rather than what they think they are expected to say. Each employee should present his or her ten most important goals to the other team members in a group meeting.

Each should write his or her goals on a flip chart and tape them to the wall in the meeting room. Everybody should then go around the room, read each person's goals, and then review them in a team setting. Questions should be asked, and comments and suggestions made to the individual whose goals are being reviewed. The leader needs to participate and have his or her goals reviewed too.

The employees should then return to work with the understanding that another meeting would be held the following week. After hearing from their colleagues and getting suggestions and criticism, they should have the opportunity to change some goals and add to them. They should be encouraged to make the goals SMART: specific, measurable, achievable, (high) return on investment, and timely. They should bring these revised goals to the second meeting and again tape them to the wall for group discussion. After this second discussion with colleagues, each worker should make a final version, a third draft, based on all the input and suggestions they received during the two meetings. These final goals should be submitted to the leader, who should sign off on them as much as possible, along with each associate.

This is a time-consuming process, no doubt, but one of the great advantages is that all members must think clearly about their goals and understand what their colleagues are doing. Each employee can see clearly how his or her actions will affect others in the group. Also, people stake themselves out in front of the team. Peer pressure becomes an ally. Working smarter should be the result of this goal-setting exercise.

· 19 ·

BUILDING CONFIDENCE

I've never believed that there was a magic formula for building confidence. I think it comes out of the process. The working equation is: Hard work equals success, which equals confidence.

There are some who believe a leader can trick subordinates into being confident. I know of a Columbia University experiment of many years ago involving twenty young people who flunked a math quiz. Ten of them were told they had flunked while the others were told they had made Cs. When they all took the exam over, the ten who had been told they'd made Cs improved more than the others. Ten of them had been conned and improved, but I think that type of confidence is short-term. The truth will be revealed at some point, and those who were conned into believing they were improving will suffer a significant setback. They could lose trust in themselves and their coach or teacher.

I believe strongly in positive reinforcement. I looked carefully to determine that we praised behavior that we wanted to see repeated. In the case of at least one player I even made a note on the top of my practice plan to try to find some reason to praise him. He did not have much self-confidence and needed a boost. His play reflected it. However, I waited for it to happen before I praised, and then I made a big show of it to make sure every player on the team heard it. I wasn't going to offer false praise because I believe it's counterproductive. Maybe something good would come of it in the short term, but not for the long haul. Years later the player might look back on the incident and realize his coach had conned him or lied to him. The truth will prevail.

Every coach wants a confident team. Players who enter a game intimidated or doubting themselves don't have much chance to succeed. There's a fine line in athletics between confidence and complacency. I wanted our players quietly confident but not overconfident because overconfidence leads to complacency. Overconfident people think they're better than they really are, and they're ripe for a reality jolt. Sometimes players act cocky to hide being scared.

While most of our teams were confident, I also liked the players to feel a little nervous before they played. In our 1993 national championship victory over Michigan, Donald Williams asked to come out of the game early because he couldn't catch his breath. He told me he was a little nervous and apprehensive. I took that to be a good sign and believed he would settle down when he went back in and would play well. He was voted the Most Valuable Player of the Final Four.

Senior leadership also was crucial in having a confident team. Those players had been in our program for four years and knew what we wanted and what it took to get it. They were able to mentor the younger players and give them a heads up on what to expect in different situations, especially on the road, where we faced hostile crowds. They told them it was okay to be nervous and to expect some adversity in the game.

I was not a locker room orator along the lines of Knute Rockne. The players would have been shocked to hear me stand before them and give a "Let's win one for the Gipper" speech. However, I did challenge them. For example, if an opponent had played harder than we had in the first half, I challenged them during our halftime talk to reverse that in the second half. On most occasions, though, I would just go over our strategy at halftime, review the first half and talk about what we needed to do in the second half, and then on road games say, "Remember, after we win the game, no celebrating on their court. Let's come back down here and celebrate the victory in our locker room as a team."

When Lefty Driesell coached at Maryland, his home crowd and band serenaded the visitors with a version of "Amen" after a Maryland victory. It was their "victory cigar." At halftime of one of our games there I told the players, "After we win this game, I'll sing 'Amen' in the locker room." The players won it, and I sang. At the halftime of our national championship game with Michigan in 1993, I told the players that the coaches would run sprints instead of the players on the first day of practice the next season "after we win this game." George Lynch, a great senior captain on our 1993 team, called on the first day of practice in 1994 to make sure the coaches had kept their promise. We had. I gave the players the whistle and let them conduct sprints, although I did tell them, "Don't run us so hard you'll kill us."

I heard about a football coach before a 2003 bowl game who arrived at the stadium early with his team. He took the players onto the field, had them kneel in a circle, and said, "I wanted to bring you out here early so we could stake our claim to this turf. This is our field, and we're going to protect it. Let's stake our claim right now, right here." Maybe this performance gave his players confidence, maybe not. If it did, it probably lasted no longer than the first hit of the game. When we played on the road, we got to the game site as late as feasible. We preferred practicing at home, where we thought we'd get in better work and have a keener focus. Sometimes our players shot on the opposing team's court the morning of the game; sometimes we didn't. It depended on what time we arrived and other circumstances. The opponent's court had the same dimensions as ours, and their baskets were ten feet high, so I saw no need to go a day in advance to get ready. It was basketball, not rocket science. Furthermore, I didn't want our players to miss any more class time than was absolutely necessary to accommodate our road trips. We believed in getting in late and getting out early—and keeping our players in class.

In our 1968 ACC championship game against NC State in the Charlotte Coliseum, we led at halftime by a few points but had played well below our standards. I thought we had played tentatively and tight. A repeat performance in the second half could have cost us the game and a trip to the NCAA tournament, even though we had won the ACC regular-season championship. There was a lot of pressure on the players. I didn't spend much time in the locker room during that halftime. "I know you guys can play better," I said. "It's your team, so sit in here for the rest of halftime and decide how you're going to do it and how badly you want to do it." I left. We played a sensational second half and won, 87–50. I later was told that two of our players, senior Larry Miller and junior Franklin Clark, led the halftime discussion and got our team fired up and ready to go.

I never was one to plan what I was going to say at halftime. It depended on how the game was going. It was important not to be redundant, and I spent most of my time on strategic matters. I'd get on the players if I needed to, but it was also important to praise them for the good things they had done, especially on the road, where they faced enough adversity without my piling on. I wasn't as critical during games as I was at practice. Players needed confidence during games more than criticism.

One of the best ways to instill confidence is through good preparation. If the players knew we'd prepared well, they had every reason to be confident. At a time-out in a crucial situation, I might say, "We've worked on this in practice. Let's take this minute to review and make it fresh in our minds and then go out and execute it. We've prepared for it." I do believe that players can gain confidence from their coach if they see he is poised and prepared.

We wanted every player on our team to feel confident and needed. It's one reason, among several others, that I never wanted a so-called go-to guy on our team. A team is more dangerous when each man on the court can score or make a play in a crucial game-deciding situation. If you have one player designated to take most of the crucial shots, the opponent knows it and could take steps to defend it. I preferred having five go-to guys on the court. Every one of our players could make the shot if left open; otherwise he shouldn't have been on the team. I didn't want our team to think it had a go-to guy. My goal was for all of them to feel they had an important role, which they did, and how could that be if one guy was designated to take all the important late-game shots? We loved playing against teams that had go-to guys. We could plan ways to defend them and force them into a lot of bad shots. It didn't bother us if a go-to player scored thirty points, as long as he shot a low percentage in getting them.

When one or two players are featured in the offense, it tends to make the others stand around and watch. How does that build confidence? It has the opposite effect. I always thought it would be hard to convince players that they should play team defense, dive for loose balls, set screens, and box out on rebounds if they never got a chance to shoot.

As I've said many times, practice is where we built our foundations, and that included building confidence. For example, I didn't use a player's name when practicing a play. Instead of calling the name of the starting point guard, I would say, "This is what our number one man needs to do in this situation." That way the reserve point guards also felt more a part of the team and gained confidence from it. After all, they were very much part of the plan.

Confidence is elusive but a great thing for anyone, not just college basketball players, to have. I see no shortcuts to get it. Hard work plus success equals confidence. It is contagious to have quietly confident people in the locker room.

PLAYER PERSPECTIVE

Eric Montross,
class of 1994, starting center on UNC's
1993 national championship team,
now a player in the NBA

———————

Success breeds confidence. Confidence wasn't taught by Coach Smith; it was instilled in our team through hours of hard work and dedication in practice to perfecting our offensive and defensive sets.

As players we knew no individual was responsible for winning the game by himself. We would win as a team, provided we did the little things that Coach Smith and the other coaches taught us in practice. I believe we all held ourselves to high standards because we did not want to let our teammates or coaches down by not rotating on defense, not hustling for loose balls, or failing to make hard cuts to get open for a pass on offense.

Our team was led by a confident and extremely competent coach. We never entered a game thinking that we would not win. This confidence was there because our preparation had been thorough and complete, and we knew it. We ran offensive sets until we could run the play without thinking about what to do next; that proved crucial to our team in late-game situations. This is when thinking about what you had to do, instead of acting on instinct, could cost the game. Toward the end of games, emotions run high, pressure mounts, and if you are not supremely confident in your abilities to execute, little mistakes are magnified and turned into lost games.

End-of-game situations never caught our Carolina teams by surprise because we prepared for them every day in practice. We knew what to do and when to do it, more by instinct than direction.

Although we looked to Coach Smith for advice during games, we did not have to think, What do we do next? He had taught us what to do, when to do it, and how to execute in these crucial late-game situations.

When we scrimmaged in practice, the score was not put on the arena scoreboard. Coach taught us, and instilled in us the confidence, that we would win if we executed our plan correctly. His players believed this implictly. This was in large part due to our confidence in Coach Smith. We knew he had taught us the way to win.

Carolina basketball featured a confident style of play, which is not to be confused with cocky. We weren't cocky, and we didn't always think we were the better team, but we *knew* that our coaching staff had prepared for any eventuality. We took that mind-set into every game, and it breeds confidence. On rare occasions when something occurred during a game that we didn't know how to handle, we turned to the best coach in basketball, and he explained it to us, told us how to handle it, and how to win.

Confidence came naturally to our Carolina teams. It was all about hard work and coaches and players who believed in one another.

BUSINESS PERSPECTIVE

Confident people are more likely to think clearly, act wisely, and execute effectively what they've learned in training and from past experiences. They're able to focus on the present by concentrating solely on the task at hand. Rather than worry, they act; they think about solutions rather than obsess about failing.

Confident people seek responsibility, initiate projects, believe in their purpose, trust their instincts, and respect their roles. Therefore they're able to focus on their work, commit to their goals, and work effectively to achieve them. Since they don't feel a need to convince people they're talented, they go about their work and lives by displaying authentic confidence and grace.

Those who lack confidence have a hard time performing. Their thinking is fuzzy, their actions are disjointed, and their objectives unclear. They might even forget what they know as well as lose their focus. They worry about outcomes and results, fret about past mistakes, second-guess themselves, distrust their decisions, and doubt their ability to do a job well. The lower their self-confidence, the more they try to exaggerate their importance. Some withdraw, others try to display confidence by showing off.

So, if it's important for leaders to help their associates build confidence, how do they go about it?

- This first step is simple: Hire confident people. They will behave confidently without coaching, helping build the confidence of those around them.
- Leaders should build their own confidence. Their decisions and actions reveal who they are, how they feel, and what they believe. Their way of communicating says a lot about their confidence. They communicate in many ways, including body language, facial expressions, posture, and movements. Also revealing are the tone of a person's voice, inflection, and delivery. Leaders can communicate confidence by their choice of words. Leaders with low confidence will create a team of employees with low confidence.
- Leaders must not fear failure. The fear of losing or of missing numbers destroys performance, effectiveness, and profits. Here are some ways to master the fear of failing:

1. Think through what the worst possible outcome could be concerning the project being worked on.
2. Predict the probability of that worst-case scenario's happening.
3. Develop a plan to implement if the worst does occur.
4. If the worst outcome becomes reality, assess whether it can be survived.
5. Once the task begins, give the best possible performance. Since that's all anyone can do, enjoy the challenge.
6. If failure results, learn from it, forgive yourself, and move on to the next task.

- To feel true confidence, people must believe the projects and activities they're working on are worthwhile and have value. The main reason speakers are nervous before talking is that they don't think what they're going to say will help anyone. If speakers don't believe that they're going to say anything that will help people in the audience, they will always feel anxious and perform poorly. Search for the value of what you do, and learn how it helps others. At that point, fear dissipates and performance sparkles. You can't do your job well unless you believe in what you're doing.
- Preparation is key for building confidence. Practice, study, drill, and work on every aspect of an assignment. Anticipate problems and what should be done to counter them if they arise. Go over different contingencies. Whether a person is taking a test, playing a game, or making a speech, thorough preparation breeds confidence.
- A leader must create a plan. People are confident when they're certain about what they are supposed to do, how

they're supposed to do it, and what other team members are going to do. Make sure the plan plays the percentages and the probabilities. Do the things that have the best chance of succeeding on the basis of a risk and reward analysis.

- Leaders should work hard in preparation, and then focus on execution. People rarely feel confident when they wing it.

- Good leaders don't reward solely for winning but also for positive steps employees take that will help the team achieve future positive results. Reward specific performance and give positive feedback when people do good jobs, even if they didn't result in immediate wins. The praise should be for genuinely good work. Phony praise can end up destroying confidence because people generally learn the truth at some point. If they discover they're not as good as they were led to believe, they don't trust themselves or their leaders.

- Confidence can ebb and flow depending on how well people know themselves: what they're good at as well as what they don't do well. People who understand their weaknesses aren't controlled by them. They can work around them, and that will help them avoid making mistakes. Once weaknesses are revealed and accepted, people can work to overcome them. Those who know themselves don't fear being "discovered" or having to pretend they're something they're not.

- "One step at a time" is good advice in most endeavors. Leaders should help their employees perfect one step, then move to the next one, en route to developing personality skills they need to work effectively. Don't expect an employee to jump from ineffectiveness to greatness at the snap of a finger. It's a gradual process, and each step done well should be praised and rewarded. It's one way good leaders help their employees build confidence.

The golfer who stands on the first tee absolutely certain that he's going to hit a horrible shot often does exactly that. Visualize performing each step necessary to execute the job well. Whatever you believe in, you will arrange your behavior to guarantee that it occurs. Develop a positive mind-set about your goals, approaches, and your employees. Everyone benefits from that attitude. Remember, if you think you can't, you're correct; if you think you can, you're halfway there.

20

EARNING THE SUPPORT
OF THE BIGGER TEAM

Frank McGuire, who brought me to Carolina to be his assistant coach in the 1958–59 season, after his Tar Heels had won the NCAA championship in 1957, resigned in June 1961 to become head coach of the Philadelphia Warriors of the NBA. He received an annual salary of twenty thousand dollars, almost twice what he was making at Carolina.

Upon McGuire's departure, Chancellor William Aycock, who had served as a battalion commander in General George Patton's Third Army, Eighty-seventh Division, appointed me Carolina's head coach, at an annual salary of ninety-two hundred dollars a year. Our contract was a handshake and a pledge from Chancellor Aycock: "Give the university a team it can be proud of, and I'll support you. Don't worry about the winning and losing. Do the things I've asked of you, and you'll be head coach here as long as I am chancellor."

Chancellor Aycock knew I needed his strong support. I was only thirty years old and lacked head coaching experience, and the basketball program was on NCAA probation as well as under severe sanctions imposed by the university. It was not the best of times for Carolina basketball. The NCAA probation was for what it called excessive recruitment expenditures, but in reality it was a very minor violation, one caused by carelessness, not intent. The university sanctions occurred after a gambling scandal hit college basketball in 1961. Although no Carolina games were cited, one of our substitutes was alleged to have been involved with a gambler. Two players from NC State were implicated in the scandal. In response, university system president William Friday canceled the popular Dixie Classic, an annual basketball tournament held just after Christmas that featured NC State, Duke, Wake Forest, and North Carolina and four of the nation's most powerful teams. Chancellor Aycock also reduced Carolina's schedule to only sixteen regular-season games and limited the number of recruits we could take from outside the ACC area to two. That was noteworthy because North Carolina's high school teams were not producing many top college players in those days. So there I stood as head coach, our team not allowed to play in the NCAA tournament, the regular-season schedule cut back drastically, and our list of recruiting prospects severely limited. Not many of the best high school basketball prospects would be interested in a program facing such restrictions. Coach McGuire surveyed this depressing landscape and tried to persuade me to go to Philadelphia with him as his assistant because he believed the problems at Carolina would be difficult to solve.

Moreover, when Frank resigned, a powerful faction of financial supporters pressured Chancellor Aycock to appoint a nationally prominent head coach. To say that this group wasn't really excited about me, or supportive, is an understatement. On the other side of the issue, many faculty members were understandably unhappy with athletics because of the NCAA probation and university sanctions and wanted to deemphasize the program. Chancellor Aycock persuaded them that big-time athletics was here to stay and, if conducted properly, could reflect the university in a positive light. "There is more coverage of athletics than all other university projects combined," he argued, "and the integrity of the university is reflected to a great extent in what happens in the athletic department." In addition to being extremely wise, Chancellor Aycock was a pragmatist.

Those were the conditions under which I became Carolina's head coach. I was confident that I could eventually get the job done, but it was no slam dunk. I knew that.

From the very beginning I was cognizant of the university's "bigger team": the faculty, staff, students, custodians, and former players. Faculty members have their own teams, the students they teach. They want them to do well, exactly what I wanted for our student-athletes. Our swords weren't crossed there. Some of our faculty members didn't care a thing about basketball, were quite indifferent to it, while others cared a lot.

I was sensitive to what the faculty thought about the university's basketball program. I regularly turned down opportunities to make money from public endorsements and other areas, and one reason was that I didn't think the compensation of the basketball coach should be out of proportion to what faculty members were paid. (For the first two-thirds of my head coaching career, I was underpaid; for the last one-third, I was overpaid.) I did want the faculty to be proud of the university's basketball program.

The faculty learned over the years that we had great young men in our program who were recruited as serious students. We knew how important it was for our players to be in class. We scheduled our practices around afternoon classes and labs. We took our long road trips when classes were out for Thanksgiving and/or Christmas. After we had built our program, we made enough money for the university that we could afford to charter flights back from weeknight games that were played far from Chapel Hill so our players could be in class the next morning. It did impress a professor to see one of our players in his seat for an eight o'clock class the morning after we had played Notre Dame in South Bend at 9:00 P.M. in blizzard conditions. We didn't come back from those trips to impress the professors; we returned early because our players couldn't be good students if they missed a lot of class time. The players understood clearly that if we spent the money to charter back after a night game, they'd better be in class the next morning. There were serious consequences to pay if they weren't.

The basketball program's success, which included the high graduation rate of our players even more than wins and losses, helped university fund-raising, enhanced morale on campus, and increased the number of student applicants. If our players hadn't been serious about their academic work, I think it would have been extremely hard for the faculty to hold a positive view of our program.

In May 1981 the university's Faculty Council passed a resolution that moved me a great deal and indicated we were performing well as part of our larger team.

Dean Smith is coach of our basketball team, and far more. The players he recruits to Carolina epitomize the concept of the student-athlete. Most graduate, many enter graduate and professional schools, all lead exemplary lives.

He carries the Carolina colors to all corners, without hint or fear of blemish. He is truly Olympian, on and off the basketball court. He serves his Olin T. Binkley Memorial Church well.

He broke the color bar in Southern sports when he recruited Charles Scott to Carolina; and he was instrumental in the efforts to open the restaurants and apartments of Chapel Hill to all members of the public.

He helped initiate a summer hot-lunch program for needy and hungry children during the early days of the War on Poverty. For his countless community efforts, quiet and steady, spanning two decades. . . .

Be it Resolved that the Faculty of the University of North Carolina at Chapel Hill express to Dean Smith its appreciation for his being a good citizen of Chapel Hill, of North Carolina, and far beyond.

I accepted the honor on behalf of our coaches and players. We were doing what Chancellor Aycock asked us to do.

———

I wanted our players to be a real part of the student body and not considered privileged because they were on the basketball team. Chancellor Aycock believed in this very strongly when he named me head coach. It's the main reason we insisted on continuing our junior varsity basketball program although no other ACC schools have done so. The players on the jayvees didn't come to Carolina on basketball scholarships, but many of them did grow up with the dream of wearing the Carolina uniform. This gave as many as twenty of them each year a chance to live that dream. They played games in the Smith Center before our varsity games, and they practiced there. They worked extremely hard.

The junior varsity members served as a tremendous bridge between our program and the student body. Some of my early Carolina teams had as many as four or five walk-ons who came to Chapel Hill without scholarships. Even after our program was well established, we almost always had one or two former jayvee players who were promoted to the varsity, and some of them were awarded basketball scholarships because of their valuable contributions to the team. The last time I checked, it cost about fifty-four hundred dollars to finance the junior varsity program for a season. They wore old varsity uniforms and traveled sparingly. What a bargain for the university!

It was even better when freshmen were ineligible to play varsity basketball and we had freshman teams. Two, three, or four scholarship players were on the freshman team with regular college students. Many lifetime friendships were forged in that arrangement, which I found to be another healthy way to bring our program closer to the student body.

For many years I met with student groups in the early fall to show highlight tapes of our team. Afterward I answered their questions and talked about our program and explained why we did certain things the way we did. The students seemed to enjoy the sessions as much as I did.

From the 1965–66 season until we moved into the Smith Center in January 1986, we played our basketball games in Carmichael Auditorium on campus. It was a great building for basketball, rich in tradition and folklore. Our players were hard to beat anywhere, but in Carmichael they were almost invincible, winning more than 90 percent of our games. The building seated only about ninety-two hundred for basketball, and our games were all sold out far in advance of the season. Because of this lack of seating, we had to limit the number of students, faculty, and staff who could get in to see the games. Some faculty members were on a four- or five-year wait list to buy tickets at the special faculty rate.

Serious discussions began concerning the possibility of raising private funds to build a new basketball arena and entertainment center, one that would seat 21,500 for our games. I was not in the front lines of those promoting this project. I even suggested that we should at least consider staying in Carmichael and taking the private money to help more important financial needs at the University of North Carolina Hospitals.

When others made the decision to go forward with the project, I saw its value. The new building made it possible for the university to more than double the number of students who could attend our games, as well as open the doors to more members of faculty and staff. We had a dedication dinner the night before the building opened in 1986. It was a black-tie affair that raised a large sum of money, all of which went to the College of Arts and Sciences.

We made sure we showed the maintenance staff and custodians at the Smith Center how much we appreciated all the unsung work they did on our basketball program's behalf. They sometimes worked the entire night through to convert the building from a concert setting to get it ready for our team to practice the next afternoon. At Christmas they bought and cooked steaks for the coaching staff and basketball office. It was always a special function, a chance for us to spend time with them and tell them how much we appreciated their work.

Of course no one was more important to Carolina basketball than our former players. They made the program. Nothing made us feel better than for them to come back and visit, or scrimmage against our current players in the summer, or work out with them. There was no generation gap between our former and current players. They were brothers linked by tradition, by the color light blue. We often saw and heard from our former players. We kept cakes, cookies, and soft drinks handy in the kitchen of our office area for them to enjoy when they returned. We also enjoyed seeing them in the office after our home games.

Many people referred to our basketball program as a family, and it was. It evolved over the years, and hearing from our former players was one of the best things about my job. I didn't begin my coaching career with the goal of staying in touch with the former players, but I sent each one a media guide each year and wrote each a personal note at Christmas. If you develop a close relationship with a player, as we did, you don't drop it just because the player's eligibility is up. You don't forget them. I wanted to stay in touch, and I'm always pleased, thrilled, and interested when our former players let me know what's going on in their lives.

As those who know me are well aware, I had absolutely no ambition to break Adolph Rupp's record of 876 college coaching victories. In fact I was so turned off by the possibility and what I knew would be the ensuing media circus that I threatened to resign before I reached that mark. That upset many of our former players, who justifiably felt they were a big part of the record. I listened when they said they wanted me to break it. They understood that I wouldn't stay around *just* to break the record, but if it happened in the natural course of my career, well enough. When we got our 877th win in the NCAA tournament in Winston-Salem in March 1997, I was thrilled and moved to see so many of our former players there for the game. I consider them a special part of my life.

Those players, our assistant coaches, secretaries, and others connected with Carolina basketball were successful, I think, in winning over the bigger team. Even if I say so myself, we tried to do it the right way, and we did. As Chancellor Aycock said, we gave the university "a basketball program that it can be proud of." We were not the most important part of the university, but we were its "front porch," as Chancellor Taylor pointed out. And as Chancellor Christopher Fordham said after our 1982 national championship, "It shows that good guys can do it the right way and still win championships." Our players graduated, and there never was a hint of a recruiting violation or any other NCAA transgression. Our fans and boosters sometimes became annoyed with me when I refused to talk about which high school players we were recruiting. There was a method to my madness because while 99 percent of our fans were proud of the way we conducted our program, I wouldn't take the risk that someone might try to induce a player to come to Chapel Hill by giving him illegal gifts.

CHANCELLOR'S PERSPECTIVE

William B. Aycock,

chancellor of the University of North Carolina
from 1957 to 1964; also honored for his career
as a professor in the School of Law

One of the best decisions I made as chancellor was hiring Dean Smith to coach the university's basketball team. It didn't take us but about ten minutes to agree on terms. We didn't sign a contract, there were no lawyers present in the room when we discussed the job, and I paid him the salary of ninety-two hundred dollars a year, which he was happy to receive. Dean and I had worked together in developing the university's position to present to the NCAA investigating committee concerning the alleged infractions, and I knew from that experience that he had the fundamental values I was looking for in our head coach, particularly at that time. I wasn't worried about his coaching ability, not in the least, because I knew that Coach McGuire thought that Dean was an excellent young coach, and as far as basketball was concerned, that was good enough for me.

By the time Dean took over the program, it was on NCAA probation and under university sanctions. I made it clear to Dean that he didn't have to win a certain number of games to keep his job, but he did have to operate within the rules and within the spirit of the rules. I knew that would be no problem for him. He grew up in a small town in Kansas, and I was raised in a small town in North Carolina. The fundamental values we had learned growing up were pretty much the same.

Many of our faculty members were wary of athletics at that time because of the NCAA probation. I promised the faculty that winning would not be the test in my decision to appoint Smith as our head coach. He wouldn't be judged solely on wins and losses. I also told them that if they had had to go in front of twenty to forty thousand people to be evaluated on a public scoreboard, many of them would not have made it.

It was incredibly important to win over the faculty and staff, and Dean knew not only that it was important but how to get the job done. He recruited young men who were good ambassadors for the university. I was a public school teacher at Senior High School in Greensboro before I went to work at the university and thus valued good teaching more than most. I wanted Dean and our other coaches to be like faculty and to think of themselves as teachers. That was easy for Dean because his parents were teachers and had set a strong example for him. Our faculty quickly recognized that Dean was an excellent teacher, one of the best on the entire campus, and he taught his players much more than basketball. He developed his students in other important areas and prepared them for life.

His teams also won a lot of basketball games, and soon many of the faculty members were among his biggest supporters. They knew that his players were students and good citizens first; basketball came well down the list of priorities he set for them. Once his teams began winning, they appeared on television often, winning even more supporters for the university because people liked the way our basketball players conducted themselves.

Dean and his players won over the larger university community, and that helped him greatly in building his program. It made the faculty proud to see North Carolina play basketball on television, knowing that those young men were serious students with the goal to graduate from a great university. My role in this simply was to give Dean a chance. Basically I told him to give us a program that wouldn't get the university in trouble. He went far beyond my expectations and gave our university a model basketball program, one that made the larger community proud and supportive.

BUSINESS PERSPECTIVE

Leaders and their team members must understand that they work for a number of teams, not just one. I find it helpful to think in terms of six different teams: the one that reports directly to you; your leader's team; the other company departments with which you work closely; your overall company team; your customer team; and the team of suppliers, service providers, and stakeholders.

Many leaders frequently make the mistake of focusing so intensely on their own subordinate team that they ignore the five others. That myopia is detrimental to the organization's success. For example, I know of a new president who had just begun his job of leading a highly technical engineering firm whose sales had plummeted in a poor economy. One of his first major goals was to cut expenses over the next nine to eighteen months so the company could maintain a base level of earnings. He told his senior officers in a meeting what they needed to do, the reasons why, and asked for their support. The board and CEO had asked them all to cut expenses.

Their first assignment was a hiring freeze. During the meeting the vice president for marketing protested the hiring freeze. He was a veteran, powerful player in the industry and the company, and he was opinionated, bright, aggressive, and argumentative. He argued that he had a senior position to fill in his division, had already interviewed candidates, and was prepared to offer the job to an old friend of his who lived on the East Coast. It was a high-paying position, and the move to the company's home base in California would require expensive moving costs as well as other compensation expenses.

The new president wasn't expecting this big a protest. Having come up through research and development, engineering, and manufacturing, he was unsure of the validity of the marketing vice president's argument. The team discussed his case at length. The president and other team members said they thought it would be best to delay this hire. The vice president argued so angrily that the president finally said, "Let's think about it tonight and discuss it tomorrow."

The marketing manager didn't relent the next day. In fact he took an even more aggressive approach. He said he wasn't going to let his department suffer by not filling this position and suggested that other departments cut their costs because his needs were greater than theirs. The president did all he could reasonably to persuade him not to make the hire and then said: "You make the final judgment, but I strongly recommend that you postpone this hiring for at least nine months to a year so we can address the issue of our expenses. Every other manager has the same argument as you. You need to focus on the company's success, not just your own unit's."

Two days later the marketing vice president told the president that he had decided to make the hire and that his candidate had accepted the job at a compensation level that was even higher than expected. Over the ensuing two weeks the president did his own research to determine whether the new position was actually needed, whether the new employee was the best match for the job and the company, and whether the compensation package was appropriate. He concluded that people within the department could handle the job for the next year, thus delaying the need to hire immediately.

Furthermore, the person who had been offered the job was a weak hire, and the compensation was much higher than it should have been. The president told his vice president for marketing to withdraw the job offer. The candidate had been let go from his previous job several months earlier, so that wasn't an issue. Nevertheless, the vice president was defiant: "I'm not going to do it. If you want to rescind the offer, you do it."

The president did. The leader of the marketing team had alienated the president and other managers throughout the organization as well as the board of directors. He had focused so intently on his own team that he had forgotten he was a member of five other teams. He was asked to leave the company several months later.

How do you build teamwork among different interdependent teams? Here are some thoughts:

- Identify what the different teams in your professional universe are, and determine which ones are critical for your immediate team's success.

- Rate the value of the teamwork you are currently getting from each of the critical teams.
- Identify the three to five key individuals on these teams whom you absolutely must work with to help you succeed.
- Assign each member of your department to be the point person to build teamwork with one person on each of the significant teams.
- Meet quarterly to allow each of your team members to present a progress report on his or her effort to increase teamwork with these outside teams.

21

DISCIPLINE MUST BE FAIR

By now, if nothing else, you know that basketball is a team game. Therein lies its beauty. If the Carolina Way meant anything, it meant that all five men had to play together in order for us to be successful. That's how we taught the game. If one man failed to carry out his assignment, it hurt the team. People *do* fail to carry out their assignments, of course. The question is, How should one respond?

As I said, our seniors made the off-the-court rules, such as where they'd like to eat on road trips, where they wanted to stay, how late their curfews were. We made it clear that we didn't want a long list of rules because we were going to enforce them. The on-the-court rules were mine, period. We didn't vote on those. If a player came to see me in my office with a suggestion, certainly I would listen. That didn't mean I would agree. We had a clear understanding about what our rules were before the first practice was held.

Discipline is very much a part of building a team. Events and actions that are counterproductive to teamwork should be punished, and the punishment must be meted out fairly, consistently, and promptly. We disciplined players for a variety of reasons: missing class; being late to practice, meetings, or classes; selfish acts; not hustling; conduct that was detrimental to the team, the university, or the individual. We believed in being on time, absolutely. No person's time is more important than another's. We wouldn't allow that arrogance in our program.

In enforcing discipline, there can be no exceptions, no favorites. Treat the players as you would your own children. If one player is punished for an act while another escapes punishment for a similar offense, team building sinks like a cement block in a fishing hole. If one of our players was eight minutes late for the pregame meal, we punished him accordingly. But it didn't stop there. We wrote down the punishment so we could refer to it the next time a similar offense took place. You can rest assured that the players knew what punishment was handed out for what offense. Word gets around in a team setting. Players accept punishment that is fair and consistent. They know when they've done wrong, and allowing them to escape punishment is another way to destroy the team. Inconsistent punishment is impossible to defend.

We punished individually and as a team. If a player missed class or made another off-the-court mistake, punishment was handled on an individual basis. For trangressions on the court, we punished the team. For example, if a player didn't sprint back on defense, the whole team ran for him. If a player received a technical foul, all his teammates shared the extra running with him at the next practice. There was one time when I didn't punish for a technical because it happened right in front of me and I knew the call was totally unjustified. All the player did was score a basket, sprint back to midcourt, and turn around. I still don't know why the official called a technical in that case, but I knew he was wrong, so I didn't punish the team for it.

We believe peer pressure is more effective in building good habits and morale than motivation created by fear, reward, or other means. Having twelve tired athletes run extra sprints because a teammate violated our philosophy certainly got the point across. The twelve innocent players were quick to tell the offender, "Get your act together. We're tired of paying for your mistakes."

Sometimes an athlete won't be affected by anything but individual discipline. I told a group of high school coaches about our policy of having players run for a teammate's mistakes. At the time our practice was to bring a chair to courtside and have a repeat offender sit in it while his teammates ran for him. That was an uncomfortable position for the guilty player. However, one high school coach told me he had given his star player a chair and a glass of water and made him sit there and watch his teammates run up and down the court for his mistakes. "We had to quit it," the high school coach said, "because our player enjoyed it. It didn't bother him at all." Well, it takes all kinds.

Early in my coaching career we made notes of violations as they occurred in practice and said we'd run sprints for them after practice. I changed that when seniors told me a few players held back in practice so they could run the sprints afterward. We found it was more effective to discipline immediately and get it out of the way. It made it easier for the players to concentrate on practice and not worry about running punishment afterward. I was a demanding coach, but the teachers that most of us remember throughout life are those who demanded much from us. I criticized and praised in my role as head coach. I raised my voice when I saw an action I didn't want to see repeated.

The desire not to let your teammates down is a powerful force. You see it in professional golf when members of the Ryder Cup team say time and again that the pressure they experience in that team competition is much more severe than playing in a major championship, when they're playing for themselves. When a six-foot putt is for teammates and country, there's more pressure than when it's just for the individual.

I never believed in dwelling on the negatives in foul shooting. If one of my players missed several free throws in a game and the media asked me about it afterward, I'd say, "I'm not worried about it in the least. He's a great free throw shooter, and he'll make them. We record his shots in practice, so I know how good he is." College basketball players on Carolina's level are world class. They should make a high percentage of shots from fifteen feet that are not guarded. If they struggled, it was more likely a psychological rather than a physical problem. I wasn't going to exacerbate the problem by talking about missed free throws. Why plant a negative seed with one of our own players?

When it comes to demanding discipline, coaches have a lot of power. All the players want to play, and the coach controls playing time. The keys, though, are to be fair, consistent, and prompt and to play no favorites. It keeps getting back to coaches' being honest with and caring for their players, doesn't it?

PLAYER PERSPECTIVES

Steve Bucknall,
class of 1989, now a professional
basketball player in Europe

Discipline was never a major issue for me or my teammates at North Carolina. There were standards we were expected to uphold, and we knew exactly what they were and what was expected of us.

Coach Smith and his assistants were careful to tell us exactly what the rules were. Also, it was clear from the beginning that punishment would occur if we broke them. No one got any favors, nor were any expected. We didn't have many rules, and the seniors helped make some of those, but the ones we had were enforced.

I had an altercation with another student from a rival school during my playing days. I was embarrassed by the incident because I had brought negative attention to my teammates, Coach Smith, and myself. Coach Smith reiterated that such behavior wouldn't be tolerated and told me to correct it immediately. Even then, when he could have chastised me, he instead counseled me and supported me to bring the matter to a successful conclusion. My punishment was severe, the kind no player desires. I was suspended for a big game that was played on national television. I recall my palms sweating throughout the game as I watched my teammates play that day.

A second disciplinary issue arose during the 1989 NCAA tournament, when a player violated curfew before a big game. Coach Smith and assistants showed great wisdom in involving the senior players in the decision process in this instance. He knew this would be the last NCAA tournament for the seniors, and a loss would mean the end to our Carolina careers, which was a very big deal. He thought the seniors should have a say in the decision. It was a very hard decision to reach because the violation by the outstanding player was not serious. Still, it was decided to suspend him for our tournament game against a very good team. Even though it wasn't in question, all involved were reminded that the Carolina program was bigger than any individual. Fortunately we still won the game. The seniors got to continue their season, as did the suspended player, who returned to play excellent basketball.

I would characterize Coach Smith's disciplinary policy as one that was administered fairly, surely, with great wisdom, and sometimes with a wounded heart. He was a caring coach, and part of that caring was making sure team rules were enforced.

Woody Coley,

class of 1977, senior managing director,
Trammell Crow Company, Orlando, Florida

———

Coach Smith's practices were orchestrated to the minute, more so than any corporate activity I have experienced. He made it clear that being on the basketball team at North Carolina was a privilege, and while it would be fun, we had an obligation to do as well as we could.

When he blew his whistle, it was "the word." At the whistle we stopped whatever we were doing, even if we were in the middle of a shot and sprinted to where he stood at midcourt. Coach established incredible discipline in everything we did. If we did not stop what we were doing at the sound of the whistle, the entire team ran. If someone used inappropriate language, we ran. If a player was late to practice, he donned a weighted vest and ran the arena stairs. If a player was late to the team bus, he did not start (even if he was a star). Pregame warm-ups were monitored by team managers. Missed layups resulted in sprints the next day. We had a lot of fun, but when it was time to be serious, there was no horsing around.

There was a consequence for any action that was deemed detrimental to the team. As players we understood it, and it became a way of life for us.

BUSINESS PERSPECTIVE

People will usually do the right thing if they know they will be punished when they don't. When there's no punishment, people tend to stray.

One reason discipline is essential is that people naturally change their jobs to suit themselves and in the process can develop bad habits. Smart discipline is the key. Leaders must have the confidence to control their employees so they in turn learn to control themselves. Discipline that is fair, reasonable, and wise is accepted, even appreciated, and results in employees' liking and respecting the leader. It also encourages them to become self-disciplined and to take charge of themselves.

If leaders don't care enough to enforce discipline, then their employees tend not to care and lose respect for and confidence in their leaders. Leaders who can't discipline employees should not be in leadership positions. On the other hand, leaders who focus too much on discipline and are arbitrary about it also shouldn't lead.

One large, well-established retail organization that employed my services had gradually declined because it didn't innovate or work smart. It became sloppy and ineffective in its performance standards, controls, and expectations.

Even though the firm was losing market share, revenue, and profits, its leaders had grown so complacent and undisciplined that they watched from the sidelines as the company continued its decline. They demonstrated no sense of urgency in identifying problems and finding solutions. They seemed to be in a state of denial.

It took me about six months just to persuade the CEO and his top eight managers to set aside a three-day retreat to talk about the problems and try to fix them before the company went under. At the first meeting I asked the chief financial officer to report on the company's financial condition. The CEO, company president, and vice presidents heard the bleak news: If the company continued its current trend, it would be out of cash and out of business in eight months. The CEO and most of the other leaders had heard the same thing a year earlier but didn't take it seriously.

The CFO admitted that he hadn't hammered this information home in their management meetings because "The other managers would have been angry at me and accused me of being negative. The CEO and the president would have been frustrated with me for being a naysayer and diverting attention away from the day-to-day business."

In that meeting I asked each of the nine officers if they believed the financial report and if they thought their company faced a major crisis. Ironically, they had planned to work the three mornings of the retreat and then play golf, play tennis, or go fishing in the afternoon. I suggested that we cancel the afternoon recreation and spend the time trying to solve the company's problems. I was an outside consultant and had no personal investment in the business, but I was volunteering to work overtime for them. They resisted and said they could talk about it over dinner. They wanted to have fun and certainly weren't burned out from too much work.

The management team members liked one another, so team building was not a major issue. Lack of discipline was. They didn't have the discipline required to face difficult problems, change their comfortable work patterns, or make the personal changes and sacrifices needed to turn their business around. They had no fear of being punished for poor performance.

They enjoyed their three afternoons of recreation and neglected the urgency of their company's crisis. The end of the story isn't a happy one. The company had to be sold for a low price eight months later. The CEO, the officers, many employees, and the stockholders lost most of their net worth, which was held in company stock. Lack of discipline had created this business disaster.

On the other hand, I know of another manager who was so focused on creating a military-style discipline for her work group that her employees lived in fear of making mistakes. They knew they would be reprimanded if they didn't precisely follow their leader's perfectionist procedures. Their response was to do as little as possible to get by, to take no risks, and never to suggest new and better ways to do things. They did exactly as they were told, period. Nothing more. And some of what they were told to do was very ineffective.

Discipline and punishment must be fair and evenhanded, or it won't work. Equal punishment for the same violations, across the board. Play no favorites and do no favors for friends, relatives, buddies, or stars of the team. No exceptions. It should be clear that the rules apply to everybody.

To keep people "nervous and on their toes," the senior manager of a scientific organization applied severe punishment for minor infractions or sometimes for no infractions. For example, in order to travel to meet with a major customer, a junior manager bought a round-trip ticket from New York to Dallas. To save the company money, she booked her return flight for Saturday morning instead of Friday afternoon, even though it would wipe out most of her weekend with her family. Her good planning saved the company eight hundred dollars on her airline ticket.

When the meeting finished earlier than expected on Friday morning, the company decided to hold another session with about thirty managers to review product offerings and marketing strategies. All this was relevant to the junior manager's work, so she asked the senior officer if she could sit in on the meeting since she wasn't flying back until Saturday morning. The senior officer, in the hotel lobby and in front of other managers, guests, and employees of the hotel, ripped her up and embarrassed her. "These meetings are carefully established for senior people," he said. "You should never ask to sit in on a meeting to which you've not been invited. Who do you think you are?"

News of his outburst quickly made the rounds throughout the company. The senior officer's reputation and ability to lead were damaged seriously. Already he was widely known behind his back as "the company's worst leader." Can you imagine being known as your company's worst leader? He thought of himself as a disciplinarian when in fact his actions produced fear and animosity among those he led.

One CEO I know gained his job through family connections.

He was independently wealthy, wasn't committed to the business, and worked only about half the time. He would step back into the business when he thought he was needed to solve a problem.

Meanwhile a senior leader of his organization was named as his chief operating officer with instructions to run the business on a day-to-day basis as well as to create a new division. Less than six months into his job, the COO upset three veteran individuals who happened to be favorites of the CEO's. The CEO had overlooked their poor work because he liked them and they were very involved in his outside pursuits of skiing, fishing, and working in his garden, and didn't reveal his poor work habits.

Furious because the COO had disciplined them, the three veterans went over his head to the CEO, who caved in to their pleas and asked the COO to let them continue doing what they had been doing, which wasn't much of anything positive for the company. The three veterans, knowing they wouldn't be punished, stepped up their assault on the COO by sabotaging him throughout the company.

The lack of courage and wisdom by the CEO in failing to uphold the disciplinary action taken by the COO had serious ramifications for the organization. The COO was very good at his job, but he seriously considered quitting because he was rendered partly ineffective by the actions of three individuals whom he was ordered not to discipline.

In this particular case the three individuals causing problems for the COO should have been dealt with firmly. But they were not, so the marketplace will enforce the discipline the CEO didn't. Playing favorites hurts everybody—the leader, the employees, the customers, and the company.

22

CONTINUOUS LEARNING

From the time I was old enough to ask questions, it seemed I was always trying to learn more about sports and how to teach them effectively. As a boy growing up, I peppered my father with questions about coaching strategy. During my college playing career, my coach at Kansas, Phog Allen, asked me to teach our offense and defense to the football players who joined our team after their season was completed. Following graduation, as I awaited my assignment in the Air Force, I helped Dick Harp, the brilliant assistant to Coach Allen, coach the Kansas freshman team and assisted with varsity practice. Coach Harp, knowing I wanted to coach, was generous, caring, and patient as he shared his vast knowledge with me.

One of the best breaks of my life came when I was in the U.S. Air Force stationed in Germany and met Major Bob Spear. In addition to being a decorated pilot, Bob was an outstanding basketball coach. He had served as Ben Carnevale's assistant coach at the Naval Academy. In the summer of 1955 the team that I played for traveled to Châteauroux, France, to play an Air Force team coached by Major Spear. Afterward, he invited me to his house to talk about the pressure defense that Kansas had played with tremendous success in 1953. We hit it off and became such good friends that soon afterward he asked me to become his assistant coach at the Air Force Academy, an offer I eventually accepted.

We started the basketball program at the new academy, which was a major challenge. The academics were demanding, and since the cadets had to fit into the cockpits of the basic trainers, we couldn't take anyone taller than six feet four. Bob was a genius at devising strategies that put his teams in position to defeat opponents that had more talent and size. He encouraged me to contribute to these strategies, and with his blessing, I implemented the shuffle offense, some of the defensive principles we used at Kansas, and the point zone. My confidence as a coach grew tremendously because of my relationship with Bob Spear.

Frank McGuire, the coach at North Carolina, hired me to be his assistant, and I learned much from him about the importance of recruiting and how to deal with players off the court.

But I can't talk about continuous learning without saying that my assistant coaches were the most important people to me in this area. I had some great ones, and we spent hundreds and hundreds of hours together studying tapes, talking basketball, drawing Xs and Os on the chalkboard, planning practice, and strategizing to make sure we disguised the weaknesses and accentuated the strengths of each of our North Carolina teams. Those were great learning sessions.

I loved thinking of new and better ways of doing things. Many of these ideas came to me during the summer, when I watched tapes and developed our overall practice plan for our next team. Sometimes my assistants hated to see me return to the office in the summer after a week at the beach. They knew I'd come back with many new approaches. They often said to me, "We're winning, so what's wrong with what we're doing now?" They would succeed in talking me out of some of my proposed changes, while others would be adopted. I placed great value on the give-and-take I had with my assistants in sessions such as these. Although the final decision was mine, the end result was vastly improved by the input from the assistant coaches. They knew I wanted them to shoot holes in my proposed changes and make me defend them. We didn't mince words.

It's amazing what I learned from studying tapes. For example, I learned that our best offensive rebounding came when our big men were not boxed out on the break, say, fifteen to eighteen feet away from the basket. With our big men so positioned, our best three-point shooters were free to stop and shoot the three in transition before the defense was set, because if the shot missed, our big men running toward the basket without being boxed out had the best chance to get an offensive rebound and score. Roy Williams, in a study of his great Kansas teams, learned that about 78 percent of his team's offense came on points scored off the break. Opponents knew Kansas would run the break, but it executed it so well that opponents still couldn't stop it.

Even after I retired from coaching, many of our former players who are coaches came back to Chapel Hill each September, and we'd talk basketball and try to figure out new and better ways of doing things. I'm sure it's true in most professions, but in basketball coaching the learning never stops. A college coach has a new team each year, and that means he has to change to take best advantage of the skills of that particular team. It's also important for the coach to know the rules inside and out, so that after deciding what his team does best, he can put his players in the best positions within the spirit of the rules to be successful. Bill Guthridge, who succeeded me as North Carolina's coach in 1997, was the assistant in charge of knowing the rules, and he was great at it. He could have conducted a rules clinic.

I also learned from my players, from both what they said in our meetings and how they responded to certain situations on the court in practice and games. People who realize the importance of continuous learning know it's important to ask questions and be a good listener.

People who want to learn pay attention to their surroundings. Things pop up unexpectedly. For instance, in a practice session one afternoon with our 1963 team, we were preparing for an opponent that had used a half-court zone press against us in the previous meeting. Most teams attacked this particular defense by sending four players to the corners of the court and a center to the foul line. We wanted to score out of this set, so we tweaked it and put our best ballhandler, who was Larry Brown, on the foul line and sent our center to one of the corners. I told the defense to show the zone press and then to shift to man-to-man. The purpose was to see if Larry would recognize the defensive switch and put us in our man-to-man delay game. Larry, who is extremely bright, didn't recognize the defense, but he did sense a scoring opportunity. He drove past his man and passed to a teammate for an easy layup. That incident in practice made me realize that this offense would work against any defense, and our famous four corners offense was born.

PLAYER PERSPECTIVE

Pete Chilcutt,
class of 1991, former NBA player,
now with RBC Dain Rauscher, Sacramento

My Carolina basketball career was one of continuous learning, lasting throughout my five years there. My learning curve certainly was a little steeper in my first year in the program, but the process never stopped. From the day I arrived on campus from my Alabama home, I learned the qualities and fundamentals it takes to succeed in basketball. As I look back on my UNC career, I realize that I grew up while in the program and learned many things that are helping me get through life without basketball.

While we did watch tapes of our games and practices at Carolina, I think we spent much less time on that activity than players at other schools. Our film sessions were brief, direct, and to the point. Coach Smith believed in short, efficient viewing sessions, which he thought were the best way for him to teach and for us to learn. It took only one instance of his throwing a player out of a meeting for not correctly identifying something on the tape to get everyone's rapt attention.

Included in the practice plans were the offensive and defensive emphases of the day. As you know by now, players were required to recite those from memory if called upon by Coach Smith. The entire team ran sprints if the recitation wasn't accurate.

You've also read about Coach's decision to give us a Thought for the Day to learn and recite. It was a key learning tool for us that had nothing to do with basketball. Some of those are still fresh in my mind. This was one method that Coach used to teach us, and it certainly helped keep basketball in perspective. As I look back on it now, I see that a secondary benefit was that it relieved the pressure on us that playing basketball at this level could bring. As much as basketball was Coach Smith's passion, he was first and foremost a great teacher whose top priority was not to win but to mold his players into good citizens. He wanted us prepared for the day we would wake up and basketball would no longer be part of our lives.

BUSINESS PERSPECTIVE

In order to survive, businesses have to change to match the changes in their external environments. I've discussed those external environments previously as well as why it's important to change with them. When a company changes its strategies, its employees must learn to do new work; that means new skills and practices.

One of the most important jobs leaders have is to ensure that each person in their organizations continues to improve and learn new skills. Many people think they are so busy that they have little or no time to learn. They prefer action to thinking. Learning requires thinking, and time must be set aside for thinking. Many leaders and workers go through their careers with a learning curve that is flatter than it ought to be or could be. They don't change much, so they don't work as smart as they could.

Leaders should create and enforce learning programs for themselves and their associates. No exceptions, no excuses.

I know of a leader who built a successful United States retail chain that had more than a hundred outlets. As he approached retirement, he promoted a younger leader to become president of the company and run it on a daily basis. It was evident after one year on the job that the new president, although intelligent, well intentioned, and hardworking, was not working smart or effectively.

She did everything fast, rushing her decisions, hurrying through meetings. She also pressured her subordinates to act too quickly, and intimidated them with her micromanaging. She was in the middle of every decision and tried to do everything herself. She was more an individual producer than a leader, and her style led her to make some big mistakes.

Recognizing her problem, the CEO began coaching her on a regular basis as she began her second year as president. He tried to teach her to slow down, be more thoughtful and thorough, study closely the consequences of her decisions, and delegate to subordinates rather than try to solve all their problems for them. He coached her to train her associates rather than try to run the whole show.

After six months of coaching, the CEO concluded that the president had not made much improvement. He asked her to serve as his assistant for a year, during which she could focus on building her leadership skills while he led the company.

In the course of that year the president met monthly with an executive coach. She also was required to gather feedback from her CEO, associates, customers, and board of directors concerning her performance, leadership practices, and decision-making skills. She enrolled in an advanced leadership roundtable, in which twelve senior officers from different companies met once a month for a year to improve their leadership skills and develop new techniques for running their businesses.

The president's initial expectation was that the "year of improvement" was a mistake and unnecessary. She couldn't spot her own weaknesses. Nevertheless, she maintained a positive attitude during the year of leadership training, which was to her credit. By the end of the year her outlook had changed; she felt fortunate to work for a CEO who had given her a chance to improve rather than fire her. She knew he'd made a wise decision.

The CEO and board reinstated her as president. They also scheduled monthly meetings for the first year to review her progress. She has now run the business successfully for two years, and the business has prospered.

In another case, a recent college graduate—smart, hardworking, eager to learn—took his first full-time job as a service representative for an automobile dealership. After eight months he loved his job and believed he had done well but felt frustrated because he had little time to improve his understanding of the business and its leadership. He arrived at work at 6:00 A.M. and didn't leave until 6:30 P.M. He wanted to read and study at home at night but was too tired and wanted some personal life.

This is the normal pattern for most people. Most leaders reflect year after year that they want to set aside time to study and learn, but there's not much energy left for it after fulfilling the many responsibilities of their jobs and personal lives.

So how can you find time to learn on a continuous basis? Most people say their best learning experiences came from their failures, but why wait to learn from mistakes? A smarter strategy is to learn on a continuous basis from daily events. Each lesson might be a small one, but soon the lessons will accumulate to become something meaningful and important to your life.

An effective technique for continuous learning is to develop what I call an Achiever's Brain Book. Keep a notebook accessible throughout the day. In spare minutes write down key things you've learned. At the end of the day add the three major experiences of the day. They might be the biggest decisions made, projects worked on, meetings attended, or interactions with others. Analyze what was done in those three instances and what the impacts or consequences were. How did they turn out? How effective were the results? Then establish actions based on what you've learned that will positively affect your future behavior.

The key to continuous learning is to articulate one's inarticulate knowledge. Do it continuously; draw lessons from your daily experiences. Lessons don't arrive on command, but you can budget a little time in your life to step back and get the perspective that leads to insight.

PART FIVE

LESSONS
LEARNED

23

DON'T DWELL
ON THE PAST

I've never been one to look back at my life and wish I had done things differently. What purpose would it serve? Life doesn't come with a mulligan. Besides, there's no guarantee we'd do better given a second chance. Mistakes are part of life, and everyone has some regrets. Press me, and I'd say if I could do it over again, I would work harder at recruiting and would scrimmage more. Having said that, I prefer to accept the things I can't change and move forward.

It's true that I regret the injuries our North Carolina players suffered over the years going into the NCAA tournament (Dick Grubar, James Worthy, Kenny Smith, Steve Hale, Walter Davis, Phil Ford, Tommy La-Garde, to name a few), but I felt sorry for the players, not for me. A coach can't control injuries.

At North Carolina we didn't spend a whole lot of time on what might have been. Injuries hit at inopportune times, and we lost some players early to the NBA, but our philosophy was to play with the players we had available and not dwell on what ifs. When one of my teams played poorly in the first half, I assured the players in the locker room that they couldn't get those twenty minutes back, no matter how much they'd like to. That half was history. "We've prepared, so let's do better in the second half," I told them. Sure, correct mistakes and learn from them, but don't dwell on things that can't be changed. Our team's Thought for the Day concerning mistakes was "Recognize it, admit it, learn from it; then forget it." We tried to live that way. Certainly we tried not to waste a minute fretting over things that were out of our control.

I have friends, close friends, who think I retired from coaching four or five years too soon. I respect their opinion, but it's *their* opinion. They look back on *my* career more than I do. Some of them had goals for me that I never had for myself, such as winning enough games to keep the record for college coaching victories for many years to come. It was never my goal to have the record, and it's not a goal now to retain it. I never even think about it unless someone asks me. College basketball should be for the players, and coaches get entirely too much attention.

A DNA of my personality would reveal that I enjoyed tweaking and putting in new things for my teams. Some were nice enough to call me an innovator, but like they say, necessity is the mother of invention. I felt I had to do some things differently from season to season to stay ahead of the pack. I certainly didn't abandon our principles, though. North Carolina had its staples. We were going to run the secondary break, share the basketball, get good shots, play unselfishly, and build our program on defense. We weren't going to change those things, no matter how predictable they might have been. If we executed them well, we'd still be successful. Neither would we forget our mission: Play hard, together, and smart.

I did honor the rich tradition that our former players built for North Carolina basketball, but tradition is a two-edged sword, as I'll discuss later in this chapter. It's certainly not good if it influences you to keep doing things the same way year after year, regardless of the circumstances.

I took tapes of our past teams to the beach each summer and studied them. Most years I'd focus on some aspect of our scheme and make it completely different. The objective was to make the best use of current personnel. We wanted to play a style each season that would give the players their best chance to succeed, to accentuate our strengths, disguise our weaknesses. The changes might have involved something as mundane as who we wanted to throw the ball inbounds after a made basket. It could have involved the signals we used to change defenses or call an offensive set. I'd bring my changes back and present them to my coaching staff and ask them to pick them apart. No holds barred. I also ran the ideas past our former players who were coaching their own teams. I sought honest feedback from all of them, and after I received it, I'd usually stick with some of the changes I'd proposed and drop others.

Even though we were consistently near the top of the nation in team scoring average, some fans and media had the impression that we preferred a ball control offense and a low score. It was the opposite of what we desired. We pressured and gambled on defense most seasons and ran the break on offense. But because so many North Carolina games were on television, people saw us go to the four corners to protect a lead late in the game and drew the conclusion, with ample help from the media, that we played that way as a general rule. Teams that have leads late in a game earn the right to dictate how the endgame is going to be played. We did it by protecting the lead with our four corners offense. The rules allowed it, and it was a very hard offense to stop. I know people didn't enjoy playing against it.

When the shot clock and three-point shot came to college basketball, beginning with the 1987 season, we weren't surprised. We were ready for those major changes. I always looked ahead and tried to forecast what was coming for college basketball. As far as the shot clock was concerned, we didn't have to change our play much at all, even though some people thought it would hurt us. We liked having a shot clock, because it meant more possessions in the game and a faster pace. We made plans for the three-point shot, both in recruiting and in the way we played. We changed things in 1987 for the three-point shot, but when the ACC experimented with the shot in 1983, we changed very little, because the experiment would not be used in the NCAA tournament. Some of the nation's leading coaches took contrasting views when the three-point shot came in. Some said they would never shoot the shot. Of course they eventually had to change, or they wouldn't have survived.

In teaching our players the best way to do certain things, I often showed them tapes of our past teams, for example, tapes of a former team that was excellent at defending the baseline drive. It was a great teaching tool. But as I've said, while we did indeed honor the tradition that our former players established, I didn't want our current players looking back on all those great teams and worrying about matching their records or continuing the many streaks of excellence that North Carolina basketball had going. That could be self-defeating. For example, before the 1990 season, North Carolina had been to a record eighteen consecutive NCAA tournaments, a number that grew to twenty-nine before it ended after the 2002 season. Bill Guthridge had joined my staff, beginning with the 1967–68 season, as an assistant coach and had never been associated with a North Carolina team that had suffered more than nine losses in a season. We also had an amazing streak of twenty-five straight seasons when we had not finished lower than third in the tough ACC. Most of those years we were first or second. We had a streak of nineteen consecutive seasons when we won at least twenty-one games, most of those featuring twenty-five or more victories.

Well, it looked as if all those streaks would end in 1990. We had a record of 17–11 with two games remaining, one at home against Georgia Tech, the other at Duke. We had to win them both to finish third in the conference. You get an idea of how tough that assignment was when you learn that both Georgia Tech and Duke made the Final Four that season. Newspaper columnists and television commentators pointed out that all of North Carolina's streaks looked as if they would end: twenty-one-win seasons, top three in the ACC, going to the NCAA tournament. Rick Fox, a great player who went on to play on three NBA championship teams for the Los Angeles Lakers, was quoted as saying, "I don't want this to be the team that stops all of North Carolina's streaks. I don't want to let all of our former players down."

It was a pervasive issue, one we had to talk about with our players. In this instance, tradition and looking back were serving a negative purpose. They were hurting us. I told the players that I didn't care about any of those past streaks and didn't want them thinking about them either. It was putting enormous pressure on them. "This is the *only* North Carolina team that I'm interested in right now," I told them. "Forget the past, and do the best you can *this* year."

I thought then, and still believe, that we had to beat Georgia Tech and Duke just to get a bid to the NCAA tournament. Of course I didn't tell that to the team. We played a great game in Chapel Hill against Georgia Tech and beat them, 81–79, thus avenging a decisive loss in Atlanta on February 1. Then we had Duke, one of the nation's most talented teams. We knew they'd be waiting on us and pointing to us because we had beaten them badly in Chapel Hill on January 17, by the score of 79–60. Somehow, with the odds stacked so high against them, our players performed brilliantly in Durham and won the game, 87–75. Talk about winning big games in the clutch! A loss at Duke, I'm convinced, would have snapped our consecutive NCAA tournament streak. It also would have dropped us lower than third in the conference. You can imagine how badly Duke's coaches and players wanted to be the team to break Carolina's streaks and how very good and mentally tough our players had to be not to let them do it.

Beating Georgia Tech and Duke left us with nineteen wins against a very tough nonconference schedule and a third-place finish in the ACC. We lost to Virginia in the ACC tournament to finish the regular season at 19–12. It earned us an eighth seed in the NCAA tournament. We were shipped to Austin, Texas, where we beat a strong Southwest Missouri State team in the first round, 83–70. That earned us the dubious right to play Oklahoma, the number one team in the nation and the top seed in the entire sixty-four-team NCAA tournament. The building in Austin was filled mostly with Oklahoma fans, but again, our players defied the odds. Fox hit a shot at the buzzer, and we won, 79–77. It gave us twenty-one wins for the season, enabled us to advance to the Sweet 16, and knocked the nation's top team from the tournament field.

Our 1985 team, the one after Michael Jordan left for the NBA, also was in perilous position of breaking what was then a twenty-year stretch of not finishing lower than third in the ACC. When we went to Duke on March 2, our ACC record was 8–5. A Duke victory would have dropped us to fourth place in the conference standings. Again, our players wouldn't let the pressure of living up to past standards slow them. Duke's rowdy crowd didn't bother them either. They beat Duke, 78–68, and tied for *first* place in the regular season. You have to tip your hat to our players. They were at their best in the biggest games. That's why those streaks were active in the first place and why so much tradition surrounded the program.

Let me make it clear that while I didn't want our players to feel pressured to maintain past excellence, I wanted, and expected, them to respect and honor that tradition. I wanted them to feel that it was a privilege to wear the Carolina jersey and that with it they were expected to play a certain way: hard, together, and smart. Those were things they could control that past Carolina teams also had done. That part of looking back was beneficial and important.

Our basketball tradition also connected our past with the present. Our former players came back to Chapel Hill often (and delighted us in doing so) and became friends with the current players. It was very seamless. Age didn't matter; eras didn't either. They were members of the same family, the Carolina basketball family. They all had worn the same jersey. After games in Chapel Hill, former players congregated in our basketball offices, where they met and became friends with the families of our current players. Everybody was on a first-name basis.

As much as I loved coaching each of my North Carolina teams and still marvel at what they accomplished, I don't pull out old game tapes and look at them. As for those friends who think I stepped down too soon?

Well, they're right if they surmise that I miss the on-court teaching, the relationship with the players, and the competition provided by the big games. But I don't miss the countless off-court demands that face the head coach at North Carolina or the recruiting. I made my decision in October 1997 to retire from a coaching job that I loved. I don't look back and second-guess myself.

I spend my time thinking about what's next. I might do a basketball training tape. My granddaughter is on a soccer scholarship at UNC Greensboro, and I hope to see her play some. I'm even thinking about learning how to work a computer. For a man who struggles to change a lightbulb, going on-line would be quite an achievement. I'm told this E-mail thing is a real advancement in communications and is here to stay. I have a computer on my desk, and it looks like a good one. I wouldn't know for sure because I've never turned it on. I guess I'm going to have to look into that.

PLAYER PERSPECTIVE

Pete Budko,
class of 1981, managing director,
Wachovia Securities

I don't think Coach Smith ever "learned" to be the coach that he was. I think he came by it naturally. He was never a "rah-rah" type of motivator. He simply cared a great deal about the people around him, and this caring gave us a quiet confidence in ourselves and our teammates. What he gave us was something that ran much deeper than the hype and emotion of game time.

Coach Smith was never one to dwell on the past. Looking back and wondering what might have been are not his style. As his players we were taught to concern ourselves with the things we could control. Since we couldn't change the past, we learned from it and forged ahead.

I will always remember some situations during the final minute or two of a crucial game when we found ourselves trailing an opponent with victory apparently out of our grasp. Instead of dwelling on what had transpired, Coach would call a time-out and, with a distinct sparkle in his eyes, say something to the effect of "Wouldn't it be great to come back and win this one?" Then he would tell us confidently exactly what we were going to do to win the game. We often did too, as incredible comeback victories are part of Coach Smith's legacy. On the occasions when we didn't win, he would tell us there were two billion people in China who didn't care one bit about the outcome of our game. Perspective! If you extrapolate those situations to the ones we find ourselves in now, you begin to get an idea how his influence has shaped our lives and careers. Identify mistakes; fix them; move on. Don't dwell on the past.

I easily could speak of the disappointments that occurred in my college career. Injuries and other setbacks caused me to move from a McDonald's High School All-American to a supporting role at Carolina. However, I will never forget a comment Coach made during the final airing of his television show after my senior season, when we finished number two in the nation. Asked about my career, Coach replied, "There are only two people in this world who know how good a player Pete can be—Pete and I." At a time when I was ready to hang up my sneakers for good, that one brief comment from him was the catalyst for me to prove to myself that I could play with anyone in the world. After recovering from my senior-year injuries, I went on to play professionally for four years in Europe, with preseason NBA stints in Dallas and Denver. I played against the best and held my own just fine. I accomplished what I needed to do in order to move on to success in other areas of my life. As I look back now, I believe Coach Smith knew exactly what he was doing when he made that comment about me.

In his own way, instead of having me dwell on the past, he planted a seed to get me to move forward, all for the good. Thanks, Coach.

BUSINESS PERSPECTIVE

Those who long for the good old days or believe things have gone downhill since then typically have quit living in the present and have given up on their tomorrow. Remember, what happens today will become somebody else's good old days in twenty or thirty years.

People can't see into the future, hear new ideas, or perceive positive events taking place around them if they are looking backward. The secret is to learn as much as possible from the past while keeping in mind that everything changes. Focus on creating positive experiences for yourself and as many others as possible. Move forward; participate in challenging activities and relationships that take you beyond your comfort zone. Read extensively, seek training and development, attend conferences, and get involved in things that force you to think differently and develop new outlooks. Surround yourself with smart, positive people so that you become like them.

Young people have educational experiences that bombard them with new ideas. Children entice parents to do things they normally wouldn't, such as meeting new friends, trying new activities, and taking fresh looks at their own childhoods and philosophies. As children graduate and leave home, as people grow comfortable in their jobs and lifestyles, there's the danger they may begin to withdraw into themselves. It's important to work harder as you grow older to make sure you are moving forward.

If you're doing any of the following things, it could indicate that you're thinking too much about the past and not enough about the future:

- Spending an inordinate amount of time longing for the past.
- Daydreaming about doing things the way you used to.
- Trying to re-create conditions you used to have.
- Always telling others how great things used to be and how bad they are now.
- Growing cynical about people and current events.
- Being pessimistic about the future.
- Brooding about how horrible people and events are now as opposed to how good they used to be.
- Dwelling on past achievements and trying to gain personal satisfaction from them instead of what you are doing now.

Here are some ways to counteract those danger signs:

- Forgive yourself for past mistakes. Learn from them and free your mind to understand that you did the best you could at the time.
- On the first day of every month, make a list of three things that you most want to learn about during the month and then make it happen.
- Once every six months, spend an hour making a list of the three best things you anticipate in each of the next six months.

- On January 1 and July 1 of each year, develop a list of the three best things that are happening to you in each of the eight domains that surround and affect your business life: competitors, cultural value shifts, economic conditions, government regulations, your partners and stakeholders, suppliers, all the people in your industry, and technical changes. Study the changes taking place in those areas and then put down on paper in your own words the great changes that are taking place in these areas. Those ideas will stay with you if you write them down.

Look to the past to learn; look forward to live.

24

DON'T FEAR CHANGE

Not every plan turns out to be a good one, even if it is well thought out and thoroughly taught. If it turns sour, there must be a willingness to change, even a desire to do so.

Such was the case in 1997, which turned out to be my last season in coaching. For virtually my entire career as North Carolina's coach, our signature defense involved calculated risk taking and synchronization. We pressured the ball, moved our defenders into passing lanes, and did enough trapping and double-teaming to keep our opponents tentative and off-balance. It was very much a team defense, an attacking defense, one that took a lot of savvy, a fair amount of quickness, and devotion on the part of the players to perform as a team. If one man failed to carry out his assignment, the defense likely failed. It was part of our overall plan. We knew if our players learned to depend on one another defensively, trusted one another, played unselfishly, and did all they could to help one another, all areas of our game—defense, rebounding, offense, team chemistry— would benefit.

The Carolina defense was beautiful to watch when we ran it correctly.

It created a fast-paced game, which we liked, and caused our opponents to spend a lot of their planning and practice time preparing for our traps and double teams. One outstanding Big Ten coach, after playing against us several times, told one of my assistant coaches that his team spent so much time in practice preparing for our changing defenses that it neglected its own stuff. A bonus was that our defense was fun for the players to execute, and we loved coaching it.

However, in the mid-1990s our personnel changed in such a way that it made sense for us move away from the pressure and double teams and go to a softer man-to-man defense with some zone sprinkled in. We used our point zone even with our pressure defensive teams, but when we made the switch to guard our basket by using a softer defense, we relied on the zone a little more. The changes were made because it gave those teams the best chance to succeed.

We had thought during the off-season planning sessions and preseason practices that with hard work, the 1997 team could return to playing the pressure defense. Most of our preseason work, which included summer planning sessions by the coaches, was geared toward returning to that style of play. Our players were excited about it, and so was the coaching staff. We believed we could make this change back to the pressure even though we had a very young team in 1997. One senior, a junior, three sophomores, and a freshman were in our top six rotation.

We had a million question marks when we opened the season against Arizona in the Hall of Fame Tipoff Classic just before Thanksgiving. We ran the pressure defense in that game, but our young players didn't execute it well and we lost, 83–72. After studying the results of that game, and even though we had invested a great deal in our plan to return to the pressure defense, I felt strongly that we needed to return to the more conservative man-to-man defense that we'd used in 1996. When Serge Zwikker, our seven-foot center who had quickness limitations, was in the game, we played a good bit of point zone.

Knowing our players had been excited about returning to our old pressure style of defending, I had to persuade them that there was more than one way to defend our basket. In the best interests of this team, we needed to play defense another way, a more conservative way. It's certainly not a bad defense; it was just not Carolina's defense, not the one we had been known for. While we were in the transition of going from pressure defense to the more conservative approach, our players responded brilliantly in December. We won nine straight games, including a win over UMass in the Meadowlands before its fans and a win at Princeton, which had an excellent team. The crowd in Jadwin Gym, which seated 6,854, was so jammed that the fire marshal stopped fans from entering. We won a very difficult game, 69–60, and afterward, Princeton's excellent coach, Bill Carmody, praised us for playing them there. "Give North Carolina credit," he said, "because most top programs won't even think about playing us in here." Southern California, South Carolina, and Louisiana State were other teams that we defeated in December through the defensive transition. Being 9–1 against that difficult schedule with our young team was impressive.

Still, I saw weaknesses, things that we would have to correct before we could compete in the ACC. We had a long way to go. The route to getting there was made much more difficult because of a major scheduling mistake that I made. As I said earlier, it was our policy to get our players a game as close to their home as possible. Zwikker had played three years of prep basketball in the Washington, D.C., area, but his native land is Holland. Instead of being at home and practicing a couple of times a day during the Christmas holidays, preferable with a young team, we made a tiring trip to Amsterdam and continued from there to Italy to play that country's national team.

Our players were exhausted when we returned home just in time to travel to Wake Forest to play against Tim Duncan and his nationally ranked team. Even though we were to beat Wake Forest two out of three that season, its players routed us in that game, 81–57. Our players lost confidence, and Vince Carter, one of our main players, was injured. I told the reporters afterward: "I had hoped to see two good teams out here tonight; I saw one. At this point, Wake Forest is obviously much better than we are, but it's a long season. I hope we can get better." A reporter asked me if our team was tired from the overseas trip. I never was one to make excuses, so I said I didn't think so. To say otherwise would have taken away from Wake Forest's great game.

With Carter still injured, we lost at home to Maryland and on the road to Virginia, two excellent teams. We were 0–3 in the ACC and the media had a great story on their hands. Our opponents in the league weren't feeling sorry for us, either. Said one conference coach, "It's about time they learned how all the rest of us have felt at one time or another." Some sharp words were exchanged by our players in the locker room at Virginia, some of which were heard by reporters. There was speculation that we would be lucky to win enough games to earn an NCAA tournament bid. The head coach was concerned too but there were signs of encouragement that the writers ignored.

We almost went to 0–4 in the ACC with our next game. We were down nine points to NC State and it had the ball with less than two minutes to play. Somehow, our players scored the last twelve points of the game and we won, 59–56. What could have been devastating to our confidence turned out to give us a big boost.

We started playing better. After finishing 3–5 in the ACC in the first half of the season, we won by lopsided scores over Florida State and Virginia to begin the second half of the schedule. "I never was one to throw dirt in their face when they were down," said Virginia Coach Jeff Jones. I might have eased up on the players a little after the 0–3 start, but once we got it turned around, I challenged them more. Someone recalled me saying one day at practice, "If we want to get to the Final Four, we need to take better care of the ball."

It was such a season of highs and lows, very tiring. We didn't lose another game in the regular season and went on to become ACC champions. In the process of putting the season back together, the players also made history by giving me 879 coaching wins, 3 more than the record previously held by Adolph Rupp of Kentucky. The players on the 1997 Carolina team, and our former players, had let me know that they wanted the record because they had been such an important part of it. While happy for them, I experienced great relief that the hoopla surrounding the record was finally over.

As I left the court and entered the tunnel toward our locker room, many of our former players were lined up to greet me. They had come from far and near to be there. I was surprised to see so many of them and recall wondering how they got tickets. I shall never forget their faces, their generous words, their hugs. I felt better about the entire record episode when I saw how much it meant to them. After all, this was their story, not mine. They had been the players on my thirty-six North Carolina teams. They had won the games. Seeing them there that day was a very moving experience, one I shall never forget.

Neither shall I forget that 1997 team. It rose from the ashes to make it all the way to the Final Four, a sensational accomplishment for a team so young and one that had faced such adversity. Would the team have had that success had we stayed with the pressure defense in light of what we learned from the opening game of the season? I don't think so. The change was necessary to get the most out of that team, to put the players in the best position to succeed.

In building a particular team in a unique set of circumstances, it's sometimes necessary to discard an original plan and go to something else, even though you would prefer not to have to do it. I'm not suggesting that you should give up on a good idea prematurely, but I am saying that being stubborn, inflexible, and refusing to change when the evidence warrants it can reduce your team's chances of succeeding.

Charles Scott,

class of 1970, All-American, NBA player,

now administrator of Fundamental Programs

for Jordan Brand, Atlanta

I was the first African American to receive a basketball scholarship to an ACC school, south of Washington, D.C., and Perry Wallace (Vanderbilt University) and I were the first two on athletic scholarships at all the predominantly white schools in the Deep South. When it came to contemplating change, I had plenty of chances to be apprehensive.

Some have called me a pioneer. That sounds like bragging, so I'll let others make that call. I do know that I was on the cusp of a changing society, and Coach Smith was great in helping me deal with a lot of issues. It began when he was recruiting me. On my official recruiting visit to Chapel Hill, Coach took me to his church to worship. That might not sound like a big deal today, but in the mid-1960s not many white men were taking African Americans to church with them in the South. I visited many schools, including Duke, NC State, and Davidson, and Coach Smith was the only coach to ask me to go to church with him.

I had no grand views of what awaited me. I did know that just because Coach Smith and my North Carolina teammates accepted me, it didn't mean the entire state of North Carolina would. On my recruiting visit to Carolina I disappeared for a couple of hours to be on my own. I wanted to walk around the town and see how people treated me without having Coach Smith or a Carolina player at my side. It was a good experience. Davidson Coach Lefty Driesell had done a good job recruiting me, and I was very interested in attending Davidson. One day Frank McDuffie, my high school coach, and I were in Charlotte and decided to ride unannounced over to Davidson to see Coach Driesell. When we dropped by the basketball office, Terry Holland, one of his assistant coaches, told us that Coach Driesell was uptown having lunch. Mr. McDuffie and I went to the restaurant, and Lefty asked us to join him. The waitress took our order, but a few minutes later we were told by a man who worked at the restaurant that we were in a section reserved for whites and we would have to move to another area of the restaurant. It infuriated Coach Driesell, who had nothing to do with it. Nevertheless it's hard to forget something like that.

Once I got to Carolina, I was often apprehensive when we went on the road to play in front of another team's fans. It was usually quite an adventure, let's put it that way. I was certainly apprehensive when we went to Kentucky in December 1968. Kentucky had the reputation for having great teams, great all-white teams at the time, and its coach, Adolph Rupp, was generally thought of then as the best coach in the country. This was only a couple of years removed from when Kentucky, with five whites, played Texas Western, with five blacks starting, for the national championship, and Texas Western won. That game got enormous national attention. So it wasn't hard to be intimidated going to Kentucky to play. The way Coach Smith prepared us for the game, though, helped ease my mind. He had Kentucky scouted perfectly. In my mind, this was a perfect contrast in coaching styles: Coach Smith, who liked to change to take advantage of game situations, versus Coach Rupp, who did things his way and was reluctant to change. For example, Kentucky liked to run one play in particular, and Coach Smith knew it. He told us exactly how the play would unfold and added that Kentucky would not change it. His scouting of Kentucky put us in position to beat its men to a certain spot on the court, and I must have drawn five charges in that game, which we won by ten points.

When we went into hostile environments to play, Coach Smith helped me greatly by treating me like everyone else on our team. If he had singled me out and prepared me in a special way, it would have stayed on my mind all the time. I would have wondered what to expect from the fans and how to react to it. Instead he treated me just like the other members of our team, and it served to help relax me because it put my mind on basketball. Respect is a very big thing with Coach. He taught us to respect every opponent and never sell anyone short.

Change certainly was a part of Coach Smith's program. He adapted better than any coach from year to year, one reason his teams won so consistently. He knew where to place his players on the court to get the most out of each man's ability. For example, he taught his great players to play better and more efficiently. Some people said, in a teasing way, that he was the only coach to hold Michael Jordan under twenty points a game. Well, ask Michael, and he'll tell you that Coach taught him to be a *complete* basketball player. He taught his great players how to score without having to dominate the basketball. He put me in a position on the court to take advantage of my quickness. The way he tweaked his four corners offense serves as a good example of what I'm talking about. Most coaches, in using that offense, would have their point guard handling the ball. However, the opponent would usually have its quickest player defending our point guard, so it would be hard to beat him one-on-one. Of course, if Phil Ford is the point guard, you give him the ball. But back then Coach Smith often used his small forward to run the four corners. We had some small forwards who were quicker than but not as big as the men guarding them, like Larry Miller, Bob Lewis, Al Wood, and me, to name some, and we could beat our man off the dribble. Coach knew it and adapted his thinking to give us the ball in the four corners.

Coach was a master of adjusting for the situation. He could make changes during the course of the game, on the spot, that enhanced our chances of winning. In my career many people recall the game I had against Duke in the ACC finals in 1969. I scored forty points, and we won by nine points after trailing at halftime by nine. Some people said it was uncharacteristic for a player on a Dean Smith team to score forty points in a game since Coach preferred balanced scoring. There were mitigating circumstances. Dick Grubar, our senior point guard and one of our best leaders, tore up a knee early in the game and was out for the season. Another senior leader and starter, forward Bill Bunting, got into foul trouble early on and fouled out with about ten minutes left in the game. We lost a lot of our offense with those two players not available. Still, it wasn't like Coach was calling plays for me or putting me at point guard so I could control the ball. I wanted the ball, sure, but the shots I got were out of our offense, and I had one of those games that young men dream about. I hit twelve of my thirteen shots in the second half. It wasn't like I was out there hunting my shot. We won our third straight ACC championship and made it to the Final Four for the third consecutive year. Adaptation! Coach was the best at it and expected his players to be too.

I learned about a lot more than basketball playing for Coach Smith. He taught us life's values: loyalty, the importance of teamwork, our obligation to follow through on our responsibilities. He stressed that if we lost, we should accept it as a loss and not blame someone else. Learn from it; hold up our end; no finger-pointing. What he taught us mirrors life, and that is what I try to teach my children today. Take responsibility for something, do it as well as you possibly can, and then accept the outcome. If you do your absolute best, you won't have to second-guess yourself, no matter what the outcome.

Coach Smith certainly didn't fear change; he brought it on. He was ahead of the times, as a coach and with his views on society. If he believed something was morally right, he would stand up for it, and he didn't worry if it was popular or unpopular to do so. It's kind of sad to see the nature of basketball today, where there are so many selfish acts and so many players putting themselves above the team.

BUSINESS PERSPECTIVE

Organizations exist at the will of their external environments. Leaders frequently lose sight of this obvious point. To survive, business leaders must see to it that their organizations create products and services of value that meet the needs of their customers at a competitive price. Those products should outperform the competitors', meet the government's expectations and regulations, and fulfill the cultural values of community and society.

I talked previously about how an organization's eight external environments continually change, making it necessary for the organization itself to change to the same degree. If the external environment changes but the organization doesn't, it will get out of sync with the external environment and at some point be faced with the need to make massive changes. Organizations must evolve—daily, weekly, annually—or they will face revolutionary changes, which are costly, risky, and often unsuccessful in saving a business. Leaders should ask themselves: What improvements can we implement this month? What can we do better? Change shouldn't be viewed as traumatic but as normal.

No organization changes unless its individuals decide to change. Unless people see a problem or are unhappy, they often resist change. People must perceive the gap between the results they are getting and those they hope to get. As long as they see no problem, there will be no desire for change.

The most effective way to create desire for change is to ensure that individuals and organizations receive constant feedback about the results they are achieving and those that are possible. To get feedback, leaders must be certain that their followers get out, talk with others, observe competitors, and see the changes taking place. They must also make sure that those they lead are continuously exposed to the external environment they serve; if they are, they will inevitably be bombarded with feedback about how things could be done better to serve their constituents.

It's important to understand that change can create problems. Change means people give up things they value and enjoy. They suffer losses, as well as gains, and those who are impacted by change tend to focus first on their losses. They must resolve those losses before they will look at or accept the gains provided by change. So it is critical for leaders to help their associates get through five stages of grief:

1. When people are forced to change and thereby lose some of the benefits of their past behavior, they tend to deny that there is a need to change. So the first stage is denial.
2. The second stage is anger and blame. Who did this? Who caused this need for change?
3. The third stage is one of resignation. People accept that the change is actually going to happen. They digest its meaning.
4. People then begin to search for alternatives. What can they do now? What are their alternatives?
5. Finally, most people enter the action phase. They move forward to turn the change into an opportunity, to make the best of their situation.

People often become stuck in one or more of these phases. Some become arrested in the stage of denial and never can see the need for change; they continue living and working as if nothing had happened. People can be permanently stuck in the anger and blame stage. Some can be frozen in resignation and just give up. Others can continue to search for things to do yet never take action. Stagnation in any of these four phases is unacceptable. If a person is stuck in one of these phases, it is critical that his or her leader helps him or her move forward.

Everything will change, so if a change is resisted in any way, the organization and its people will become obsolete.

Leaders should select for their teams individuals who have proved capacity to change. You can predict a person's ability to change by answering these questions: (1) Is this person curious?; (2) does he or she like to learn?; (3) does he or she listen well to ideas different from his or her own?; (4) is he or she humble enough to understand he or she doesn't have all the answers?; (5) is she or he resilient?; (6) does he or she like to test new ideas?; (7) is he or she willing to admit he or she is wrong when necessary?

Those who lack these qualities tend to be stubborn and closed-minded. Thus it's highly likely they will lose their effectiveness as the conditions surrounding them change. In business, those who do not adapt to new technologies and those who have trouble adapting to cultural changes, such as gender and racial equality, suffer devastating consequences. So will the company.

So what to do? A few suggestions:

- Schedule quarterly meetings with your subordinates in which they're asked three things they've improved in the past three months and three things they intend to improve in the three months to come. Hold them accountable for their suggestions.
- Ask your customers at least once a year what are the problems affecting their business that will have an indirect but real effect on yours.
- Ask your customers at least once a year how you can improve your work to help make them more successful.

25

THE OLYMPICS:
WHEN WINNING *WAS* THE GOAL

I had never even thought about coaching the U.S. Olympic team, but when the committee that selected the head coach called me in 1975 and asked if I would accept the position if it were offered, I happily replied I would.

I was named eighteen months prior to the Summer Games of 1976. Since my first job was to name two assistants to help me coach the team, I immediately called John Thompson, a close friend and an excellent coach, and he accepted my offer. One of my former players and assistant coaches, Larry Brown, who had Olympic experience as a player, could not accept an offer to assist because he was coach of a professional team. In those days professional coaches couldn't coach the USA basketball team in the Olympics. We used amateur players and college coaches. I'm happy that Larry gets his chance in 2004 as the deserving head coach of America's Olympic team. As it turned out, I had an excellent coach a few steps from my office, Bill Guthridge, one of my North Carolina assistants. He was thrilled to join John and me on the United States staff.

When I told the committee that I would accept its offer to be head coach, I told the members that it should be a one-term appointment. It's such an honor to coach Olympians that I believed, and still do, that it should be shared with as many coaches as possible. Henry Iba had coached the three previous U.S. Olympic basketball teams and did a great job, but that was a term that spanned twelve years. I was committed to giving everything I had to the job, because I knew it was extremely important for the USA to win in basketball, especially in 1976, but I didn't want to continue in the role beyond that. Our Olympic basketball coaches now are appointed for one term, which is for the best.

I scouted the Pan American Games, which were held in Mexico in the summer of 1975. It gave us a preliminary idea of what we'd be up against in the 1976 Olympics in Montreal, and it provided a glimpse at what our talent pool would be. I also went to Belgrade, Yugoslavia, and was very impressed with the Yugoslavia team.

The next spring, seventy to eighty United States players were invited to our Olympic tryouts in Raleigh, North Carolina, on the NC State campus. We were disappointed to learn that many of the best college players in America, including some with great size and talent, such as Robert Parrish and Leon Douglas, declined invitations to try out for the team. It severely depleted our talent pool, especially with big players. However, there was no time to worry about what we didn't have, however, because our group of twelve had to be selected in a hurry, and then we would have only six weeks of practice to become a team.

The selection committee of basketball people chose fifteen players as team finalists and gave me the authority to cut three. Once that was done, four North Carolina players wound up on the roster, and a total of seven from the Atlantic Coast Conference. Although the committee had chosen the fifteen players, with input from me, I was roundly criticized, especially on NBC, for having four of my own players on the team. "If the USA loses," one NBC sportscaster said before the start of the games, "Dean Smith will have to answer why so many players from North Carolina and the ACC are on the roster."

I paid no more attention to this "expert" than I did to others in the media who criticized the roster composition. We had work to do, a lot of it. Phil Ford, our great North Carolina point guard, didn't play his best early in the trials, and I did tell the committee how important I felt it would be to have Phil on the team. I would have been deeply disappointed if Phil hadn't been selected. Others from North Carolina on the team were Walter Davis, six-five, a great talent and team player, Mitch Kupchak, six-ten, and Tommy LaGarde, six-ten. We certainly would have been vulnerable without Mitch and Tommy; not only were they terrific players, but we needed their size. We were a small team with them; without them, we wouldn't have been nearly as strong.

The players from the ACC were Steve Sheppard of Maryland, who was great for our team chemistry, Kenny Carr of NC State, and Tates Armstrong of Duke. The other five were Adrian Dantley of Notre Dame, Scott May and Quinn Buckner of Indiana, Ernie Grunfeld of Tennessee, and Phil Hubbard of Michigan.

In selecting an Olympic team of twelve, I didn't want the twelve *best* players. I didn't want twelve who thought they should be playing. In a conversation I had with Mr. Iba at the Oklahoma City airport before our team was selected, he warned that the hardest thing would be to find the right kind of leader to be the eleventh and twelfth men on the team. In the best of worlds, these two would know in advance that they wouldn't play much but would work hard in practice and meetings to make the team better.

College players were excited to be on the team because they saw it as a great honor. In many ways I am sorry that we changed our rules to allow professionals to play on our Olympic team. Sure, other nations use their professionals, but we would still be very competitive with just college players, and they would be thrilled to be there. We're missing something with the current system, in my opinion.

We went to North Carolina's home gymnasium, Carmichael Auditorium, for the six weeks of practice. It was summertime, North Carolina summers are hot and humid, and Carmichael had no air-conditioning. With only six weeks to build a team, we worked the players extremely hard. One of the players left the team in Raleigh because he didn't like all the running we required. "I'm a basketball player, not a track star," he groused, and ran off into the sunset. Another player I had hoped would be named hadn't made his time in the mile run and came to me to protest having to continue to run it until he made his required time. He got nowhere with me, so he called his college coach, looking for help. He didn't accomplish anything with that call either. He finally made his time. Once we got to Chapel Hill for the six weeks of practice, one of the players seemed to have a poor attitude. I pulled him aside and said, "The rules say we can't take more than twelve players to Montreal, but they don't say we can't go with eleven, which is what we're going to do if you don't shape up." He had an immediate attitude adjustment, enjoyed the experience, and helped our team.

I've said many times in this book that I didn't talk to our North Carolina players about winning. Instead we talked about the process of playing hard, together, and smart. Those were things we could control. But with the Olympians, from day one I let them know that winning was our only goal. That was why we were going to Montreal. It was why we were going to work hard and prepare. In my mind, this was not a contradiction of what I believed. Circumstances demanded a different approach from what I took with my college teams since "the season" was only eight weeks long. We also told the players that the best way to win the gold medal was to play unselfishly, hard, and intelligently.

Winning the gold medal in basketball was especially important to the United States in 1976 because we had lost it, or had it taken from us, for the first time ever in the 1972 Olympics. An extremely controversial call by an official gave the gold medal to the Soviet Union. Knowing they had been denied their rightful place as champions, all the American players on the team refused to accept the silver medal. The United States had stewed over that injustice for four years and wanted the gold medal back on its soil. Sure, that added pressure to our assignment, but it also made our mission very clear. The only way for us to succeed was to win. We constantly drove the point home to our players: win, win, win.

Why did I treat this team differently from one of my Carolina teams? Because we represented a nation, not a university, and our goal was clearly laid out for us. We'd had no say in establishing it. Second, I hadn't recruited this team. I hadn't asked their parents to send them to our university and in turn promised that we would see to it that they received a good education and a chance to play in a great program. This team was selected by a committee, with input from me, and was assembled with the sole purpose of winning. Finally, I had this group for only six weeks of intense practice, not for four years. I wasn't responsible for these players' education or seeing to it that they went to class. I wasn't going to build relationships with them the way I did with my North Carolina players. My job was to make them Olympic winners. Nothing else would do.

Our 1976 Olympic team became an unselfish team, very much so. But it wasn't my goal when we set out. My goal at the beginning of the process was to win, period. If winning would have been enhanced by allowing one player to dominate a game by himself, I might have let him. Still, the players knew from the first day of practice that if they didn't play hard and unselfishly, I would bench them. I told them on the first day, "We're together as a team to win the gold medal." I also told them there would be no all-tournament team selected, no most valuable player named. One group would stand together as a team on the platform to receive gold medals; twelve players would be called the best basketball team in the world. Only one team would be there. There would be no individual awards. College basketball could learn a thing or two from this way of doing it.

During our six weeks of practice we played exhibition games against the Denver Nuggets and some other NBA players who wanted to help the Olympic team prepare. We were doing well in this competition, and it helped our confidence. After playing against a professional all-star team in Hartford, the great Julius Erving said, "You guys are going to be good."

My friend Al McGuire, the Marquette coach, didn't think we had enough size to win against teams such as the Soviet Union and Yugoslavia. "Dean has no aircraft carrier" is the way Al put it, meaning we had no true center. Red Auerbach, the great Boston Celtics coach, also expressed worry about our lack of a true center. All that helped our motivation.

As soon as we hit Montreal, I showed our players the tape of the 1972 Olympic gold medal game, in which the United States had had the gold taken from it. It fired up our players, and we went out and had a great practice. All our practices in Montreal were very good, in fact. I thought we were ready to play, but in basketball you never know, and we were going against the best players the other nations had. Most were professionals and were older and more experienced than our players.

Our first game in Montreal was on July 18, 1976, against Italy. We were very good in winning 106–86. We shot 54 percent from the field, and our smallish team controlled the rebounding, 41–16. Four of our players scored in double figures, and Ford had seven assists.

I didn't allow our players to stay at the arena to watch the other games because I didn't want them to become either intimidated or overconfident. I wanted them to get their scouting report from the coaches and prepare from there, not from what they might see in a particular game. However, back in the Olympic Village, the Yugoslavia–Puerto Rico game, won easily by Yugoslavia, 84–63, was on television. Our players watched, and when we played Puerto Rico on July 20, we were not as mentally ready as we had been for Italy. We struggled for most of the game, but we prevailed, barely, 95–94. I believe the close escape helped us prepare for the other games. It got our attention.

The next day we played Yugoslavia, which had a great team and was led by Drazen Dalipagic, who is in the Naismith Hall of Fame. Had he not become homesick, he would have become a great player in the NBA. Still smarting from our close call the day before, our players were terrific. We shot 56 percent, again had four players score in double figures, and won, 112–93.

Our next game, set for July 22, never took place. We won by forfeit over Egypt, a team that wouldn't have given us much of a challenge anyhow.

In the competition on July 26, something occurred that worried me. We were very good in defeating Canada, the home team, in front of its crowd, 95–77. We were going to play in the gold medal game, our sole goal from the outset. However, we had put so much emphasis on getting the gold medal back after the 1972 fiasco that our players had their hearts set on playing the Soviet Union. But when the Soviets and Yugoslavia played on July 26, Yugoslavia won, 89–84. It surprised some of our players, but not the coaching staff. Yugoslavia had proved in recent competition that it had a better team than the Soviet Union.

Psychologically we feared a letdown. We told our players that our goal all along had been to win the gold medal, and we weren't concerned with which team we'd have to beat to get it. The last team in our way was Yugoslavia, very talented and focused. Forget the Soviet Union. It wasn't good enough to hold up its end of the bargain. Yugoslavia was.

We played the Yugoslavians on July 27, and our players were determined and skilled. We shot 57 percent from the field and won the game, 95–74. It was our world championship, our gold medal game. Our mission was accomplished. The United States had reclaimed the gold medal in basketball, and while it didn't erase the injustice done in 1972, it helped. I made sure that all twelve players on our team got into the gold medal game.

We were fortunate to win many championships at North Carolina, but this one was different. For one, I had more "alumni" and "assistant coaches" than I did at North Carolina: every citizen of the United States. Having a team for six weeks with the clear goal of winning six games against the best players in the world was a completely different experience from having a team for an entire season. I was asked afterward if I'd had fun coaching the Olympians. Well, it was a big relief to win because the stakes were so high. I had fun coaching all my teams, but I didn't think about that until afterward. So, as I look back, the answer is yes, it was fun. I enjoyed the experience. I was also asked what it was like handling the pressure of coaching this team when nothing was acceptable but winning. I didn't dwell on it. Just as I had with all my North Carolina teams, I worked too hard on what we needed to do to be successful to worry about the pressure. Larry Keith, a Carolina graduate who worked for *Sports Illustrated,* said to me after the Olympics, "If you had lost with four Carolina guys on the team, the critics would have killed you." I certainly never spent a minute thinking or worrying about that.

I've always thought that the game of basketball should belong to the players and that too much attention is placed on the coaches. So I loved the gold medal ceremony. Our twelve players stood on the platform and, one by one, received their gold medals. John, Bill, and I stood off to the side and watched. Coaches weren't on the platform and didn't receive gold medals, which I think is appropriate. Still, when the national anthem was played and our flag was raised with our players on the platform, standing there as one team and as champions of the world, it was a very moving experience for us as well as them.

The players did what we asked of them: They won. And although winning was the only goal, as I looked back and saw how it had transpired, the entire experience was even more satisfying. This group of twelve, representing college teams all over America, came together as one and won one of basketball's most prestigious prizes.

They did it by playing hard, playing together, and playing smart.

PLAYER PERSPECTIVE

Phil Ford,
class of 1978, former National College Player
of the Year, NBA rookie of the year, NBA all-star

I've known Coach Smith since I was seventeen years old. He recruited me when I was a high school player. I played for him for four years, was his assistant coach for ten years, and played for him on the U.S. Olympic basketball team in 1976.

I know him well. When he recruited me out of high school, through my playing career under him at North Carolina, and later as his assistant coach, I never really heard him talk to any of his teams about winning. Instead he talked about doing our best, improving each day, playing hard, smart, and together. As players we believed in Coach Smith and knew that if we did the things he told us to, we'd end up winning most of our games. We understood that winning would be the by-product of doing the things that he asked us to do.

That tone changed fairly dramatically when I was one of the players selected to play for him on the U.S. Olympic basketball team. It's important to understand the circumstances as they existed in 1976. For the first time ever, the United States had lost in Olympic basketball to the Soviet Union in 1972, in a game that had a most controversial ending. It was pretty apparent that the United States had that game taken from it. Our nation wanted the basketball gold medal to return to America. Anything less would have been considered a failure. Furthermore, the committee that selected our twelve-member Olympic team put seven players on it from the Atlantic Coast Conference, including four from North Carolina. Coach Smith was criticized for that, although he had only one vote. Some others in the sports media, as well as some respected coaches, said we couldn't win because we didn't have a true center because many star college players decided not to try out for the Olympic team that year. This criticism got the attention of two of my North Carolina teammates, Mitch Kupchak and Tommy LeGarde, who were determined to show that they could do the job at center, which they went on to do. The pressure on us to win was substantial.

Unlike today, the United States did not use professional basketball players on its Olympic team in 1976. That meant our team was young and inexperienced compared with some of the best international teams, which did use professionals. Some of those teams also had played together for five years or longer. Time playing and practicing together, plus their considerable skills, made them formidable competition.

When we Olympians arrived in Chapel Hill to begin practice, it was the first time I'd heard Coach Smith talk about winning. In fact he talked mostly about winning, saying winning the gold medal would be the only satisfactory conclusion to our quest. Even then he said the way to win the gold would be to play hard and unselfishly, to give ourselves up for the team. He emphasized that individual statistics would mean nothing. The only way our team would be remembered, he said, was if we won the gold medal. Individual success would be measured by our team's success and in no other way. I can honestly say that to this day I don't even know if they kept game statistics at the Olympics. I know I didn't see them or look for them and I don't recall any of our players doing so either. Our goal was to play together and win. Personal statistics weren't part of the picture. Coach did a good job of getting that point across, and the players deserve credit for honoring it.

On the court Coach Smith didn't change much from the way he taught us at North Carolina. He was always intense and serious about practice, both at North Carolina and during the Olympics. Practice was his forum to teach. He used the time wisely. During our six-week practice session at Chapel Hill, we had an exhibition game one night against the Denver Nuggets of the NBA. A construction project in Chapel Hill delayed Walter Davis, two of our teammates, and me, and we arrived at the pregame meal about thirty seconds late. Coach was angry. None of us started that game. When I finally got in, I played as hard as I could to make up for being late. It was the only time I was late for anything as a North Carolina player or assistant coach.

Our Olympic team got better and better the longer we were to-gether, a compliment to Coach Smith's teaching ability. We ended up being a very unselfish team and returned the gold medal to the United States. Winning it didn't mean as much to me then as it does now. I was just a college sophomore at the time, and my perspective then wasn't what it is now. The older I get, the more important the gold medal is to me. It's quite an honor to play for your country.

Coach Smith handled winning the Olympics the same way he handled it at North Carolina: by thanking the players and giving us the credit. However, I think he took great satisfaction in watching his Olympic team, with players from different backgrounds and programs, blend as one to play hard, smart, and together. You see, the philosophy is sound, no matter what stage it's played on.

BUSINESS PERSPECTIVE

What can we learn for business from how Dean coached the Olympic team? Leaders are often faced with similar experiences. Managers are challenged with leading an "instant organization" to launch new products; open new stores, offices, or plants; carry out major fund drives; execute special projects; or merge companies. Managers face eight major challenges when leading such tempo-rary teams.

- The project team must perform well immediately.
- The consequences of succeeding or failing are significant.
- The team's life is short term.
- The team members are typically experienced professionals who are competent and successful in their own specialties.

- Team members work under different leadership styles with their own loyalties in their "home" organizations.
- Therefore, team members are typically difficult to manage.
- The team leader must reconcile, in short order, disparate expectations, needs, backgrounds, and goals for the project.
- The leader must create a total commitment to the team's short-term goal while getting team members to park their egos and agendas at the door.

To successfully lead a temporary organization, the leader must define the goal clearly, establishing the expectation that "we will succeed, no excuses."

The employees on such a team must work hard, smart, and together from day one to succeed. There's no time for handholding or complaining. Dean's methods and philosophy in coaching the Olympics serve as a wonderful road map to how to successfully handle such leadership assignments.

- He clearly defined the team's goal, the work that had to be done, and every person's role. There was no ambiguity. Instead, he got the team to focus on the goal and how to succeed.
- He selected excellent assistant coaches and had a major role in selecting players whom he thought would put the team ahead of individual honors and recognition. He dedicated himself completely to helping the team accomplish its goal.
- He told the players that there would be no all-star team named at the end of the Olympics. The winning team would stand as one to accept the gold medals.
- He convinced players from starkly different backgrounds

and basketball systems that the best way to win the Olympics would be to play hard, together, and smart.

- He stuck to his guns. He trusted his experience and wisdom and didn't allow critics or the pressure of the situation to cause him to alter his approach to executing a successful game plan.
- He placed the players in the spotlight while he and his assistant coaches labored in the background.
- He convinced the players to buy in to his philosophy and to trust it. The confidence with which he conducted himself spread throughout the team. The players and the coaches worked hard, but also had fun acting as one team that was on a mission to return the gold medal in basketball to the United States.

26

HOPES FOR THE FUTURE

College basketball is a beautiful game, and we should do all we can to protect it and make it better. Are there excesses? Absolutely. The sport is commercialized and became so when television, led by ESPN, began showing so many games. CBS is in the midst of an eleven-year contract to televise the NCAA men's basketball tournament, for which it paid a whopping $6.2 billion. Does anyone believe a network is going to write a check for that amount of money without gaining some concessions?

When study committees such as the Knight Commission on Intercollegiate Athletics complain about college athletics' being too commercial, only two sports are ever cited: men's basketball and Division 1-A football. Maybe commercialization is not *all* bad either, because colleges depend on those two "revenue" sports to fund all the sports that college athletic departments try to maintain. That's an expensive undertaking. To pay for it, it takes the money generated by football and basketball gate receipts, television revenues, and donations from alumni and boosters, which give them the right to purchase season tickets for football and men's basketball.

Even then, many Division 1 athletic programs are having to drop some "nonrevenue" sports because they can't afford them.

College athletic departments are not taking the money generated by men's basketball and Division 1-A football and banking it. The revenue goes to help student-athletes. How would the Knight Commission, or any other study group, recommend that those "nonrevenue" sports be financed if not by men's basketball and Division 1-A football? If it wasn't for the commercialization of those two sports, how would the other teams on campus be subsidized? How would Title IX requirements be met? It's much easier to cite problems than it is to create effective solutions.

Most "reform" measures passed by the NCAA are designed to save money, not to help the student-athlete. There's a history that proves the point. While I have hopes for the future, I confess that in many areas the outlook for reform is dim. Nevertheless, here are some suggestions:

- A $2,000 stipend for Division 1 men and women basketball players on full scholarship, as well as Division 1-A scholarship football players. From the late 1940s until 1972, a full athletic scholarship included $15 a month for "laundry and incidentals." The NCAA convention of 1972 eliminated it and passed other cost-saving measures, most of which hurt athletes, especially those from poor families. Economists would agree that $15 a month in the 1950s would amount to about $2,000 a year in today's economy. That money should be restored. The money to pay men and women basketball players on scholarship should come from the $6.2 billion CBS is paying to show the men's tournament. Money for football players should come from funds derived from the twenty-eight bowl games that are played at the end of the season. To avoid abuse, the checks should be written by the NCAA, not the individual colleges. If there is a consensus that this money should be based on need, then only the very wealthy should be excluded.

- A year in residence requirement for Division 1 basketball players. Each new basketball player who arrived on campus—a high school graduate coming as a freshman or a junior college or four-year college transfer—would have to be a full-time student for a year before being eligible to play varsity basketball. Except in rare instances the transfer student from a four-year college already has to sit out a year before playing for his new school. There's a precedent here from football, where 90 percent of the freshmen are redshirted, or held out of playing in games their first year, to give them time to mature physically. A year in residence would be all to the good for the student. It would give the freshmen time to adjust to the academic demands of college life without the pressures, travel, and practice time involved in varsity basketball or football. Fewer classes would be missed. Furthermore, the graduation rate for junior college transfers on athletic scholarship at four-year colleges is only about 20 percent. It would help those students academically if they sat out a year at their new school without facing the time-consuming pressures of playing in games. In other words, treat the junior college transfers as we do transfers from four-year colleges. Also, some colleges now recruit junior college transfers as a quick fix. The NCAA has experienced many abuses in recruiting involving junior college transfers. The athletes could spend Thanksgiving, Christmas, and spring break at home with their families. It would reduce the temptation for coaches to seek a "quick fix" in recruiting, and this would in turn reduce the number of illegal recruitments. It would reduce the transfer rate and improve graduation rates for basketball players, areas of concern always cited by study committees. Many athletes now leave after their freshman seasons because they are unhappy with their playing time. They wouldn't be so quick to leave at the end of their sophomore years, after they'd made friends on campus and grown comfortable with the school academically.

- Admission requirements for athletes set by each college or university. The NCAA should continue to establish the academic curriculum for high school students who hope to qualify for Division 1 athletic scholarships because it helps high school students prepare better for college. Here's the kicker: The NCAA should tell Division 1 schools that the lowest 1 percent of freshman admissions can't be recruited athletes. We would then help a small group of students who couldn't help us in athletics. That also would take care of the lame excuse presented by some coaches that just being on a college campus helps a young athlete, even if he or she has no chance to graduate. We all know that current NCAA admission standards requiring a certain SAT score, a certain grade average in core courses, and other requirements are not working. In order for the recruited athlete to remain eligible, he or she should make normal progress toward a degree, and that should be determined by each individual university.

  (I served on a cumbersome twenty-nine-member blue-ribbon NCAA committee in 1998–99 that was charged with making suggestions to reform intercollegiate athletics. Also on the committee were C. M. Newton and Terry Holland, both of whom coached and served as athletic directors on the Division 1 level and before that had been college athletes. The three of us campaigned hard for the three reforms listed above—and didn't get to first base. The committee left the difficult questions unanswered and accomplished virtually nothing, although it spent more than three hundred thousand dollars in the process.)

- Full-time officials for the top conferences in Division 1 men's basketball. We still have many officiating issues in college basketball. Officiating is so important in college basketball that we owe it to the players to have the games fairly and competently officiated. If conferences such as the ACC Big Ten, Pac-10, Big 12, Big East, SEC, and Conference USA had full-time officials, it would improve the game greatly. The officials would have time to study tapes, go to training sessions held by supervisors, and be assigned to games in different parts of the country so they wouldn't become so familiar to the same coaches and players. In the conferences below the biggest ones, the officials would continue to be assigned as they are now. They would continue with their regular jobs, with officiating as an avocation.

- Continued study of the college game and suggesting appropriate rules changes. I can't think of any major rules change that has not been good for the game.

- When the three-point shot came to college basketball in 1987, the arc was placed close to the basket, as it should have been. We wanted it to be a genuine part of the game. Now, sixteen years later, the shot has become too prominent in college basketball. It's not at all unusual now to see college teams take more than half their shots from beyond the arc. It's time to move the line back, at least nine inches to meet the international distance. In fact I wouldn't mind seeing it moved back to the NBA distance. The game is not as pretty or as exciting as it was because of all the outside shots. And while we're changing the configuration of the court, I like the international three-second lane.

- Keeping the NCAA tournament field at sixty-five teams. Underdogs still have a chance to win. Single elimination does not always identify the best team, but it does create great excitement. Underdogs would almost never beat a better team four out of seven, but in college basketball, the way the rules are, anything can happen in one forty-minute game.

- Reducing the shot clock from thirty-five to thirty seconds.

- Change of the NBA rule to allow teams to play any defense they chose. I think it would create more excitement and less predictability.
- More tolerance of others. I did not want our players to be critical of teammates. It's not the best way to build team chemistry. Furthermore, in our society, the tolerance level for others is frighteningly low.

For our great country, I should like to see us:

- Fight the War on Poverty with more money and determination because it certainly hasn't been won. Neither has the War on Drugs. It seems to me that we should attempt to rehabilite first-time drug offenders rather than put them in prison with hardened criminals. Just imagine what we could have done in those two crucial areas of our society if we had spent the money here rather than on the war with Iraq.
- Dramatically improve the pay and social status for teachers to be on the same level with doctors and lawyers. Each of us can recall the positive effect a great teacher had on our lives.
- Abolish the death penalty. We're the only industrialized nation in the world that continues to kill people via the death penalty.
- Use our taxes to care for every one of our citizens. It's ridiculous that a human being is denied hospital care because he or she doesn't have health insurance. We need universal health care. It's long overdue. Canada and Great Britain have worked out good health coverage for all.
- Band together to help one another and keep our country great.

At age seventy-two, I'm still not in the practice of blueprinting my life. I have a small office in the Smith Center, and I come to it most days when I'm in town. While I will leave early on occasion to play golf, I stay busy.

My great family is doing well, for which I'm grateful. And I stay in touch with many members of my extended family, former Carolina basketball players. These men have brought great happiness to my life. Ninety-six percent of them earned their college degrees, and one-third of those continued their studies at graduate and professional schools. It's the way a teacher's career should be judged. Our former players are doing great things for people in all walks of life.

The Carolina Way isn't the only way, that's for certain. But playing hard, playing smart, playing together certainly worked well for us.

Our trophy case is full, but far more important, our Museum of Good Memories runneth over.

PLAYER PERSPECTIVE

Richard Vinroot,

class of 1963, Vietnam war veteran,
former mayor of Charlotte, former Republican
nominee for governor of North Carolina,
currently an attorney in Charlotte

Coach Smith's interest in his players and his hopes for our future did not end when we used up our basketball eligibility. He kept our best interests at heart forever. Once a player was a member of his team, it was a lifetime deal.

For example, star players and others talented enough to have a chance to play professional basketball needed to choose agents to represent them, no easy thing to do. It's a tricky path to navigate. Coach Smith warned the players not to talk to any agents on their own. The basketball office was going to be the gatekeeper.

Some agents were good, some were not, and Coach Smith, on behalf of his players, took it on himself to sort it all out. He had prospective agents and attorneys come to Chapel Hill in the spring to present their credentials and answer questions from a panel of experts. The player was there, of course, along with his parents or guardians, Coach Smith, and some loyal advisers. Coach Smith invited me as an attorney and former player to sit in on some of these sessions, and I was honored and delighted to do it. One of Coach's closest friends, the late Bill Miller, a brilliant accountant, sat in on most of them. Some others close to the program, such as Paul Rizzo, the former IBM vice-chairman, Paul Fulton, president of Sara Lee Inc., Jack Evans, a faculty representative of athletics, Angela Lee, who worked in the basketball office and had a law degree, and Bob Eubanks, former chairman of the university's board of trustees and a very smart financial analyst, were among those whom Coach had sit in and listen to and question the agents and their representatives.

The agents entered the conference room one at a time, and each had one hour to make his presentation, after which we would question him thoroughly. The agent was told not to contact the player again. After the question and answer period, we'd tell Coach Smith, the player, and his parents or guardians what we thought about the agent's presentation. After hearing from all of them, we would leave, and Coach Smith, the player, and his family would talk further. Eventually the player and his family would tell Coach which agents he'd like to talk to again by telephone.

Once an agent was chosen, Coach Smith laid down the law: If the player was mismanaged in any way, the agent would never get close to having a chance to represent another North Carolina basketball player—ever. Coach even took it another step by warning the agent that if he messed up in representing the Carolina player—Coach would make sure his scores of coaching friends would learn of it.

Coach Smith kept his nose in the players' business long after they had left North Carolina, making certain they were being treated properly. If things didn't go well, he was quick to jump back in and help in any way that he could. This was necessary because the UNC players who went to the NBA faced so many financial temptations. People tried to approach them constantly with get-rich-quick schemes. We can only imagine the number of financial propositions that Michael Jordan must have received, for instance. He probably was offered some kind of a deal daily. Coach Smith spent an amazing amount of time staying interested and involved in their business transactions. He was determined not to let anyone take advantage of his players.

If he thought a lawyer was overcharging one of them, he would check on it and see that it was corrected. He continues to worry about us as we embark on our careers, not just the professional basketball players, but all of us.

In December 2002 we had a well-attended reunion of Coach Smith's first five North Carolina teams. We enjoyed a fine dinner at a Raleigh steakhouse, his treat, and Coach spoke for a few minutes and predictably took the blame for us not winning more games, even though we probably overachieved. Billy Cunningham, one of his truly great players, stood and said that he is asked all the time to describe what separates Coach Smith from other coaches. Billy says he explains it this way: "Coach Smith realized when we played for him that we probably would have forty or fifty years left to live after we left his program. He prepared us for that life, and he cares as much about us now as he did during the four or five years that we played for him. That's what separates him from other coaches."

Part of Coach Smith's legacy is that he had high hopes for the future of all his players, and he has never quit caring.

BUSINESS PERSPECTIVE

Jerry Bell's Hopes for the Future

After working for many years with talented leaders and their teams from around the world and in a variety of organizations, I believe I have gained a deep appreciation for Dean Smith's leadership principles. My hope for the future is that all leaders and workers will consider these lessons and reap the benefits. From my own experience, here are some of the profound truths I think the Carolina Way represents:

1. Leaders in all professions, industries, and organizations throughout the world must come to understand that about 95 percent of *all* people are good people who have good intentions, who desire to be helpful and productive. About 5 percent are negative people, and only about 1 or 2 percent of these are truly mean. It's possible for leaders to approach their work with this understanding and not be blinded by the perception that most people are ne'er-do-wells, lazy, selfish, and greedy. Believe in people and help others achieve their goals.

   A small percentage of harmful people exists in all walks of life. When a handful of leaders at Enron, WorldCom, or Tyco destroy their organizations and the lives and careers of the other 99 percent of hardworking, dedicated, honest individuals who worked in those firms, we shouldn't assume that all business leaders are greedy crooks who lack humanity. When leaders in the Red Cross, the United Way, or the Catholic Church gain notoriety because of a few damaging people, we should know that they don't represent the other

95 percent or more who work in and lead these organizations.

2. Leaders should focus on strengthening their own personality characteristics as early as possible in their careers, so that their contributions and opportunities for success and happiness will be enhanced. Many leaders make the error of being so busy doing their jobs that they put off doing the work necessary to overcome their personal weaknesses and to develop their strengths. When they reach their late fifties or sixties, after thirty or forty years of suffering because of their ineffective personality patterns, they will have missed all those years of opportunities for improvement and done thirty or forty years of damage to others. Only then do leaders often realize their faults and start to work to build their strengths and overcome their weaknesses. I hope we'll all learn to invest more of ourselves in developing personal skills and do so faster. As leaders we should spend time and money helping our followers develop their personality strengths so they can build our organizations, maximize our success and happiness, and help us increase our contributions.

3. Leaders need to lead balanced lives. They must give themselves more years to reach their professional and business goals so they don't burn themselves out and miss life while achieving success. A common mistake for leaders throughout the world is that they lose their personal lives by being over-committed at work. In many ways, this diminishes their families, destroys their love relationships, damages their health, and restricts their joy. Then, when it is too late, they discover that they should have spent more time in each of these pursuits, been more balanced, and just worked a few more years instead of postponing living until they retire early.

4. Leaders should devote good effort to enhancing what I call the seven skills of effective communication: listening, delivering ideas, confronting people, being open and nondefensive, developing a sense of humor, honing their presentations, and understanding the nonverbal behavior patterns of ourselves and others. These are significant skills, yet most of us perform them less effectively than we should and could. They are essential to leading effectively. We should devote time in our elementary schools, high schools, colleges, and organizations to building mastery of these seven communication skills.

5. The value of leadership should be prized. Those who do it well should be honored. Major accolades are awarded in the arts, humanities, and government service, but few focus on leadership excellence. Leadership is one of our highest callings and most challenging of the performing arts. I think we should raise it to a position of greater honor in and of itself and establish it as a noble goal toward which to strive.

The Carolina Way worked for Dean Smith's Tar Heels in basketball and led to extraordinary success over nearly four decades. Given the chance, similar principles and ethics can work for the rest of us too.

ACKNOWLEDGMENTS

I thank my former players at North Carolina and the Air Force Academy for the many great things they accomplished as players and in their careers, as well as what they did for me during my college coaching career. I am grateful to all of the coaches for whom I worked and played and to those who assisted me at North Carolina. Special thanks to former UNC chancellor William Aycock, who trusted me enough to hire me to be North Carolina's head coach, and to Carolina Coach Roy Williams, who wrote the preface for this book. We couldn't have gotten along without all the people who worked in the basketball office at North Carolina over the years. To my own family, much love and gratitude.

—Dean Smith

I would like to thank Linda Hobson for her excellent editing and thinking; Sharon Kolk for her leadership; Doris Elkin, Barbara Hoover, Lynn Oddenino, Kristen Leonard, Amy Hagen, Jess Stansell, Mitzi Johnson, and Sarah Svendsen for working hard, together, and smart at Bell Leadership; coaches Dean Smith, Bill Guthridge, Matt Doherty, Phil Ford, Dave Hanners, Pat Sullivan, and Randy Wiel for their teaching and friendship and for allowing me to work with them during many exciting basketball seasons since 1992; Dr. Earl Somers and Dick Baddour for their insights into sports and coaching; to my business clients for their wisdom; to my students and colleagues in the Kenan-Flagler Business School at UNC-CH for their spirit of inquiry; and to my family—Tina, Kathryn, Sharon, Dave, Christine, Caroline, Dean, Lou, and Florence.

—Jerry Bell

Sincere thanks to the former Carolina players who graciously spent time explaining to me how the Carolina Way worked for them and affected their lives in such a positive manner. Most still carry the lessons learned from Coach Smith with them in their daily lives. They represent a terrific and impressive group of successful men. My thanks also to Linda Woods and Ruth Kirkendall, administrative assistants to Coach Smith, who were always available for encouragement and a helping hand.

—John Kilgo

INDEX

Profits, versus factors leading to profits, 43–46
Public embarrassment, avoiding, 135, 157
Punctuality, 84, 200, 222
    See also Lateness
Punishment. *See* Discipline
Pyle, Ernie, 61–62

Racial integration. *See* African Americans
Recruitment, 88–100
    bad hire, cost of, 94–95
    business application, 93–96
    coach's view of, 88–91
    effective hiring interviews, 95–96
    first African Americans, 297–301
    freshman, expectations of, 105–6
    high school athletes, negative traits of,
        104–5
    high school students' visits to school, 98–99
    home visits by coach, 92–93, 99–100
    and honesty, 91, 97–103, 127–28
    media attention to, 106–7
    overrecruitment, 91
    player characteristics, 89–90
    player participation in decisions, 99, 126
    player-prospect interaction, 98–99
    player's view of, 92–93
    of unselfish players, 141–42
Reid, J.R., 231
Responsibility
    versus blame, 136, 146, 300
    of coach and losing game, 65, 159
    of representatives of university, 200–201
    and roles, 132–40
Rest time for players
    during practice, 30
    player's view, 182–83
    tired signal, 180–87
    water break, 75, 207
Rewards, 155–60
    bonus, basis of, 37
    business application, 160
    coach's honor role, 178–80
    coach's view of, 155–57, 178–79
    at completion of project, 119
    earned during practice, 77, 105–6
    luxury hotels and trips, 155–56, 158
    player's view, 157–60, 179
    team performance-based, 142–44, 246
    to unselfish players, 178–79
Rituals
    anxiety-reducing, 39–40
    applause for teammates, 168–69
    benefits of, 39–40

and confidence building, 239
    functions of, 155
Rizz, Paul, 324
Rockne, Knute, 238
Roles, 132–40
    business application, 137–40
    coach's view, 132–35
    defining in meetings, 217
    job-person fit, determination of, 138–40
    player's view, 129, 135–36
Running
    not running as reward, 77, 105–6
    for physical conditioning, 81–82
    signal to stop, 183
    for violation of rules, 63, 262–63, 266
Rupp, Adolph, 254, 296, 298
Ryder Cup, 40, 263

Salary, team performance-based, 142–44
Scott, Charles, 148, 150, 251, 297
Scrimmages
    blue-white scrimmage, 133
    and practice, 78–79
    reducing boredom, 115
Season, length of, 111–21
    boredom-reducing activities, 112, 114–16
    business application, 117–21
    coach's view of, 111–13
    miniseasons approach to, 120–21
    planning breaks for employees, 120–21
    player's view, 114–16
Seikaly, Rony, 231
Self-discipline. *See* Focus
Seniors
    business application, 176–78
    coach's view, 172–74
    as confidence builders, 238
    and discipline process, 263, 265
    as leaders, 172–78
    and off-the-court rules, 261
    player's view, 174–75
    special honors for seniors, 172–74
Shaffer, Charles, 69, 80
Sheppard, Steve, 306
Shots, grading by players, 145
Smith, Dean
    biographical information, 9–12, 248–50, 271–72
    breaks Rupp's record, 254, 296
    coaching, basic principles, 9–20
    connection with former players, 64, 66–69, 159,
        254, 296, 324–25
    hopes for future, 317–23
    on leadership, 3–4